Born to Fly

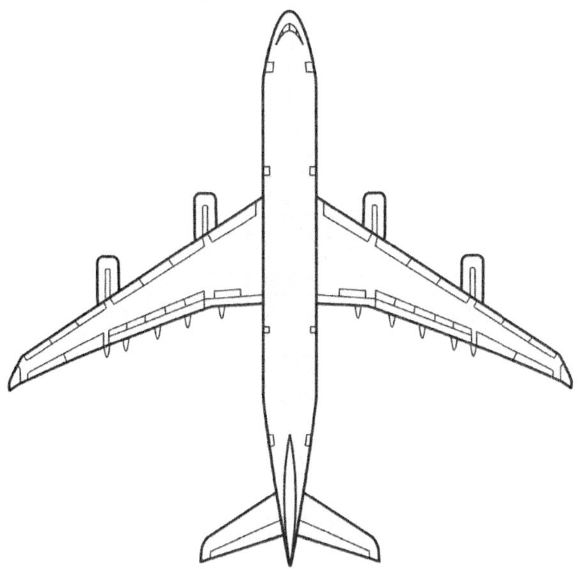

Bob Williams

From Hangar Floor to Chief Pilot

SunRise

SunRise

First published in Great Britain in 2023 by SunRise

SunRise Publishing Ltd
124 City Road
London EC1V 2NX

ISBN 978-1-9144893-6-5

A CIP catalogue record for this book is available from the British Library.

Typeset in Minion Pro and Impact.

Contents

To my lovely wife, Sara. Thank you for everything.

Chapter One

I was born in Crickhowell, South Wales, in 1948, the same year that Wilbur—the last surviving Wright brother—died. Both my parents were Welsh, my father having spent his childhood in Pontllanfraith and my mother in the neighbouring town of Blackwood. Aviation was always a part of my background; my father volunteered to join the RAF on leaving school and was trained as an aircraft engineer at RAF Halton in Buckinghamshire. He completed his training in 1936, and was assigned to 18 Squadron, operating Hawker Hind and Hawker Hart biplanes.

My father's first flight became a family legend. As part of their induction, RAF personnel were taken on familiarisation flights. In the open-cockpit Hawker Hind, the pilot sat in the forward cockpit and an observer/gunner sat in a separate cockpit behind. A machine gun was normally attached to a rail that ran around the top of the rear cockpit, but for the familiarisation flights, the gun was removed. The passenger was dressed in a cumbersome flying suit that had a leather strap that hung from the waist. Once aboard, the free end of the strap was attached to the gun rail by a dog clip. No sooner was my father airborne than the pilot began to throw the aircraft around in the hope of frightening his passenger.

Far from being scared, Dad was loving every minute of it. In fact, the more extreme the manoeuvre, the more he seemed to enjoy it. This made the pilot more determined to increase the fear factor, so he introduced some negative G by pushing the stick forward, knowing it would cause

The Hawker Hind was part of the RAF's expansion in the mid-1930s and was the RAF's last biplane light bomber

Dad to float up from his seat until his leather safety strap stopped him from being ejected from the cockpit. Dad soared up until his knees were almost level with the top rim of the cockpit and then his safety strap snapped! He immediately splayed his legs apart so that they were pressed against the sides of the cockpit which prevented him from being ejected any further. However, he had risen so high that he was unable to grab the gun rail—even with his arms at full stretch—only his lower legs were keeping him in.

Fortunately, at this point, the pilot turned to look back, expecting to see the terrified face of his passenger. Instead, he saw his passenger's legs and then, looking up, saw the rest of him suspended in space. By carefully reapplying positive G he was relieved to see my father float back into his cockpit and grab hold of the gun rail, which he continued to hold tightly until they landed. He once told me that he was surprised they hadn't found impressions of his fingers in the rail. Far from putting him off aerobatics for life, he later got his pilot's licence, and there was nothing he enjoyed more

The Bristol Blenheim was a British light bomber aircraft which was used extensively in the first two years of the Second World War

than putting an aircraft through its paces with a series of aerobatic manoeuvres.

In 1940, 18 Squadron (then operating Blenheim bombers) was sent to France as part of the British Expeditionary Force. They suffered appalling losses and by June, what was left of their aircraft were flown back to England. The ground personnel, including my father, were ordered to destroy any equipment that could be of use to the enemy, and then get home as best they could. So it was, that Dad found himself on the beach at Dunkirk—along with hundreds of thousands of other men—waiting to be evacuated by 'Little Ships' to the temporary safety of England.

He was one of the lucky ones and his squadron regrouped with Blenheim Mark IV bombers and began making night raids on German airfields. One of their more unusual missions was to fly overhead the airfield at Saint-Omer-Longeunesse, where they dropped a box by parachute containing a pair of legs for Wing Commander Douglas Bader. He had earlier been shot down over France and had lost his artificial limbs in the process.

On humanitarian grounds, an arrangement was made with his captors via the Red Cross organisation, to allow replacement legs to be parachuted in for him to use while in a prisoner of war camp.

In March 1942, my father was given embarkation leave and on 19 March, he and my mother got married. My mother's brother, Bryn, was a vicar and conducted the ceremony. He too had quite a war, having joined the Royal Navy. He volunteered even though, as a clergyman, he was exempt from military service. He became a gunnery officer and on his first voyage sank a German submarine. He was subsequently mentioned in dispatches by the king for his bravery during passages on the much-feared Russian supply convoys.

In October 1942, 18 Squadron was posted to Algeria. Once again, they suffered dreadful losses as their Blenheims were no match for the Luftwaffe's fighters. On 4 December, Wing Commander Hugh Gordon Malcolm led thirteen Blenheims in an attack against an enemy fighter airfield. The bombers did not have a fighter escort, but initially had the benefit of low cloud cover to help shield their approach. Unfortunately, the clouds cleared when the formation was still some distance from the target, but Malcolm chose to press on with the attack. German fighters intercepted them and every one of the vulnerable Blenheims was shot down and destroyed. Wing Commander Malcolm was just 25 years of age at the time of his death. He was posthumously awarded the Victoria Cross for his bravery.

As Rommel's forces were driven back, the squadron repeatedly moved forward along with the advancing allied ground forces. By August 1943, they had left the African mainland for the island of Sicily and in October 1943, they had advanced to Brindisi on the Italian mainland. From there they conducted bombing operations over northern Italy.

Finally, VE Day arrived and the war in Europe was over. The squadron moved briefly to Aviano, in northern Italy and later to Hassini, in Greece. My father then returned to England and the squadron was disbanded. He spent a period as an instructor at RAF St Athan in South Wales before being demobbed. While my father was overseas, my mother had been conscripted into the civil service and transferred to London. She spent most nights in an Anderson air raid shelter in the garden of the house where she was living. Two nights a week she had to stay at the office on fire watch as this was compulsory at all public buildings. When the air raid sirens sounded, the gang on duty was supposed to run up to the flat roof of the building where there were buckets of sand, water, and stirrup pumps. I don't think she or any of her colleagues held out much hope that they would be able to tackle any major fires, but they all went through the motions.

Upon leaving the RAF, my father decided to join the nascent British airline industry; the same industry that he and I would spend our careers working in. In the years following the Second World War it would grow from almost nothing to an industry that, today, employs over a million people and contributes more than £22 billion to our national wealth. In 1945, the British government wanted to establish a regular air service between Britain and South America because of that continent's abundant food and mineral resources. They also planned air links to Bermuda and the Caribbean, and a new airline, British South American Airways (BSAA), was created.

The man put in charge was Air Vice Marshal Donald Bennett, the decorated wartime pilot who had created Bomber Command's famous Pathfinders' squadron. Bennett was both a pilot and master navigator who, quite literally 'wrote the book' with regards to airborne navigation. His book had been required reading at all the RAF aircrew training facilities. During the war, Bennett had recognised that to improve Bomber Command's success rate, it was vital for the aircrew to accurately locate and identify their targets. His idea was to take the cream of the crop from the RAF's navigator training schools and assign them to a specially created squadron nicknamed the Pathfinders.

On every bombing raid, the Pathfinders would go

ahead of the main bomber stream, locate the target, and drop coloured marker bombs and incendiaries to clearly highlight it. It was a brilliant idea and greatly improved Bomber Command's success and efficiency. After the war, when the authorities were looking for someone with a proven track record as a leader and a determined 'can do' attitude when it came to difficult projects, they chose Bennett as the head of British South American Airways. Unfortunately, this was to be as difficult a project as it is possible to imagine.

From the start, it was made clear that the new airline was to operate only British aircraft. The intention was understandable, but from a practical point of view made little sense. Because of the very long distances to BSAA's planned destinations, the British aircraft then available were totally unsuitable. American manufacturers were producing aircraft that were much better suited to long range flights; partly because distances between some city pairs in America are very long, but also because America had been quick to recognise the need for fast transport links to far flung parts of the world. Purpose-built, modern airliners were the answer, and the United States produced several including the Douglas DC-4, the Lockheed Constellation, and the Boeing 377 Stratocruiser.

BSAA, however, wasn't allowed to buy any of them, and the alternatives were not great. The Avro Lancastrian was—literally—a converted Lancaster bomber. The subsequent Avro York was an improvement, but it also owed much to the Lancaster. It had a cruising speed of 200 knots and a range of 2,600 nautical miles but it was unpressurised and had to fly through bad weather rather than above it. These slow, noisy, unpressurised machines were not suited to long haul flights and some of the routes planned for BSAA would be at the very limit of their range.

Don Bennett was both determined and goal-driven, but he could also be stubborn, abrasive, and short tempered. With a reputation for straight talking, he made a lot of enemies during his time in the Royal Air Force. He was used to getting his own way and, once he had an

Stargirls (Stewardesses) of British South American Airways in front of a BSAA Avro York

objective in mind, he would move heaven and earth to achieve it. He set high standards, possessed boundless energy, and expected everyone else to keep up with him. He also tended to disregard any rules that he thought would impede his ability to get the job done. Sadly, over a period of just twenty-nine months, BSAA suffered ten crashes, eight of which were fatal, and questions were soon being asked in the House of Commons. Bennett said that accidents were to be expected on such challenging routes and he made public criticisms of the inquiry set up by the government. This led to him being fired and replaced by Air Commodore Herbert Brackley.

Bennett decided to start his own airline, Airflight Ltd, to take advantage of the lucrative freight charters that were being offered during the Berlin Airlift (1948–1949), and he asked my father to leave BSAA and join him. Although many people found Bennett difficult to get on with, he and my father had a mutual respect. He used to

BSAA crews with Avro Tudors at the end of the Berlin Airlift

call Dad 'my imperturbable Welshman' and they enjoyed a good working relationship. Consequently, Dad decided to accept his offer.

Following the Berlin airlift, Bennett's Avro Tudors carried out trooping flights for the British government and numerous ad hoc charters under the name of 'Fairflight.' Dad was crewed with Bennett on several memorable trips, including one in October of 1949. They flew from London to Johannesburg taking settlers to South Africa. When they landed at Palmietfontein, with sixty-nine passengers, it created quite a stir as this was the biggest single passenger load ever flown into the country. The last leg of their journey had been from Dar-es-Salaam and had taken just over seven hours. Their arrival was reported in the *Rand Daily Mail* and a journalist had noted the Tudor's already 'chequered' safety record. Bennett was quoted in the paper as saying, 'The Tudors are fine aircraft and ideally suited to the South African service.'

Sadly, just five months later, the safety of the type was again brought into question in the most dramatic way. On Saturday 11 March 1950, the Welsh rugby team were due to play against Ireland in Belfast. Anticipation was high, because if they won the match, they would become triple crown champions. A Fairflight Avro Tudor V had been chartered to take seventy-eight rugby enthusiasts from Llandow airport in South Wales to watch the game in Belfast. They were to fly out on Friday and the same aircraft would be flying them back to Wales on the Sunday. My Father was delighted to be one of the crew members for that flight, because they would be staying over in Belfast with their passengers and would also have tickets to watch the game. As a keen rugby man, my mother's brother Bryn was very envious and joked that he wished Dad could smuggle him aboard the flight.

The day before the flight was due to leave for Belfast, my mother was lifting something heavy at home (not fifteen-month-old me!). Suddenly, she felt a sharp pain and it was obvious that she had badly injured her back. With her immobilised, and bed-ridden, my father had no option but to take himself off the crew list for the flight and arrange for someone to take his place. The Welsh team won their match and became triple crown champions, so the seventy-eight Welsh Rugby supporters were in great spirits as they boarded the aircraft for their return flight. As they approached Llandow, several people on the ground watched the aircraft make its descent. It appeared normal

Daily Mirror

MON MAR. 13 1950

ONE PENNY

FORWARD WITH THE PEOPLE

No. 14,412

Registered at G.P.O. as a Newspaper.

THE WORLD'S WORST AIR DISASTER

80 ARE KILLED WHEN FOOTBALL FANS' PLANE CRASHES

EIGHTY PEOPLE WERE KILLED YESTERDAY WHEN A BRITISH TUDOR V AIR LINER—PREPARING TO LAND AT A SOUTH WALES AIRPORT—FELL LIKE A STONE INTO A FIELD NEAR THE HAMLET OF SIGGINSTON, GLAMORGAN.

Only three men survived. Two walked out unaided.

It was the worst disaster, either for airship or airliner, in the history of world aviation.

Eighty-three people were aboard. The seventy-eight passengers were Welsh Rugby enthusiasts returning from Dublin after seeing the Wales-Ireland match at Belfast on Saturday. Seventy-five passengers (including six women) were killed, together with all five crew (including the air hostess).

At half past three, womenfolk, waiting happily in the sunshine at Llandow Airport, watched the long-nosed silver machine their husbands and sons had chartered approach them in a long glide.

They gave a cheer. They saw it climb a little and level out. Then it appeared to pause in its flight; a wing jerked earthwards; and for a brief instant they saw the huge machine falling to earth.

There was a thud. The noise of four engines suddenly silenced, left only the ... of the airport crash tender's bell and the groans and cries of the

ily Rand Mail

JOHANNESBURG, MONDAY, OCTOBER 10, 1949.

AVM Don Bennett (left) and my father (right) arrive at Palmietfontein near Johannesburg

at first, until they saw the aircraft's nose pitch up, following which it stalled and crashed to the ground. With a death toll of eighty, including all five of the crew, it was then the world's worst air disaster and a very narrow escape for my father. The investigation into the crash was inconclusive, but the probable cause was that the aircraft had been incorrectly loaded, putting the centre of gravity too far aft. When the pilot selected full flaps and reduced speed on the approach, the aircraft became uncontrollable in pitch and stalled. Yet again, the Avro Tudor was on the front page of newspapers around the world.

Nevertheless, Airflight Limited, under the leadership of Don Bennett, continued to work their Tudor aircraft very hard and my father was forever flying off on yet another trip overseas. Because he was based at Blackbushe airport in Hampshire, my parents needed to find somewhere to live in that area. Unfortunately, at the end of the Second World War, housing was in short supply. The constant bombing of British towns and cities had, of course, destroyed many buildings and, with raw materials and labour in short supply, opportunities to rebuild them had been limited. Some new towns were being built (such as Harlow) but supply was falling far short of the demand—especially in Hampshire—so my father came up with a temporary solution for our family: a large caravan.

A short distance from Blackbushe airport, is the sleepy but attractive village of Eversley Cross. In the grounds of a house owned by a farmer named Yeomans was the large caravan that became our new home. It was an isolated spot and a rather lonely existence for my poor mother when Dad was away on trips overseas. She would take regular walks along the narrow country lanes, pushing me along in my pushchair and chatting away to keep me entertained. Apart from calling into the general store in the village, she met few other people.

When my father wasn't flying, he would be working at the maintenance hangar at Blackbushe airport. He owned an old Austin car and, because the airport was a short distance away, this meant he could nip home for lunch. I used to go down the long gravel driveway to the point where it connected with Chequers Lane and wait for Dad's car to appear. When it did, we had a routine. He would stop alongside the gate, wind down the window, and ask, 'Can I give you a lift young man?"

I would then jump up onto the running board of his car and hold on to the window frame. Dad would wrap his arm around my shoulders to keep me secure and then we would drive (at a very sedate walking pace) up the drive to the caravan, while he asked me what sort of a day I was having, and I asked him if he had fixed any aircraft. For a toddler, this was the most exciting thing imaginable, especially when my mother pretended to tell us both off for being so irresponsible.

Years later, my mother used to tell an amusing story from our time at Eversley Cross. She always complained that my father was incapable of talking to very young children (including me) in a way that they could understand. What she meant by that was, if a small child asked him a question about something, he would answer it accurately, but without any attempt to 'dumb it down' so that the young person could understand.

Once, when the three of us were walking, an aircraft flew overhead, and I was immediately excited by this. I pointed and asked what it was. My father replied (correctly) that it was a Gloster Gladiator; a biplane that was still occasionally seen in the skies. My mother turned to my father and told him off: 'Oh for goodness' sake, he doesn't want to know who built the thing. Just tell him that it's an aeroplane!' Weeks later, my mother was pushing me along the road in my pushchair, when she saw one of my father's work colleagues—a pilot—walking in the opposite direction. They stopped to chat for a moment and just then, an aircraft flew overhead which happened to be a Gloster Gladiator. I sat up excitedly in my pushchair, pointed at the aircraft and exclaimed 'Oh look Mum. A Goster Gadilator!' Apparently, the look on the pilot's face was a picture and he said something like 'he's definitely an aviation man.' After that day, the Gloster Gladiator was always known as a Goster Gadilator in our family.

The trips that my father went on were long, arduous, and occasionally hair raising. On one occasion, he and Bennett were on their way to Bahrain where they planned to make a refuelling stop. As they flew across Saudi Arabia, they encountered a sandstorm so extensive they were unable to go around it, or over it. By now, the British aviation authorities had insisted that the Tudors flew unpressurised, because of previous unexplained accidents. One theory during the accident investigations pointed the finger at the pressurisation system. Could it have subtly depressurised when they were flying at high altitude, thereby rendering the occupants unconscious? Could it have caused the fuselage to rupture resulting in an explosive decompression at high altitude? As nobody could come up with a conclusive answer—and to avoid having to ground the aircraft type indefinitely—the temporary solution was to allow it to continue to fly with the restriction that it must remain unpressurised.

Faced with a veritable 'wall of sand' ahead of them, Bennett had climbed the aircraft to well above the altitude at which supplementary oxygen (or pressurisation) was required, but they were still unable to get above the huge sandstorm. After some time in the choking atmosphere, they eventually flew into clear air. A short time later, they reached the point at which they should begin their descent before approaching Bahrain. When Bennett tried to close the throttles (thrust levers in American parlance) they couldn't be moved. The sleeve valves that the throttle levers operated had become completely clogged by sand particles. The four engines were literally stuck at cruise power! Better to be stuck with too much power than too little, but the problem was, how to bring the aircraft down? Put it into a dive by lowering the nose and it would, of course, start to descend. However, if you didn't reduce engine power at the same time, then the aircraft speed would increase more and more until it became dangerous.

The solution was simple but terrifying: come overhead the airfield and then select the fuel mixture control levers to the cut off position on all four engines! My father, having cut off the fuel supply, listened as the engines spluttered and died. The silence was deafening. They were now in a very large, ungainly glider and Bennett began to skilfully manoeuvre the aircraft in a series of descending turns. He was carefully assessing their altitude versus their rate of descent and their distance to the touchdown point on the runway. He judged it perfectly and brought the aircraft in to land at exactly the right spot on the runway. Having pulled off a flawless dead stick landing, he turned to my father and said 'Come on Bryn. We need to get these throttles working properly again. Then we must get refuelled and on our way.'

My Dad stripped the throttle mechanism, washed all the sand out using petrol, reassembled it, function checked it all for correct operation, supervised the refuelling, and they were on their way again. The imperturbable Welshman and his fiercely determined boss were airborne on the next leg of their journey. Anybody would have thought that landing an airliner with all four engines shut down was a perfectly normal procedure!

Bennett's airline had been given the job of delivering mail to the US military personnel who were fighting the war in Korea. They were to take the mail as far as Japan and the US military would take it on from there. Bennett was determined to get the consignment to Japan in record time and my father knew that meant they were in for an exhausting journey, but little did he realise just *how* exhausting. Today, there are strict rules and restrictions with regards to how many hours flight crews can remain on duty. There are also maximum limits on how many flying hours they can clock up in a month or year. In 1951, when they set off on their mail flight to Japan, there were no restrictions at all on aircrew flying limits. Bennett was a man who liked to break records and that was going to keep my father busy. The whole trip was completed by a single crew, and they arrived back at Blackbushe seven days and three hours after leaving. During that time, they had completed 130 flying hours: an average of over eighteen hours airborne time every day for a week! Years later, my mother told me that Dad was so tired when he landed back at Blackbushe, he couldn't even speak properly. Today, pilots are limited to a maximum of 100 flying hours in a month.

Chapter Two

At the end of 1951, Freddie Laker purchased Don Bennett's Fairflight and combined it with two of his existing businesses, naming the new company Air Charter Ltd. Laker was still only twenty-nine years old and he made my thirty-three-year-old father his chief engineer. Fairflight had a lucrative contract carrying cargo between Berlin and Hamburg in what became known as the second Berlin airlift. Air Charter was soon operating more than seventy flights a week between Berlin, Hannover and Hamburg.

Following the 1951 general election, the Conservative party was returned to power, and they favoured a mixture of public and private sectors in the aviation industry. They didn't want to upset the secure status of the two state run airlines, but they did want to help the struggling independents by offering them trooping contracts. It wasn't long, however, before independent airlines started to gain a reputation for poor reliability and timekeeping. Then, the disappearance of a Skyways York over the Atlantic, with the loss of all the troops and families on board prompted questions about safety.

Never one to miss an opportunity, Freddie Laker fitted an Avro York with rearward facing passenger seats, a configuration that he knew won favour with the military on safety grounds. He also promised that his engineering and maintenance company, Aviation Traders, would set up stores of aircraft parts at strategic locations along the proposed air routes. Not surprisingly, Freddie won the contract.

By this time, we were living in Harlow and my father, as Freddie Laker's chief engineer, was working both at nearby Stansted airport and at Aviation Traders' maintenance facility at Southend airport. In September 1953, Laker bought ten Avro Tudors at a bargain price. He extensively modified them and, following a series of very through test flights, the Tudor regained its unrestricted passenger carrying Certificate of Airworthiness. He also bought all the unserviceable Tudors on the British register to break them down for use as spare parts. Everyone now hoped that the chequered history of the Avro Tudor was old news and that Freddie's trust in the type would prove to be justified.

In April 1954, that hope was seriously challenged when one of Laker's Tudors was flying over central France. The aircraft unexpectedly yawed and then banked violently, following which it went into a steep spiral dive. The aircraft lost seven thousand feet before the captain was able to regain control and pull out of the dive. When they eventually landed, there were signs of wrinkling on the wings and fuselage that clearly showed the aircraft had been over stressed during the recovery from its near fatal dive. It had been a very close call. When news of the incident reached Aviation Traders, the initial reaction had been 'Oh no! Not another incident involving the Tudor?' Laker instructed two of his senior pilots to immediately begin test flights in his Tudors to try and establish the cause of the incident.

They succeeded and discovered that the problem had been caused by carburettor icing. To everyone's relief, it was concluded that the aircraft hadn't been to blame. It was obvious that if the pilot had been more vigilant and had exercised better engine management then the incident would not have occurred. Freddie was never one to miss an opportunity for good publicity. He put out a press release claiming, '… Possibly the most important piece of recent British aircraft detective work will be demonstrated at 3 pm Sunday afternoon at Stansted airport.' The Tudor was given a clean bill of health, once again.

Freddie was now determined to increase his presence in Berlin and to set up a permanent base there. The German city was an incredibly busy and important aviation hub and of course had a huge military presence. Military personnel, equipment and supplies, all needed to be moved by air. Freddie told my father that he wanted him to move to Berlin and set up an engineering base there. Far from being a short-term assignment, Freddie made it clear that he wanted my father to remain there and run the maintenance base for the foreseeable future. In other words, it was to be our new home. So it was, that with very little time to prepare, my father, mother and I left England to live in Germany.

I was about to fly for the very first time. I knew that it must be special, because none of the kids I played with in our neighbourhood had ever been in an aircraft. When I told them that I was going to be flying to a foreign country, I discovered that none of them had done that either. The upcoming flight had the 'wow factor' and clearly made them envious. When I mentioned which country we were going to, that resulted in a 'wow' of a different kind. It was, of course, just over five years since the end of World War Two, and the Germans had been the big, bad enemy. In the minds of young kids, the idea of a British family going to live there seemed very strange. I remember being confused by the shocked reaction from some of the older boys in my circle. Clearly, they had a better awareness of recent history than I did. At my tender age, my parents had obviously sheltered me from the unpleasantness of world wars, knowing that I would be made aware of it soon enough as I grew up. So, as far as I was concerned, my parents and I were merely setting off on a new and exciting adventure, and I was going to fly in one of Dad's aeroplanes!

I was to travel in an Avro Tudor freighter from London's Stansted Airport to Tempelhof Airport in Berlin. It was noisy, freezing cold and, without doubt, the most exciting and wonderful thing I had ever experienced in my five years of life. My mother and I sat in the rear of the cockpit. Behind us, the cargo compartment contained a couple of

Merlin engines, some aircraft wheels and tyres and many crates of assorted spares. My mother was absolutely terrified throughout the whole flight—visibly shaking and crying on take-off—but she tried her very best to hide it from her 'little boy' who, annoyingly, was having the time of his life. I remember being very confused because—having seen her crying—I asked her what was wrong. When she smiled and said she was fine and just a bit excited, I accepted her lie without question and went back to taking in all that was going on around me. Absolutely everything about that flight thrilled me. The noise, the smells, the vibration, the turbulence, all of it. That was the day I became hooked. I had been bitten by the flying bug; a bite from which there is no cure.

We landed at Tempelhof in a snowstorm and looking back at the event with adult eyes, I'm certain that it must have been touch and go whether we landed that night. I know that the snow was falling heavily, the visibility was very poor, and the clouds seemed to be sitting directly on top of the airport buildings. Of course, by this time, I had decided that pilots were superhuman and could land no matter what the weather. After the engines stopped and the small forward crew door had been opened, we felt the freezing cold conditions and braced ourselves, ready to step outside.

Then, a problem arose. The ground crew had brought the tallest set of passenger steps that they could find and wheeled them up to the crew door. Unfortunately, the nose of the Tudor, due to the aircraft's tail wheel configuration, stood very tall and towered above aircraft that had a tricycle undercarriage. The steps stopped many feet short of the door sill. The ground crew indicated that we would have to disembark via the freight door which was located near the rear of the fuselage. My father shouted down that we couldn't get to the rear door until the freight had been unloaded and that was going to take quite some time. The aircraft was so full of cargo, that it wasn't possible to get from the cockpit area back to the rear. The person standing on the top of the steps looked at me standing in the doorway and then said to my Dad, 'you'll have to drop the lad down to me.' Before I knew what was happening, Dad dropped me down into the guy's outstretched arms. It will come as no surprise when I say that my Mum needed a lot more persuading to take that 'leap of faith' but eventually she did. It certainly wasn't the most elegant of arrivals.

Berlin was a huge culture shock. When we first arrived, Freddie Laker had authorised temporary accommodation at the hotel Tuskulum on the Kurfürstendamm. This was one of the main streets running through the centre of the city and quite unlike anything my parents had seen in Britain. Pavement cafes, restaurants, bars and—most significantly—a justifiable reputation as 'the city that never sleeps.' British pubs closed for the night just as the bars and nightclubs in Berlin were getting going. Of course, it took a while for my parents to adjust and get a feel for how things were done there, but they acclimatised quickly.

My father threw himself into his work, he had to get the Air Charter maintenance base fully operational. In the meantime, as the company was only going to pay the bill for the room at the Tusculum hotel for a limited period, the pressure was on to find somewhere else to live. With Dad busy at the airport all day, my Mum was left to try and find us a home. The head barman at the hotel was a man by the name of Wolfgang and he was fluent in several languages including English. He also had a very engaging personality and sense of humour which made him popular with the many airline personnel who frequented the hotel. He was a useful guide-cum-interpreter-cum-negotiator for Brits who were trying to find a home in the city. My parents befriended him, and he helped find us somewhere to live. He remained a good friend and later became manager of the Tusculum hotel.

At the end of World War Two, the city of Berlin had been divided into sectors, each sector being controlled by one of the Allies: the Russians, Americans, British and French. Our new home was a flat on Heerstraße, which was in the British sector and near to the Olympic stadium that had been built for the 1936 Olympics. The apartment block was owned by a doctor, and I became friendly with his son who was the same age as me. The flat next to ours was occupied by the famous opera soprano, Rita Streich, and her husband Deiter.

There was a large expatriate community in Berlin at that time and civilian airline personnel were entitled to enrol their children at the British military school. Also, airline personnel and their families were allowed to use the many facilities that had been set up for the military forces. These included the officer's club with bar and restaurant, golf course, tennis courts, sailing lake, and a swimming pool where I subsequently learned to swim. Life in Berlin for us, wasn't too tough at all.

My parents quickly established a large circle of friends amongst the expatriates. Some were from the airlines; some were in the military, and some were teachers at the English Military School. Everyone in the city seemed to have an attitude towards life that suggested they should 'live for today, because there may not be a tomorrow'. After all the years of wartime austerity, expatriates in Berlin quickly turned into party animals. Stories my parents told me in later years, made it sound like they had a great time.

Meanwhile, we kids were enjoying ourselves too. Berlin used to experience Siberian winters and Mediterranean summers. In winter, the temperatures plummeted, and the city authorities would flood the public tennis courts to turn them into ice skating rinks. Building rubble from bomb sites would be piled high, forming man-made hills that would then get covered in snow. These made perfect toboggan and ski slopes. Dad bought me a terrific wooden toboggan with steel runners, and I soon put it to good use. Once the summer arrived, we practically lived in and around the swimming pool at the officer's club during our free time.

My conversational German had got pretty good by this time, mainly from playing with the kids in our neighbourhood. One of the first German phrases I learned was *hande hoch*, which means hands high—as in the command 'put your hands up'—and was particularly useful when playing cowboys and Indians. It's interesting that when playing together, kids will learn a foreign language quite quickly and naturally by trial and error. There is no fear of making a grammatical error or mispronouncing a word, you just want to make yourself understood and to make new friends. I was no different and became so proficient that I was able to enrol at the local school where the teachers only spoke to us in German. The 'English kid' was managing to integrate.

Dad often worked incredibly long hours at the airport, but I particularly remember one occasion when I started to wonder if he was ever going to come home. Apparently, one of the Tudors had been grounded with a technical problem. I don't recall what the problem was, but it must have been a serious and unusual one because Air Charter had been in contact with the Avro engineers back in England to get an idea what the remedial action should be and how long it was likely to take. I believe that the answer was that the engineering work was likely to take five days. When Freddie Laker was given this news, his reaction had been 'I can't have that bloody aircraft on the ground for five days. It is fully committed with freight work, and I need it back in the air.' He told Dad to pull out all the stops and do whatever was necessary to get the job done.

When an engineer worked their normal shift and then continued to work right through the night to complete the job (in other words worked a double shift completing twice as many hours as usual) this was known as working a 'ghoster.' Presumably, the person was so knackered at the end of the job that they looked like a ghost. Anyway, whatever the reason, my Dad was no stranger to them. Nevertheless, this job made a ghoster look like child's play. After two days and nights without sleep, mid-way through the third day, he phoned Freddie Laker to say that the aircraft was fully serviceable, and was back in the air, having just taken off.

Freddie was so grateful that he told my Dad to take them all to a venue of his choosing and to 'give them the best bloody night out they have ever had.' Whatever they ate or drank, he was paying for the lot. This was typical of Laker and, one of the reasons that people couldn't do enough for the man. When people went above and beyond the call of duty for him, he always recognised the fact and saw to it that they were justly rewarded.

Stories of that night have become the stuff of legend. One engineer who danced a Highland fling on a glass-topped table, ended up wearing the table frame, surrounded by a sea of broken glass. When my father went to settle the bill, he offered to pay for any accidental damages, but was told, 'Your party has spent so much money tonight, that it won't be necessary to concern yourself with such trivialities.'

A memorable event occurred at our flat one night. It was late and suddenly there was a frantic knocking at our door. Our neighbour, Rita Streich, stood there looking very frightened and asked to come in. She explained that the Czechoslovakian philharmonic orchestra were currently in Berlin playing concerts as part of a European tour. The orchestra's conductor was a man Rita had met when she sang in an opera in Czechoslovakia. The man had decided that he wanted to escape from Communist rule in his country and to defect to America.

He and all the other members of his orchestra were closely guarded throughout their tour to prevent any attempts to defect. However, on this night, once everyone had returned to their hotel rooms, he had seen an opportunity to escape and seized it. When Rita met him, months before, in his own country, she had said something along the lines of 'If you are ever in Berlin, you simply must call on my husband and I, as we would love to see you again.' Now, the man was here, shaking like a leaf and looking absolutely terrified. She had immediately knocked on our door because she didn't know what to do. My Father quickly ushered them into our flat and closed the door. Once the man had explained his intentions, my father contacted the American embassy and relayed the story to them. A short while later, two officials from the Embassy arrived at our flat and briefly questioned the man who, by now, was close to total panic. Once satisfied that he was a genuine

An Avro Tudor V of Freddie Laker's Air Charter

defector, they announced that he must immediately come with them to the American Embassy. At this point, he became hysterical and refused to leave, saying that he now believed the two officials were not Americans at all, but were in fact communist agents who had come to take him into custody. It took a long time and a lot of reassurance to calm the poor man down and convince him that the two men really were who they said they were. Finally, the three of them left our flat in the small hours of the morning. Many weeks later, we received a postcard from America. The handwritten message simply said 'I have arrived safely in America. Thank you for everything.'

Throughout our time in Berlin, my fascination with aviation continued to grow. I was thrilled whenever my Dad took me to the airport to show me where he worked. We would be picked up from the flat by one of Air Charter's German drivers and taken to Tempelhof. Once there, Dad would proudly show me around the hangar, introduce me to some of his colleagues and show me around the aircraft that were undergoing maintenance work. I remember being particularly intrigued one day by an aircraft that was undergoing retraction tests. For this, the aircraft had been raised clear of the ground on huge hydraulic jacks. Then, the landing gear was retracted and lowered several times to ensure that it was operating correctly. We stood very close to it, with me nervously holding Dad's hand, and I watched in fascination as, with much noisy whirring and whining of hydraulics, the aircraft's landing gear slowly retracted into the wheel wells. Then, with more clunks and whines, they reappeared and gently lowered themselves into the extended position. It was more fun than an electric train set!

Hangar visits were great, but even better than that, was going on a flight. Several times, Dad arranged for me to go with him on a freight flight. If there was a short round trip from Berlin to Hamburg or Hannover, then I would be placed aboard as an item of unofficial freight. I sat in the cockpit throughout, and I remember on one flight, Captain Bob Langley sat me on his knee and told me to take over the controls because he was 'Tired and needed a break.' He then closed his eyes and pretended to go to sleep. I nervously looked across at the first officer who was sitting in front of his controls, but he held both his hands in the air and said to me 'The aircraft is all yours. You're in charge now.' In fact, the autopilot was engaged, but I clung onto the control wheel in front of me absolutely convinced that I was flying the plane. I couldn't stop smiling for the rest of the day.

On one occasion, I was on board an Avro York with my mother and father, and we were seated back in the cabin. This aircraft was configured to carry passengers rather than freight and if I remember correctly, we were about to fly to England on leave for a few days. The aircraft was holding clear of the runway and the pilots were increasing the power on the engines to check the magnetos as part of the pre-take-off checks. I noticed that my Dad suddenly looked up during the mag checks and started to frown and listen attentively. When I asked him what was wrong, he quietly said in my ear 'I don't like the sound of that number three engine.' There followed a period with the number three engine being run at a much higher power setting (presumably with the fuel mixture leaned off) and then it seemed that the pilot must have been satisfied, because the aircraft started to line up on the runway. However, I noticed that Dad was still frowning. The engines came up to full power, the brakes came off and we started to roll. As the aircraft picked up speed, the tail wheel lifted off the ground and then suddenly … bang! The power reduced on all the engines, the tail wheel thumped back down, and the brakes were applied hard. As the aircraft came to a halt, I looked at Dad for an explanation. He smiled at me and winked as he said, 'Told you I didn't like the sound of that number three engine.' He then discreetly unfastened his seatbelt and headed up to the cockpit. I turned to my Mum and said excitedly 'Isn't Dad brilliant? He knew that was going to happen before it even went bang'. My Mother just looked like she needed a cigarette.

One day, quite unexpectedly, my father received a phone call from the independent airline Dan-Air. They were looking for a chief engineer and wondered if he would be interested in applying. He said that he was happy in his current job but thanked them for their interest. Not wanting to take no for an answer, they asked when he was due to be in England again. As it happened, we were just about to return to England for a holiday and when he

Dan-Air's first aircraft: a DC-3 accepted in lieu of a debt from Meredith Air Transport

told them this, they invited him to call into their City of London head office in New Broad Street. Feeling that there would be no harm in spending a couple of hours meeting them, and also feeling curious to hear what they had to say, he agreed on a time and date. Little did he realise that he was about to start a new chapter in his career.

The name Dan-Air was derived from Davies and Newman, the two directors who headed a firm of shipping brokers. In 1953, Dan-Air Services Ltd was registered as a subsidiary of Davies and Newman Ltd. Initially they owned a single Douglas DC-3 which they had inherited from Meredith Air Transport as collateral against money owed to Davies and Newman. At that time, the airline was based at Southend airport and operated ad hoc charters. In 1955 the airline moved its base to Blackbushe airport in Hampshire and established an engineering base at nearby Lasham airfield. By now, they owned two DC-3s, one Avro York and were acquiring three more Yorks from the RAF.

My father met the directors, and they outlined their plans. He was very impressed by all that he heard, and at the end of their meeting they offered him the position of chief engineer with an attractive salary and employment package. Dad spent some time mulling it over. He enjoyed working for Freddie Laker and moving across to Dan-Air, which was very much in its infancy, would be a gamble. All the same, the airline had good financial backing from the shipping division, and they had ambitious plans for expansion. He carefully weighed up the pros and cons, and then accepted the job.

As part of his relocation deal, the company provided us with a temporary home (a bungalow) until such time as we could find somewhere permanent to live. Dad's office was at the company's engineering base at Lasham airfield, and the bungalow was just a few miles away. However, knowing that he would also be spending time at their operating base at Blackbushe airport, they decided to buy a house called Tudor Lodge in the village of Blackwater, a small town in the northeast of Hampshire. It was a lovely home and I have very fond memories of the place. Blackwater was a quiet little village back then and we soon made friends and settled in.

By now, the airline owned two DC-3s, four Avro Yorks, a Bristol freighter and a de Havilland Heron. They were operating inclusive tour charter flights and had begun their first scheduled service route from Blackbushe to Jersey. I travelled as a passenger with my parents on the DC-3 which flew the inaugural service, returning later the same day. I wasn't too sure why the Dan-Air people on board were so excited about the trip, but I was very amused by all their antics when we got back to Blackbushe. There was a reception committee waiting in the terminal building with much cheering and popping of champagne corks when everyone disembarked. I decided that if this was normal behaviour on scheduled passenger services, then I was all for it.

Chapter Three

When the family had settled at our new home in Blackwater, I started at a new school. Over the years, my parents spent a lot of money on my education, but to my eternal shame, I wasted their investment. My dedicated avoidance of study and hard work was only exceeded by my determination to have a good time throughout my school years. Soon after settling in Blackwater, I was enrolled at Yateley Manor preparatory school in Hampshire. Fine establishment though it was, I seemed hell bent on proving they couldn't make a good student out of me. One thing I did learn, however, was that having a sense of humour was an asset and coming out with an amusing quip or response usually got me out of most tricky confrontations with the teachers.

One teacher, whose name I have forgotten, seemed immune to any attempts to make him smile and his classes were very serious affairs indeed. One thing he would not tolerate was for anyone to talk during his class. God help the hapless student who leaned over towards their neighbour to whisper something or other. This teacher had incredible hearing and I swear he would detect a pin drop from a hundred yards away. He would then spin on his heel and hurl a board rubber at the person who had spoken. His aim was remarkable and unless the intended victim had incredibly quick reactions, he never missed his target. For those not familiar with board rubbers, I should explain that they were used for erasing the chalk 'scribbling' from a blackboard. They were basically, a wooden block about six inches in length, that had a felt strip attached to one side which was used to rub the chalk off the board. The wooden block, when hurled at you, was very hard and very painful. This teacher was incredibly accurate and, if it had ever been introduced as an Olympic sport, I'm absolutely convinced he would have won a gold medal in the event. Needless to say, in today's world he wouldn't be winning any medals at all but would probably be locked up for child assault. Thankfully, I had very quick reactions and managed to duck out of harm's way whenever I was his intended target. Who knows—he may have been responsible for honing my quick reactions and excellent peripheral vision?

The headmaster of the school was a sports fanatic and his enthusiasm quickly rubbed off on me. His true love was rugby and I remember that when he refereed our games, he used to award classroom credits if we made a strong tackle against an opponent. His definition of a 'strong tackle' may well have been categorised as a bone jarring, life threatening assault by some more timid members of society. Indeed, they might have suggested that his credit scheme encouraged violent and aggressive behaviour. However, I certainly found it useful in offsetting some of my classroom debits for misbehaviour.

His other love was cricket, and while I was no good as a batsman, I was a useful bowler. An uncle of mine had shown me how to bowl a 'spinner' and this, coupled with the fact that I am left-handed, proved to be very unsettling for some of the batsmen. I earned myself a few very useful classroom credits for consistently bowling people out. However, my enthusiasm for cricket took a bit of a hammering one day. Midway through a match, I was fielding close to the receiving batsman, when he took a mighty swipe at the ball and connected with it beautifully. I remember raising my hand in front of my face as I started to throw myself to one side. I woke up on the bed in the Matron's office. There were several concerned looking people staring down at me, the matron and headmaster being amongst them. However, no sooner had I regained consciousness then their concern faded. I was told I was 'absolutely fine' and should now 'run along and get some fresh air.' Different times, as they say. My two black eyes and split lip got me a lot of street cred amongst my classmates, but at the same time severely dented my confidence in my own invincibility. It was the last time that I stood close to a batsman when fielding.

In 1960, the Government closed Blackbushe airport to commercial flights. Many independent airlines, including Dan-Air, had to find a new home. I was then in my final year at Yateley Manor preparatory school. I had literally come bottom of my class in the previous term, having done no study at all. If pupils had been graded on how much clowning around they did, then I would have scored far better, but unfortunately for me, they seemed to concentrate more on academic prowess and exam results. I finally woke up to the fact that if I didn't apply myself and do well in my end of term exams, I was going to be hard pressed to get into a decent school after leaving Yateley Manor. I put in a short but determined burst of hard work and study, which resulted in me getting good exam marks, coming second in my class and also being awarded a certificate for being the school's 'most improved student of the year.'

At the age of twelve, I got my first car. It cost £10 and was a magnificent 1935 Austin 10 with black paintwork (of course), flared wings topped with huge chrome headlights, a fold open windscreen and a roller blind for the rear passenger window that could be operated by the driver. Sheer luxury. Sadly this twelve-year-old who was addicted to 'Hot Rod' magazines from America, decided to modify the car. The wings were removed, the bonnet was removed, the engine block was painted with silver paint (influenced by the chromium plated engines depicted in Hot Rod magazines) the sidewalls of the tyres were painted white, dramatic red flames were painted down the sides of the car and finally, the exhaust silencer was removed in order to make the engine sound 'great.' I now had myself a totally unique Austin 10 Hot Rod. We named the car 'Fred', but

I've long forgotten why. Our house had a 150-yard drive running from the front gate down past the house to some garages and stables. There was space to turn around at both ends of the driveway (although the lawn edges suffered at the gate end if I wasn't careful.) According to the trip gauge on the car, I eventually clocked up over 600 miles on that driveway.

I sat a school entrance examination which resulted in me being awarded a place at Salesian College grammar school for boys. The college was in Farnborough, close to the airfield that hosted the world-famous air show. It was also the home of the Royal Aircraft Establishment (RAE), the Empire Test Pilot's school and the Air Accident Investigation Branch (AAIB). People literally came from all around the world to study and work at Farnborough because the RAE was held in very high regard by the world's aviation authorities.

With it being a new school for me, I initially got stuck in and performed well. However, once I had got the lay of the land, I soon slipped back to my old ways. Having fun and avoiding work was the top of my agenda. A couple of weeks before the end of term exams, I would frantically read and study until late into the night, trying to cram the whole term's work into my head just long enough to sit the exams. This worked well in the first year but was doomed to failure thereafter. Worse still, I had taken to playing truant on a regular basis, because hanging out in coffee bars and cinemas was much more to my liking than sitting in a classroom.

I was able to forge my father's signature perfectly, so I told my parents that the school had dropped the idea of producing weekly reports due to lack of parental interest. Unfortunately, I soon came unstuck. To my horror, my parents went to a school parent's evening where one of my teachers said, 'Robert has done reasonably well during the term bearing in mind how often he has been absent due to illness.' I was in deep trouble and was grounded for some time. Not surprisingly, they kept a watchful eye on me following that episode, but this had the effect of making me a resentful school attendee and I became rebellious. From that point, I was almost permanently in trouble. On Monday mornings, I often had to visit the headmaster's office for 'six of the best'.

I left the college with practically no qualifications. Bearing in mind the extent of my laziness, it was no surprise. Ironically, after my determined efforts to avoid any academic studies, I had to throw myself into studies anyway when I enrolled for night classes at Farnborough Technical College. I needed passes in mathematics and physics because I wanted to apply for an aircraft engineering apprenticeship. A burst of enthusiastic studying at night school followed and I finally got my qualifications. My career in aviation was about to begin.

In September 1965, I was one of twelve people who were selected to start a four-year aircraft engineering apprenticeship with the independent airline, British Eagle. The company had been formed after the war by Harold Bamberg, who proved to be a true pioneer in the travel industry. He began operations flying two Halifax bombers that had been converted to carry freight. These aircraft were used to transport fruit and vegetables around Europe. However, Bamberg's big break came when the Berlin Airlift began and, seizing the opportunity, he quickly acquired two more Halifaxes. All four aircraft then flew around the clock throughout the airlift. In 1951, having by now acquired a fleet of nine Avro Yorks, he was awarded a trooping contract flying between the UK and Singapore. The following year, Eagle moved to Blackbushe airport and built up a large fleet of Vickers Viking aircraft which they used for scheduled services.

Bamberg then bought out two travel companies, the Henry Lunn travel agency and the Polytechnic touring association. These were merged to form a new travel company he called Lunn Poly. Now Eagle became the first airline to be vertically integrated with its own travel agency and they pioneered all-inclusive package holidays. Through Lunn Poly, the British traveller could now book both their flight and accommodation as a combined package. The

Harold Bamberg on the flight deck of a British Eagle Britannia

idea quickly took hold and was a great success. In 1957, Bamberg formed Eagle Airways (Bermuda). Using a fleet of Vickers Viscounts, the company operated scheduled services between Bermuda and New York. The network was extended to include Montreal, Baltimore and Washington. Eagle then acquired the first of six Douglas DC-6 aircraft for use on long haul operations.

When in 1960, Blackbushe airport was closed, Eagle transferred their operation to London Heathrow. For some time, Eagle had been lobbying the Government to end the statutory monopoly enjoyed by the two state owned airlines, BOAC and BEA, on all scheduled domestic and international routes. Now they were joined in these lobbying efforts by British United Airways and the combined clout of these, the two largest independent airlines in the country, resulted in the Civil Aviation (Licensing) Act of 1960 being passed. Much to the annoyance of BOAC and BEA, this act abolished their monopoly.

1960 was the first time that more passengers crossed the Atlantic by air than by sea, a fact which alarmed the Cunard Steamship company. Determined to move with the times, Cunard bought a sixty percent shareholding in Eagle and formed a new company, Cunard Eagle Airways. In anticipation of being granted traffic rights for transatlantic scheduled services, Eagle put in an order with Boeing for two brand new Boeing 707 aircraft. This act, along with the Cunard merger, really made BOAC sit up and take notice. They were further annoyed when Bamberg pulled another clever trick out of the bag. He now owned some Bristol Britannia turboprop aircraft, which he promptly put onto the Bermuda register, which got him around restrictive licensing provisions normally imposed by the British Authorities. Because Bermuda was a British colony, no reciprocal approvals were needed from the overseas authorities. Now Cunard Eagle could fly scheduled services across the Atlantic to Bermuda and link up with Eagle Airways (Bermuda) schedules to America and Canada.

In 1961, Cunard Eagle became the first British independent airline to be awarded a licence to operate scheduled services from London and Manchester to New York, Boston and Washington. BOAC was furious and immediately lodged an objection. The licence was subsequently revoked, pending a review. Bamberg then put his first Boeing 707 onto the Bermuda register and started operating it between Bermuda and New York. Unknown to him, at the same time, BOAC secretly approached Cunard with a proposal to start a joint venture. To make the proposal irresistible to Cunard, BOAC offered to pay 70% of the required capital and to dedicate eight of their Boeing 707s to the operation. In plain English, Cunard had been made an offer they couldn't refuse. Bamberg was so disgusted that he bought back control of Cunard Eagle airways and formed a new company British Eagle International Airlines.

When I joined British Eagle in 1965, the company was operating seventeen Bristol Britannias and seven

A Bristol Britannia of British Eagle

Vickers Viscounts. They had orders in place for three BAC 1-11s and two Boeing 707-320s. Although I wasn't aware of it at the time, the company was in dispute with the Government and HMRC over a fourteen percent tax that was payable on imported foreign aircraft. This was a measure that had been put into place by the British government to encourage British airlines to buy British made aircraft. Eagle maintained that they should be excused from paying the levy on the grounds that there were no British made alternatives to the Boeing 707. At first, the government pointed to the Vickers VC10, but it was quickly demonstrated that the Boeing 707-320 had a greater payload and range than the VC10. When this argument appeared to cut no ice, Eagle pointed out that BOAC had been granted a waiver when they purchased their Boeing 707-336s, thereby setting a precedent. Incredibly, this point was also ignored by the authorities, and they continued to refuse to exempt the company from the import duty. In view of this refusal, Eagle put a delay on the delivery of their first Boeing 707.

Meanwhile, the twelve newly arrived apprentices were blissfully unaware of such highbrow negotiations.

All we knew was that we were starting a new adventure working for one of Britain's leading airlines. Starting any new job is exciting but starting a new job in aviation in 1965 was *really* exciting. The advances that were being made in aviation were just incredible. Passengers were now travelling in pressurised cabins flying high above the weather and covering ground at the rate of one mile every seven seconds. The American and Russian manned space programmes were well underway, and a supersonic passenger aircraft called Concorde was being developed that was due to fly in less than four years. Anything seemed possible and we were now part of that incredibly optimistic and ambitious industry.

We began our basic training at a school in Pinkwell Lane, Hayes, a short distance from Heathrow airport. We spent our time in a workshop using basic hand tools to make various test pieces out of steel or aluminium. With a chunk of metal fastened into a vice, we were tasked with hack sawing, chiselling, hammering, drilling and filing the bloody thing into a particular shape of carefully measured dimensions, so that it could be fitted exactly into another piece of metal that you had previously hack sawed and filed to some different carefully measured dimensions. As I was destined to be an aircraft engineer specialising in electrics—as opposed to engines or airframes or instruments—I failed to see how these metal-modifying skills were going to be useful. However, I was sensible enough to keep my opinions on the subject to myself. Thankfully, basic training was short, and we soon moved on to better things.

The four-year apprenticeship was designed to give us some experience of working in each of the airline's engineering departments. For example, a couple of us might be assigned to the powerplant bay for a few weeks. We would watch and learn as qualified engineers carried out various tasks on aircraft engines. Then the qualified engineers would get us to carry out the same tasks while they watched us closely to make sure we did everything correctly. It was a case of 'I'll show you how to do it, then you show me that you can do it.'

After a spell in one department, you would be assigned to a another for a short period: the instrument workshop, or the safety equipment workshop for example. It was a good system and gave us an excellent overview of the whole engineering set up. The company had three hangars located side by side and numbered two, three and four for some unfathomable reason. Each month we would spend three weeks working in the hangars. For the remaining week we attended a technical college in Southall, where we studied for a national certificate in aeronautical engineering (ONC and HNC). The week at technical college felt like being back at school again which, in effect, it was. Working in the hangars, on the other hand, was very new and exciting. We were standing slap bang in the middle of the busiest international airport in the world, and it felt good. During idle moments, I would stand outside the Eagle hangars and watch all the aircraft taxiing past and taking off and landing, and it felt good to know that I was a very small part of the action.

I'm sure the engineers and supervisors that we worked with were frequently exasperated by our ignorance, clumsiness and naivety, but they rarely showed it. The team of people they had at British Eagle's engineering base were, almost without exception, a pleasure to work with. There was also time for some fun now and then and all of us apprentices were put through 'initiation ceremonies' of various sorts. For example, the engineer you were teamed up with would rummage around in his toolbox for a moment and then suddenly exclaim 'Oh Hell, I've run out of long weights! Nip across to the storeroom and tell them you need a long weight, will you?'

When you asked, 'What's a long weight?' he would reply 'Don't worry, the storeman will know what you mean.'

You would dutifully trot across to the stores and relay the message to the storeman. He would give you a serious look for a moment and then he would disappear out of sight into the back of his storeroom. After you had been waiting for what seemed like an age, he would reappear. Looking you straight in the eye he would ask 'Was that long enough?'

You'd reply, 'Was what long enough?'

He would smile and say 'You asked for a long wait. Was that long enough?' Once it had finally dawned on you, you wandered off hoping that your blushes weren't too evident.

We all spent some time doing a stint in the wheel bay. This department dealt with wheel rims, brake units and, of course, tyres. Moving heavy brake packs and aircraft wheels and tyres around was physically very demanding, but the guy in charge of the place was a great bear of a man and incredibly strong. He could pick up all these heavy objects and throw them around as if they weighed nothing at all, which left you feeling like a wimp. Because of his great height and size, he looked very intimidating, but was in fact a gentle giant and would go out of his way to help anyone who needed it. I did, however, see the not-so-gentle side of him on one occasion. A guy who had a reputation for being a bit of a bully, was giving an apprentice a very hard time. Our gentle giant quietly told him that he was out of line and should back off. The guy made the mistake of saying something along the lines of 'Sod off, it's got nothing to do with you.' There was a moment of stunned silence.

The two men were outside the wheel bay at the time, standing next to a huge zinc tank. A drainpipe led from the hangar roof and was directed into the tank so that it collected any rainwater. A sturdy steel beam was suspended above, and this had a pulley and chain mechanism attached to it. When a new tyre had been put onto a wheel rim, it would be inflated using a high-pressure air hose and then the whole wheel assembly would be hoisted up using the pulley and chain and lowered into the water tank. They could then check for signs of bubbles appearing around the tyre, which would indicate a leaky seal. Our gentle giant didn't need the chain on this occasion. He grabbed a handful of the man's clothing and using just one arm, lifted him high into the air, and then dropped him fully clothed into the water tank. Without a word, he then turned on his heel, walked back into the wheel bay and got on with his work as if nothing had happened. None of the apprentices were bothered by that man again and although it may have been my imagination, I'm sure that he always gave that water tank a very wide berth whenever he walked past it.

Before I started my apprenticeship at Eagle, I had been living with my parents, who had by now moved to Camberley in Surrey. Once I started work at Heathrow, I needed to be closer to the airport and so I found some digs in Stanwell, Middlesex. The house belonged to a lovely elderly couple who made a great fuss of me. In the mornings, I came downstairs to an enormous, cooked breakfast, which was enough to feed an entire army. Fortunately, I was a very brave soldier and managed to eat it all without complaining. In the evening, another enormous meal would round the day off nicely and on Thursday evenings, they would even turn on *Top of the Pops* on BBC Television for me to watch. In other words, they spoiled me rotten.

I suppose there was a bit of a downside, in that the house was very close to the airport. While this was convenient in terms of catching a bus to work in the mornings, it also meant that you were more than aware of aircraft noise. At this time, all the long-haul airlines using Heathrow were flying very noisy aircraft. Boeing 707s and Douglas DC-8s might have been exciting examples of the early jet age, but they could make a person's ears bleed! The aircraft, being heavily laden with fuel for a transatlantic crossing, used nearly all the available runway to get airborne, and their climb performance left a lot to be desired. When I was lying in bed in Stanwell, it sometimes sounded like they were about to fly through my bedroom window. Eventually, repeated exposure allowed you to sleep through it all.

I won enough money on the premium bonds to buy a humble Austin A35, it was mine and I was the king of the road. I found that if I took the engine up to maximum revs in every gear, braked late and cornered fast, then I could give most people a run for their money. My reign of terror on the roads had begun; we apprentices tweaked and tuned our cars and motor bikes, fitted noisy 'straight-through' exhaust systems and generally behaved like we were Formula One drivers. During lunch breaks it wasn't unknown for some of us to have races around the perimeter road at Heathrow airport and on one memorable occasion, one of the guys completely miscalculated the final bend and his car crossed the finishing line on its roof. The engineering supervisor who was overseeing our group of apprentices at the time, ingeniously (and generously) turned the situation into a training exercise. We were all tasked with the job of making our colleague's car roadworthy again by the end of the day. We succeeded and although the bodywork clearly showed the battle scars, the car itself was mechanically sound by the time we had finished. News of our perimeter road races started to leak out and it wasn't too long before police cars started to appear at random but frequent intervals. They put an end to the Heathrow Grand Prix and the speed of cars driving around the airfield returned to a sensible level.

One job that we all hated was crawling up into the sharply tapered tail section of the Britannia. The rear cargo hold was below the floor of the passenger cabin, and you could move further aft along a catwalk by lying on your back and shuffling your body towards the tail. The problem was that you were lying directly beneath the toilets with their unavoidable drips and odours. It was affectionately known as 'Piss alley' and the phrase an apprentice did not want to hear was 'Right lad, it's your turn to go down Piss alley.'

In late 1968, the company was running an in-house course on the Boeing 707 to enable some of their engineers to gain a licence on the aircraft type. It was felt that it would be a good idea to include a couple of apprentices amongst the eager students and I was one of them. I had completed three years of my four-year apprenticeship and it was exciting to find myself on such a course. The syllabus was very detailed and the amount of information we were being given was rather intimidating. We each had an enormous manual sitting on the desks in front of us and they were full of detailed text and diagrams revealing the inner workings of the Boeing. A little voice in my head had been asking 'how the bloody hell am I

British Eagle aircraft parked at Heathrow following the failure of the company in November 1968

going to remember this lot?' but the question quickly became irrelevant.

On Wednesday 6th November 1968, I was seated at my desk and our instructor, John O'Nions, was at the front of the room explaining the intricate workings of the Boeing's electrical systems. Suddenly, someone stuck their head around the door and said, 'Sorry to interrupt, but I thought you ought to know that there is going to be a meeting over at the Eagle hangars.' He then paused before adding, 'apparently, we have gone bust.'

I remember it feeling like a bad dream. A huge crowd of familiar faces had gathered in common disbelief and shock. British Eagle was no more. I vaguely recall that some made stirring and heartfelt speeches saying that it was not going to happen and that they were prepared to forfeit their pensions to keep the company afloat. These sentiments were greeted with rapturous applause and shouted cries of agreement. However, everyone knew in their hearts that they were noble but futile gestures; the company had failed and over two thousand people lost their jobs that day. My big question was, 'Who the hell is going to employ someone who is only three quarters of their way through their apprenticeship training?'

Miraculously, there *was* someone: The Civil Air Transport Industry Training Board; a government body that I hadn't known existed but was my saviour. They took all the British Eagle apprentices under their wing and ensured that their training would be completed and financed in full. To say that we were relieved and grateful would be an understatement.

I completed the fourth year of my training at the same establishment my father had trained at all those years before, RAF Halton, in Bedfordshire. Each day, we would rendezvous in the car park of a hotel on the Bath Road, right alongside the runway at Heathrow airport. From there we would be driven in a chartered bus to RAF Halton. After a day of 'teach, learn and apply' (the Halton motto) we would be returned to Heathrow. They were long days and I usually spent most of the return bus journey dozing in my seat.

The training facilities at Halton were excellent and we were taught by both civilian and RAF instructors. We spent time in classrooms and workshops as well as working on military aircraft in the hangars: Hawker Hunter jet fighters, English Electric Canberra bombers, and an Avro Vulcan which seemed huge compared to the other aircraft. Sadly, none of these aircraft were going to fly again and the only aerial activity on the base was confined to small single-engine training aircraft. We spent some time stripping and reassembling various components on the Hunters and Canberras and, on one occasion, towed a Canberra out of the hangar, started it's Rolls-Royce Avon engines using the rather scary cartridge starters—a bang, followed by a loud whooshing sound and lots of smoke—and then carried out engine runs, during which the engines were taken up to maximum power and noise. Great fun! The day finally came when we had completed our four-year apprenticeship, all we needed to do now was get a job.

I completed my training at RAF Halton. One of our instructors (Eddy) is seated at the front in the centre and I am in the second row, last on the right. The aircraft are Hawker Hunters.

The Civil Air Transport Industry Training Board had arranged interviews for us with several airlines and my first was with Monarch. When we got to the Monarch base at Luton airport, we were greeted by a familiar face. Jim Rainbow had been our boss at British Eagle. Now he was the boss at Monarch Engineering and here he was, giving us a warm welcome. This eased the tension somewhat and made us feel less nervous about the interview ahead. As we took a walk through the hangar, we saw an ex-British Eagle Britannia that was now resplendent in Monarch airlines livery. I also recognised a few of the engineers who were working on her as they were former British Eagle employees. There was another ex-Eagle Britannia parked outside and the more I looked around, the more the whole set up looked like British Eagle Two. Everything the same but painted a different colour. The aircraft, the ground equipment, the vehicles, the passenger steps, the stewardesses' uniforms; everything was yellow. If you stood still for too long, you were in danger of being painted yellow. I was offered a job, but I left Luton feeling uncomfortable. It just reminded me so much of British Eagle, that I couldn't shake off the feeling that if Eagle had gone bust, then surely Monarch would end up going the same way. My misgivings were confirmed when Monarch *did* go bust, forty-eight years later! Just goes to show how little I knew about the airline business.

A few days later, I went for an interview with the American airline TWA, who had a small maintenance base at Heathrow at the time. They also offered me a job, but pointed out that it was only likely to be for the upcoming summer season and there was a good chance that I would be laid off for the winter. Not an attractive prospect.

It was third time lucky for me. I went for an interview with the British Overseas Airways Corporation (BOAC). Of course, being BOAC, the interview was followed by another interview and that one followed by yet another. Finally, having jumped over all their hurdles and fooled all their interviewers into thinking that I knew what I was talking about, they offered me a job, which I gratefully accepted. but I had one more hurdle to clear. When noting down all my personal details, they asked me what union I belonged to. When I replied that I had never felt the need to join a union, there was a stunned silence for a moment. They then told me that BOAC's engineering division was a closed shop, meaning that all engineering employees had to be in a union. When I casually replied that at least now they had given me a good reason to join a union, there was another stunned silence. I was told that I would have to formally apply for union membership, then go before a review board who would examine my case and deliberate as to whether they would accept me for union membership. If my application was rejected, then BOAC would not be able to offer me a job.

I went humbly before the review board, said yes sir and no sir in all the right places and, to my relief, was accepted into the union. As I was being employed as an electrical engineer, I became a member of the electrician's and plumber's trade union. This was unofficially known as 'Flash and Splash.' I was delighted when, some months later, the closed shop was ruled to be illegal. As soon as that was announced, I left the union and started my charitable donations.

It was in this climate that I started working for BOAC. I soon encountered petty posturing by trade union officials and a couple of occasions where actual strike action was imposed. The demarcation between trades had reached a laughable level and I remember one occasion when I was working on an aircraft in the hangar. I had been tasked with changing an electrical actuator and when I was midway through removing the old unit, I became aware that I was being watched by someone in the background. On looking around, I could see a person who I knew to be a militant union man glaring at me. He said, 'What do you think you are doing?" I replied that I was changing an actuator. He then said, 'How did you gain access to it?' I replied that I had undone several screws on the access panel and removed it. His response was, 'Do you realise that is a job for an airframe fitter?' At first, I thought he was joking, but when I laughed, he made it clear that he was deadly serious. In fact, he insisted that I replaced the panel and secured it with the screws. He would then call for an airframe fitter to come and take it off again. I don't think he appreciated my reply (which I'll admit was rather rude) and he launched into an irate 'do you know who I am' tirade and followed it up with the threat to bring all work on the aircraft to a halt. By now a few other people had started to take an interest in what was going on. Then, one of our supervisors sidled up to me and quietly said, 'Better do what he says Bob. We don't want this to escalate into industrial action.'

I replaced the panel and then watched as another engineer removed it again. I completed my work on the 'electrician's bit of the aircraft' and, with the crisis averted, everyone drifted away again. Presumably someone was later called to replace the access panel, but to be honest I had really lost interest by then.

I was based at Technical Block B, at London Heathrow airport. This was a large complex in the maintenance area, close to Hatton Cross. The hangar that I worked in was reserved for BOAC's Boeing 707 aircraft. On the other side of the building was an equally large hangar reserved for the Vickers VC10 fleet. All the engineers were 'fleeted', which means they either worked on VC10s or Boeing 707s, and I was a Boeing man. BOAC operated Boeing 707-336 aircraft, with Pratt and Whitney JT-3D engines and the 707-436, with Rolls-Royce Conway engines. They were rotated on a regular and routine basis for major overhauls. Once they were brought into the hangar, engineers worked on them around the clock until they were ready to be rolled out again.

Aircraft don't make any money when they are on the ground, hence the need for twenty-four-hour maintenance work. There were three work shifts: early, late, and night. We would work seven days consecutively on early shift, from 06:30 until 14:30. This was followed by three days off. Then we would work seven days on late shift from 14:30 until 22:30, followed by four days off. Then we switched back to early shift again and so on. Meanwhile, the night shift workers stayed permanently on the same shift, working from 22:30 until 06:30. This was the 'Vampire shift' (people with a chalky white complexion who only appeared at night). In this way, work on the aircraft never stopped and jobs were merely handed over from one shift to the next. It is an extremely disciplined and methodical process, and if a member of the public saw the extent to which an aircraft is stripped down and taken apart during a major maintenance check, they would understand the need for such a disciplined approach.

Whenever one of the Boeing 707s had undergone a C check (a very comprehensive check) it had to undergo a full air test before being returned to passenger service. These air tests were carried out by BOAC pilots who were specially rated for the task. A couple of ground engineers were taken on the flight to observe the performance of the aircraft and its various systems. They would write notes as the flight progressed and the operating crew—two pilots and a flight engineer—would add their own comments and observations. Once the air test had ended and the aircraft had returned to base, the crew would give a thorough verbal and written debriefing to all interested parties. Provided the aircraft had performed well and had met the required performance criteria, then it's C of A (Certificate of Airworthiness) would be renewed, and it could be returned to passenger service.

These air tests were not for the faint hearted and nervous flyers need not apply. In fact, I was surprised just how many of my engineering colleagues flatly refused to go on air tests when asked. This suited me because I could volunteer without fear of competition. The aircraft were really put through their paces and taken to the very limit of their safe handling envelope. For example, an engine would be shut down in flight, then the aircraft's rate of climb through various altitude bands checked and timed. At a predetermined stabilising altitude, a second engine would be shut down to see if the aircraft could maintain altitude on its two remaining engines. After all the engines had been restarted, the aircraft's low speed handling would be explored, and the aircraft slowed until the stick shaker operated, warning that the aircraft was close to stalling speed. After recovering, the aircraft would be accelerated to the other end of the speed envelope by taking it up to MMO. This is the percentage of Mach where a change to the handling characteristics takes place as localised airflow approaches the speed of sound, creating shock waves that alter the aircraft's controllability. The 707 had a quirky and alarming characteristic in the form of a sudden and violent 'Mach tuck' if MMO was inadvertently exceeded. The aircraft's nose would suddenly pitch down, causing the speed to increase further. If the pilot failed to respond immediately and correctly, this could result in a further rapid speed increase, loss of control and structural breakup. Not to be recommended.

When the Boeing 707 first appeared on the aviation scene, a gentleman by the name of D P (Dai) Davies was

A Boeing 707-436 of BOAC

the head of the flight test team at the British Civil Aviation Authority. He carried out a series of test flights in the 707, prior to the type appearing on the British register and made several mandatory modifications. Some of these were very significant, such as the fitting of a larger vertical fin to improve the handling at Vmcg (Velocity of Minimum Control on Ground). During the take-off run, Vmcg is the minimum speed at which the aircraft remains controllable by using the primary flight controls alone in the event of an engine failure on the ground. Davies disputed the Boeing figures and felt that a slight increase in the size of the vertical fin was required. Boeing eventually agreed with his findings and the larger fin became standard on all subsequent 707s and were retro fitted to the early model aircraft already flying. He also insisted on fitting a 'stick nudger (not to be confused with a stick pusher) for all British 707s.

One of the items on our British air tests, was to switch the yaw dampers off and then deliberately induce a Dutch roll. Once the out of phase gyrations had increased to a 'sporty' level, the yaw dampers were switched back on to check that they ironed out the yawing and rolling gyrations. During my spell on the 707, Dai Davies conducted one of the BOAC air tests. Knowing that the Dutch roll manoeuvre was his pet thing on the 707, the rest of the crew were apprehensive, and he certainly didn't disappoint anyone. Dai carried out a series of ever increasing rolling and yawing manoeuvres, until the aircraft was adopting the sort of attitudes and bank angles that most people thought a large transport aircraft was incapable of. Eventually, the flight engineer let out a loud expletive, reached up to the overhead panel and switched the two yaw dampers back on. As the aircraft began to recover, he muttered 'this bloody thing isn't cleared for aerobatics you know!' Dai gave him a withering look but decided to let it go. The rest of the crew breathed a sigh of relief and made a mental note to buy the flight engineer a beer when back at Heathrow.

I really loved doing air tests and found them exhilarating. It was always fascinating to discover just how manoeuvrable a large passenger aircraft is and how much it can be thrown around when 'the gloves are off.'

While I was working in Technical Block B on the Boeing 707, a huge building was being erected nearby, intended to house the giant Boeing 747 that was about to take the aviation world by storm. It is hard to explain to a person who grew up routinely seeing Boeing 747s flying around, just what a huge leap in size that aircraft was when it first appeared on the scene. BOAC took delivery of their first Boeing 747 in April 1970 and I distinctly remember the first time I saw one up close. Everyone knew that it was going to be big, but just how big still came as a shock. It seemed enormous, which of course it was. I climbed aboard and walked around the inside of the aircraft as if in a dream. Before long I found myself working on the 747 more often than I worked on the 707. No matter how often I saw it or worked on it, the Boeing 747 never got any smaller. You got used to seeing it, but you never stopped marvelling at its sheer size.

Chapter Four

When my Dad joined Dan-Air as their chief engineer, the company's chief inspector was Frank Horridge. They became good friends and shared a love of flying small aircraft. Frank had started a company at Lasham airfield called Air Tows which, as the name suggests, towed gliders up to their desired altitude. As Lasham was the busiest gliding site in the UK, Frank's aircraft were kept hard at work. He was also a director and part owner of the Three Counties Aero Club, based at Blackbushe. I had worked there as a holiday job during the summer when I was a schoolboy and got to know the chief instructor, Derek Johnson, and his wife, Elsie, who was the receptionist and admin person. They were a lovely couple, and I really enjoyed their company. I spent the days working in the hangars at the western end of the airfield with an engineer called Pete Townsend. Now, several years later, I came to a firm decision. I wanted to learn to fly.

I was about to celebrate my twenty-first birthday. My parents offered to pay for some flying lessons and I couldn't have asked for a better gift! On 3 February 1970, I took my first lesson, with Derek Johnson, in G-AXBE, a Beagle Pup. I was totally hooked; I loved every second of it and didn't want it to end. *This* was what I really wanted to do. I didn't want to fix aircraft any longer, I wanted to fly them!

To save money, I switched from the Beagle Pup to an older Piper J3 Cub. In this aircraft the student pilot sat in the rear cockpit, with the instructor seated in front—

I learnt to fly at the Three Counties Aero Club at Blackbushe. Initially on a Beagle Pup (above) and later on a Piper J3 Cub (below)

when it came to flying solo, this had to be done from the rear cockpit, so it was better to get a student used to flying from that position to begin with. Anybody who has flown a tailwheel aircraft will confirm that they are a good deal trickier to handle on the ground than tricycle gear types. Both take-off and landing require your full attention and some nifty footwork, particularly when landing in a crosswind. My instructor Derek Johnson used to joke that the landing wasn't over until you had climbed out of the aircraft and returned to the clubhouse. What he meant by that, of course, was that pilots have been known to make an excellent approach and touchdown on the runway, but then allow their concentration to wane just a little as the aircraft begins to slow down. Next thing they know, the tail has started to swing and before they can catch it, there is a screeching of tortured tyres. They have performed a ground loop and find themselves facing the way they have just come. I'm delighted to say, thanks to Derek's timely prompts and warnings after I landed, I never did suffer the embarrassment of a dreaded ground loop.

Derek was an excellent teacher, and it was only after I encountered less talented instructors in later years that I appreciated just how good he was. One of his greatest gifts was the ability to know exactly how to get the best out of a student. I was a rather shy person back then and lacked self confidence in everyday life. Derek somehow knew how to build my confidence subtly and progressively. He knew when praise was appropriate and when criticism should be metered out. He knew when I needed a kick up the backside because I wasn't applying myself enough, but he also knew when I needed encouragement when I was feeling despondent, such as in my early untidy landing efforts. Most of all, he achieved all this in a relaxed atmosphere of good humour and enjoyment. Derek loved flying and it showed. That love of flying was extremely infectious and I will always be very grateful to him.

They say you never forget your first solo flight, and it's true. On 28 March 1970, Derek said we were going to practice some take-offs and landings. After we had done a couple of touch and goes, he said 'make the next one a full stop landing.' When we had landed and stopped, he told me to taxi back to the holding point in preparation for another take off. Once we were at the holding point, he climbed out of the aircraft, turned to me, and said 'Off you go then. Just one circuit and then back to the parking apron. Remember, if you aren't happy with the approach at any stage, then go around and try again.' Suddenly, there was no bulky figure impeding my view ahead and I didn't have to crane my head from side to side to see the instruments. It was just me, solo, and I remember it alright; it was fabulous.

The instructors at Three counties Aero Club knew only too well that I was keen to fly as often as possible. They also knew that I could rarely afford it, so they put some free flying my way now and then. Occasionally one of the club's aircraft had been taken to Lasham airfield for maintenance. One of the instructors would phone me and ask if I was available to fly the aircraft from Lasham to Blackbushe. They would then take me by car to Lasham and drop me off there to fly the aircraft back to Blackbushe. It was a very short distance between the two airfields, but they wouldn't complain when it took a surprisingly long time for me to complete the journey. They knew I had taken full advantage of my 'free' flight and just so long as I didn't take too long, they said nothing.

My love of aerobatics had initially been sparked by Derek Johnson, who hadn't needed to be asked twice when I suggested he demonstrate some aerobatic manoeuvres at the end of one of our flying lessons together. I now booked myself some aerobatic lessons with him—exercise twenty-one in official parlance—and we flew several times together in Beagle Pups and a Tiger Moth. I absolutely loved the feeling of freedom and control when swooping and soaring through a series of loops, rolls and stall turns. Flying aerobatics calls for greater feel and co-ordination on the controls than more sedate and conventional manoeuvres, and when you hit the sweet spot and get it just right, it is immensely satisfying.

Mind you, get it wrong and it is stomach churning and embarrassing in equal measure.

I began to think about my future. I was getting no satisfaction at all from my job at BOAC. I was a poor engineer and couldn't get motivated at all. Conversely, every time I took to the air at the controls of an aircraft, I felt as though I'd come alive. I absolutely loved the physical act of piloting an aircraft and, what's more, I thought that I might be good at it. To fly for a living, I needed a Commercial pilot's licence and that cost a shed load of money—much more than I could afford. There was only one practical solution: I needed to get sponsored by an airline.

At this time, BOAC and BEA had their own pilot training school at Hamble, near Eastleigh in Hampshire. Cadet pilots at the school were nicknamed 'Hamble Hamsters' and were much envied by wannabe commercial pilots. The training facilities at the school were excellent, but what made the trainees so envied was that successful graduates came out with a commercial licence and a job at either British European Airways (BEA) or British Overseas Airways Corporation (BOAC) the two government owned airlines. Sadly, I was told that BEA and BOAC had overestimated the number of pilots they needed and, as soon as the current course had completed their training, the college would to be temporarily closed.

I discovered that three independent airlines were offering pilot sponsorship schemes and I applied to all three. I heard from the first that they had already filled the places on their scheme for the current year, but the second airline I applied to, Dan-Air, invited me to an interview with Captain Arthur Larkman and Captain Bob Atkins. They were Director of Flight Operations and Chief Pilot respectively and I was very nervous as they questioned me. Midway through the interview, one of them—I can't remember which—asked me if I knew anyone in Dan-Air. After a brief pause, I said that my father was Managing Director of Dan-Air Engineering. There was another pause and then Arthur Larkman smiled. I left their office feeling very unsure of the impression I had made. Nevertheless, I soon received the best possible news; I had been offered a sponsorship under the following conditions:

- The airline would pay for all my training for a commercial pilot's licence and instrument rating.
- If, at any stage of the course, my training was terminated because I failed to reach the required standard, I must repay all outstanding costs.
- Upon successful completion of my training, I would be offered a position as a pilot with Dan-Air.
- I had to repay all my training costs in full to the airline within ten years (interest free).
- I had to agree to stay with the company for a minimum period of five years.
- If I left after that time, I had to immediately repay any outstanding training debt.

I immediately signed the agreement, before they had a chance to change their mind. The next step for me was to decide which training establishment I was going to choose. There was a large pilot training school called Oxford Aviation Training School based at Kidlington. I had sent off for an information pack and it all looked very impressive, but the prices were also impressive and, bearing in mind I would have to repay the training costs in full, it made sobering reading.

An alternative was Air Service Training (AST) in Perth, Scotland. There was really nothing in it as far as cost was concerned, but there were differences elsewhere. Whereas Oxford used Piper aircraft, at Perth they used Cessna 150s for single-engine flying and Cessna 310s for multi engine. However, what really attracted me was AST's location: Oxford wasn't many miles from where I had been living and working but Perth was way up in Scotland. The comparative isolation appealed to me for one very good

reason. I realised that I was really going to have to knuckle down and apply myself if I was going to get through the course. I can resist anything except temptation and knew that I might easily get distracted from my studies if I was near friends and familiar pubs and clubs. Scotland it was then!

While working my notice period at BOAC I was acutely aware that once I received my final pay cheque, there would be no more money coming in for some considerable time. Accommodation and food were covered by the course fees at Perth, but all other expenses were going to be coming out of my savings. Although I had been earning a good salary at BOAC, I was far more skilled at spending money than I was at saving it, so there wasn't much in the kitty. As soon as I finished my last shift at BOAC, I sold my car to top up my meagre savings. The car had been nothing to write home about, so the money I got for it did little to swell my bank account. I consoled myself with the thought that I wouldn't have the time or the opportunity for any socialising in Scotland anyway. On a cold and overcast day in November 1972, I boarded a train and began the long journey to Perth and the start of a new aviation career. I was simultaneously nervous, excited, and very keen to get started.

Air Service Training marketed themselves as 'Britain's

Air University.' They had been established for many years and trained both pilots and aircraft engineers. They had contracts with several airlines around the world and the cross section of students reflected this. We were all living on the airfield in identical accommodation blocks that looked rather like an army barracks. We each had our own room with bed, desk and built-in modular shower unit. They were like the rooms you might find in a budget hotel—cheap but not cheerful—and this was to be my home for many months.

On my first day I was issued with the required books, and I staggered back to my room clutching a pile of manuals so high that I could barely see where I was going. The thought of having to read, absorb and memorise the contents filled me with dread.

At that time, only five of the students at the school were British. Now that I had arrived, that made six of us. There were students from the Caribbean, Australia, the Middle East, South Africa and a large group from Nigeria, but the biggest group was from Japan. With so few British students, I had met all of them by the end of the first day. Two of them had already started the course that I was due to join so we quickly swapped names and background histories. Joe was English, married and self-sponsoring his way to a commercial licence. Hugh was Scottish, single and also self-sponsoring. Hugh was living with his parents, who had a home close to the airfield, and Joe's lovely wife had secured a job at a hotel in nearby Perth so that she could be close to her husband while he was doing his training. Her job included free board at the hotel, so that was where they were both going to be staying. Unusually, both those guys were living 'off camp' while all the other students were staying in accommodation blocks on the airfield.

I met the other three British students later in the canteen. One was just days away from completing his course and was waiting his final flight test before being awarded his instrument rating. He had been sponsored by Cambrian Airways and was destined to fly the Vickers Viscount on domestic scheduled services. The next guy was another self-sponsoring student by the name of Rick Smart, who was also nearing the end of his course. The last of the half dozen was Dougal, who was a bit of a character. He too, was a self-sponsored student. Who would have thought that so many people had enough dosh to put themselves through a course for a commercial pilot's licence? I had met five on my first day!

There are several ground school subjects that are covered in the syllabus for the commercial pilot's licence and a high mark is needed to obtain a pass in each one. The rule at the time was that if you failed two of the many subjects on the exam syllabus, you could keep the passes and resit the failed subjects. However, if you failed more than two subjects, it was a total wipe-out and you had to resit the whole lot again. This had been Dougal's downfall. Apparently, he had passed every single subject at one time or another but had never managed it with less than three 'fails' along the way. Consequently, his ground studies kept reverting back to square one. I got the impression that the school was worried he would end up in the Guinness Book of Records for failed exam attempts.

The next two guys I met lived at the other end of my block. They had started at the school a couple of months before and were, therefore, old hands and knew their way around the place. They quickly became my closest mates at the school. Greg Harrison was from Botswana and was being sponsored by the International Civil Aviation Organisation (ICAO). Alex Hamel Smith was from Trinidad and was sponsored by British West Indian Airways (BWIA). They were both great guys who helped to relieve the tension and I was really glad to meet them. Not long afterwards, we had a late starter who joined our little team. He was Bob Smart, an Australian who was great company and soon became a welcome addition to our gang. I can honestly say that those three guys helped to keep me sane throughout my time at Perth. The course there was intense and inevitably there were periods of ups and downs. Thankfully we were rarely synchronised when it came to the 'downs' so whoever was suffering the temporary crisis could be bolstered by the other guys. Hours spent in the classroom felt like days and were very hard work, but hours at the controls of the aircraft felt like minutes and were very good fun. I knew the technical studies were a very necessary part of the course, but it was the act of physically flying the aircraft that gave me the buzz. Unfortunately, it wasn't too long before I was faced with something that I had never encountered before: a full-blown personality clash.

There were some great instructors at AST but, unfortunately, the one assigned to me wasn't one of them. I shall rename him Mr Sourman, but AST students of the time will know exactly who I'm talking about. The cockpit of a Cessna 150 is very narrow. In fact, it is the narrowest of all the general aviation aircraft types; a mere 38 inches wide. Consequently, two average sized people need to show each other a little consideration when flying, otherwise they will be quite literally rubbing shoulders. Sourman was a large man, but he made no effort to budge up or keep his arms close to his sides. He would wriggle himself into a comfortable position and then his student had to squeeze into what little space was left. My first flight with him was on my birthday, the fourth of December. We carried out some general handling exercises. A few days later, we flew together again, and this time did some spinning and stalling. It must have impressed him because at the end of it he said that I should apply for a shortened flying syllabus in recognition of my previous experience. I told him that I had already done so and that it had been approved.

I think we probably did a couple more trips together before it all started to go downhill. By then, I had discovered that Sourman had a simple instructing technique. If I was flying the aircraft well, he would sit in stoney silence. He never praised a well-handled manoeuvre or nicely flown exercise and I'm pretty sure that I managed to achieve one occasionally. If he was frowning and silent, I knew I was doing a good job. However, if I did something that was not to his liking, he shouted, and if this didn't do the trick, then he would shout even louder. I don't think anybody responds well or performs well under those conditions. I know that I did not, and I would get so wound up before flying with him that I just wasn't performing well. I would psyche myself up before each flight and tell myself 'OK, I'm going to show him how to fly a bloody aircraft perfectly today.' But it never happened. By the end of each flight, I would be totally demoralised. My dislike of the man began to grow, and I couldn't help thinking that he could learn a great deal about instructing techniques from Derek Johnson, my old instructor at Blackbushe.

Our flying sessions were a mixture of dual, with an instructor aboard, and solo when we set off on our own. Needless to say, with my deteriorating relationship with Sourman, I didn't look forward to the dual sessions, but found the solo trips a blessed relief. There were occasions when we didn't exactly stick to the flying syllabus, but instead added some exercises of our own creation. This usually happened when a few of us had gone off to do some solo flying in our separate aircraft. We would have prearranged our plan of action and soon after taking off and leaving the vicinity of the airfield, we would rendezvous at a particular location and then set off for some fun. Low flying around the hills and valleys was always a thrill or, alternatively, we would head for a loch that was in an isolated spot. Picking up to maximum speed as we descended towards it, we would fly low across the water and then skim over the top of the trees at the far shore. For obvious reasons, this was known as a 'Dambuster beat up.' Of course, I wouldn't have dreamed of doing anything so childish or irresponsible, I'm merely recording what others occasionally did.

My last recorded flight with Sourman took place on 14 June 1973. By that time, I had been flying with him for over six months and things had gone from bad to worse. I had grown to hate the man and it had become blindingly clear that he felt the same way about me. My colleagues Greg, Alex and Bob were acutely aware of the friction between Sourman and me because you could cut the atmosphere with a knife whenever we were in the same room together. My flying skills had deteriorated, and I was even having trouble concentrating on my ground studies. I knew that I had to do something about it.

Bob Critchley was the chief flying instructor, and I went to see him in his office. I had been pacing the floor in my room for ages, as I decided what action I needed to take about my predicament. Once I'd made my decision I went to Critchley's office and knocked on his door. Now that I stood in front of him, I was as nervous as hell, but determined to have my say. I told him that I just couldn't get on with Sourman and far from learning and improving under his instruction, the opposite was happening. Critchley then told me that Sourman had already had a word with him about me and he had concerns about my performance and my attitude. He had even had a moan about my appearance, saying that I could do with a haircut and needed to smarten up a bit.

Bob Critchley then spent a few moments telling me what an experienced instructor Sourman was and how he had successfully trained loads of student pilots over the years. Just when I thought he was about to tell me that I was entirely to blame for the situation, he went on to say 'Well, it seems that there is a personality clash between you two, so I shall be assigning you to another instructor.' The feeling of relief that I experienced was enormous. I felt as though a weight had been lifted from my shoulders. With the change of instructor, it was as if a magic wand had been waved over my head. No longer did I have to squeeze into a cockpit alongside the dreaded Sourman. My self-confidence soared and I began to enjoy my dual flying again.

Once a student pilot has learned the basics of flying in visual flight conditions, then the next step is to learn how to fly in Instrument Meteorological Conditions (IMC). In other words, how to fly the aircraft on instruments and without any visual reference with the outside world. A pilot can lose sight of the horizon if the aircraft enters cloud, or the visibility deteriorates. Once that happens, it doesn't take long before the pilot becomes disoriented. The sensations felt through the 'seat of your pants' can trick you into thinking that the aircraft's attitude has altered in some way. If you turn your head, this can trigger the sensation that the aircraft has started to turn left or right. Normally a glance out of the window would reinforce or reject that belief that you are turning. Without that visual cue to help you, confusion, disorientation and vertigo will set in. Many aircraft have crashed over the years when a pilot has become confused in this way. The solution is to master instrument flying.

Losing sight of the 'real' horizon out of the window is replaced by referring to an 'artificial' horizon mounted in the aircraft's instrument panel. A seat of the pants sensation that the aircraft has started to climb can be checked by referring to the altimeter and vertical speed indicator. A perceived turn can be checked by looking at the compass and turn indicator, etc. To correctly interpret all the various instruments is very difficult at first and it takes a great deal of practice in order to be able to fly accurately in this way. One very useful tool for learning instrument flying is a flight simulator. Nowadays, the simulators are remarkably realistic and can reproduce an aircraft's handling characteristics over a range of flight conditions. At Perth however, they were using very antiquated and basic device called a Link Trainer—popularly known as the 'sweat box.'

The student would climb into the cramped and claustrophobic 'box' or cockpit and the canopy would be slid into place over their head. There were no windows, so the pilot couldn't see anything outside the cockpit. They had a radio link with an instructor who sat outside the sweat box and two-way conversation was established using headsets and microphones. The instructor would act as your air traffic controller and would issue clearances and instructions for your simulated flight. It was hard work at first, but gradually it all started to make sense. After a while, I really started to enjoy the challenge of accurately flying the increasingly complex exercises that were thrown at us by the instructors. Next, of course, you started practicing your instrument flying in the real thing. In other words, in the aircraft.

I really enjoyed the challenge of instrument flying and although the old Link Trainers were useful for learning the basic principles and techniques that you needed to employ, the satisfaction came from doing it 'for real' in the aircraft. When you went flying to practice your instrument skills, the instructor would either clip a screen into place on the inside of your windscreen or you would wear a training hood that restricted your field of vision to just the instrument panel in front of you.

While I was at Perth, they took delivery of a brand-new Aerobat that had been built in Reims, France. There had been times in the past when students wanted to see how high they could climb in a single-engine Cessna and, over time, the altitude record had been broken again and again. I reckoned that a brand-new Cessna, with only delivery mileage on the clock, was going to give us the best possible aircraft for a record attempt. I asked Alex to be my safety pilot and he said he was up for the challenge. Off we went for our mutual instrument flying exercise. Fast forward to the point where we had reached 10,000 feet. I turned to Alex and said 'okay, I'm going to stay under the hood and continue to fly with reference to instruments only. If my flying starts to get a bit ragged and inaccurate, then that will be an indication that I am suffering from hypoxia due to the lack of oxygen at high altitude. As soon as you see signs of that, you shout out that it's time to quit. Does that sound like a plan?' He said it did, although, at this stage, we would have been hard pressed to spell hypoxia, let alone actually recognise it.

The flight droned on, and we slowly climbed ever higher. I had been trying to locate and use thermal activity over the Cairngorms, but there was little sign of that. I had checked for carburettor icing periodically as we had climbed through some cumulus clouds, but now we were in clear skies with the clouds well below us. To cut a long story short, we got the aircraft up to an altitude of 16,200 feet. Alex took a photograph showing the altimeter and the aircraft's registration, G-BAIN, and we congratulated each other on being the new altitude record holders at AST Perth.

It had taken us so long to complete the climb, that we were in danger of getting back late from our planned session. To make things worse, as we descended through a layer of cloud, the windscreen was so cold from our time spent at high altitude, that ice formed and completely obscured our forward view for a while. Eventually the rather feeble cabin heater/windscreen defroster did manage to clear enough ice from the screen so that I could see where we were going. After landing, we hastily removed the rest of the ice before anyone saw it. However, because we had been forced to stooge around a few miles from the airfield, waiting for the cabin heater to clear the ice, we were quite late back to base and got a tremendous bollocking.

Chapter Five

A big moment during your pilot training is the day you fly a twin-engine aircraft for the first time. Now, you feel you are really moving up to the next level. The school at Perth had a fleet of Cessna 310 aircraft: a sexy looking beast with a long, streamlined nose, raked wingtip fuel tanks and an overall look that seemed to shout speed! The two Continental engines had a powerful sounding growl and when taken up to full power for take-off, they gave out a very loud and satisfying roar. The aircraft could cruise up to 180 knots, but at the school we operated them at a reduced power setting for fuel economy.

Apart from the fact that it had twice as many engines as a Cessna 150, it was a far more complex aircraft with variable pitch propellors, retractable landing gear, airframe and prop de-icing and full IFR radio navigation equipment. A veritable mini airliner. It was also a very stable aircraft which made it an excellent instrument platform. Once the power was correctly set and the aircraft had been carefully trimmed, it stayed put. This was a very welcome characteristic for a pilot who was trying to get their head around the demands of instrument flying.

The instructor that I was teamed up with was Hector Skinner. He was excellent and had the ability to really put me at my ease, while at the same time keeping the pressure on just enough to ensure that I didn't feel tempted to give less than one hundred percent effort. He gave praise when praise was due and criticism whenever that was appropriate. An excellent balance and one that gets the very best performance from a person. Thank you, Hector!

If the Cessna 310 had a weakness, then it was the landing gear. The nose leg looked rather spindly and, as it turned out, was. Pretty much every single aircraft in the Perth fleet of 310s had done a wheels-up landing at some time or other. This wasn't because anybody had forgotten to put the gear down prior to landing, but when the gear had been selected down on the approach, one or more of the gear legs had failed to extend or lock in the down position. When a pilot selected the gear down, they looked for 'three greens.' The green lights that illuminated when all three gear legs were locked correctly in the 'down' position. If a green light did not illuminate, it meant that there was a problem. There was a backup system whereby you could manually wind the gear legs down using a handle under the pilot's seat. If the leg was quite simply jammed for whatever reason, then neither the electric motor nor the mechanical crank handle would solve it. That resulted in a gear up landing. I witnessed one of these not long after I had arrived at the school.

We were in a classroom doing ground studies when the word went around that one of the 310s had a gear problem. There were three people on board, an instructor and two students, and they had circled around for some time trying various methods to extend the gear successfully, including pulling positive G manoeuvres, but to no avail. Eventually the instructor shut down one engine and then turned it over on the starter motor to get the two-bladed prop horizontal. This would ensure that it remained clear of the ground and would remain undamaged on touchdown. He then came in for the landing, by which time a large crowd had gathered and fought for a good ringside seat. As he crossed the runway threshold, he shut down the remaining engine, motored the prop into the horizontal position and then landed. He did a great job. Nobody was hurt, the aircraft was relatively undamaged and after the engineers had replaced some skin panels and a couple of radio aerials, it was back into service in no time.

For multi-engine training at Perth we used the sleek and stable Cessna 310. If it had a weakness, it was the nose wheel

My very first flight in a 310 at the start of my twin-engine training was great fun and I thoroughly enjoyed it. However, when we selected the gear down on the approach to land, we only got two green lights instead of three. We recycled the gear up and then down again. Same result. Only two greens. I then cranked away at the manual gear extension handle and this time we were successful. With three greens we made a normal landing and completed a successful training detail.

There were three runways at Perth, two were asphalt, and the third was grass. There was a suspicion that the grass runway was knocking hell out of the landing gear on the 310s and causing all the gear problems. It was decided that the grass runway should not be used by the 310s unless the direction of strong winds put the asphalt runways out of limits. This seemed to do the trick, because there were no more wheels-up landings for the remainder of my time at Perth.

The flight training throughout the course is intensive. By the end of it, a student pilot will have clocked up over two hundred hours in the air; mostly in single-engine aircraft. It will have included a minimum number of hours flying at night and a minimum number of hours instrument flying. There will have been hours spent in the flight simulator and around thirty hours flying a complex aircraft with multi engines, variable pitch propellors and retractable landing gear. There will have been numerous flight tests along the way, including general flying tests, night flying tests and an initial instrument rating flight test. Finally, on 24 January 1974, Captain Rees of the Civil Aviation Authority was the examiner who passed me on my initial instrument rating flight test. I had done it. The Civil Aviation Authority issued me with a commercial pilot's licence and instrument rating (CPL/IR) licence number: 90703.

I drove away from Perth in my newly acquired mark one Ford Capri which was loaded up with all the junk I had collected over the previous year. I was heading down to London where Margaret, my Australian girlfriend was living. She was sharing a place in Barnes with a couple of other girls, and we were planning a party to celebrate my escape from a Scottish jail. I had a long drive ahead, about eight hours, but felt on top of the world.

I had first met my girlfriend a couple of months before I moved to Scotland to start my training. One night I had been on a pub crawl with a few friends and one of

UNITED KINGDOM

CIVIL AVIATION AUTHORITY

COMMERCIAL PILOT'S LICENCE

AEROPLANES/~~HELICOPTERS AND GYROPLANES~~

Licence No. 90703

Name WILLIAMS
Robert John

Address
90 Watchetts Drive
Camberley
Surrey

Nationality British

Date of Birth 4 December 1948

Place and Country Crickhowell United Kingdom

Issued in accordance with the provisions of the Civil Aviation Act, 1949, and of Annex 1 to the Convention on International Civil Aviation signed on 7th December, 1944, and subject to the terms and conditions of the Air Navigation Order for the time being in force, the holder is entitled to exercise the privileges of a Commercial Pilot's licence ~~until~~ from

30 January 1974 to 29 January 1979

Signature of Issuing Officer
For the Civil Aviation Authority.

Date and Stamp 30 January 1974

The holder may, at all times, re-enter Great Britain and Northern Ireland upon production of this document.

Signature of Holder

TL Form 150/3

the places we visited was a hotel called the Duke of York, in Yorktown, Camberley. There were two Australian girls working at the bar there and we enjoyed a bit of banter with them before setting off on the next leg. A couple of pubs and several drinks later, I persuaded my friends that we should return to the Duke of York to further improve Anglo-Australian relations. That was where it all started and, as the saying goes, one thing led to another. Now, well over a year later, my romance with Margaret was still on, and I was about to start my new career as an airline pilot.

As with most things in life, timing is important in aviation. That well-worn phrase 'in the right place at the right time' is always applicable. I had now successfully completed the training for my commercial pilot's licence and was about to start work with Dan-Air, one of the leading independent airlines in Europe. They were going to put me on an in-house type rating course for the Avro 748 aircraft and they had told me that once I completed my conversion training, I was to be based at London Gatwick. Life was looking pretty good but, unfortunately, one thing that wasn't so good was my timing.

At the end of 1973, The Organisation of the Petroleum Exporting Countries (OPEC) agreed to stop selling oil to nations that had supported Israel and the Yom Kippur war. The countries initially targeted were the USA, Canada, Japan, Netherlands and the UK. In the space of just a few weeks, the price of a barrel of oil had increased by over 200%. In America, because of a weakening dollar, the price had increased by 300%. This had a massive effect on both the airline industry and me: Dan-Air cancelled all their planned courses until further notice. Suddenly, I was a pilot whose feet were staying firmly on the ground!

I took unpaid work at Dan-Air's pilot training centre in Horsham. Because of my engineering background, I might be of some use working with the simulator engineers at the centre. It sounded like a good idea in principle, but I was about as much use to the simulator engineers as a submarine in a desert. On one of my days off, I went to Blackbushe airport to look in on the guys at the Three Counties Aero Club where I had trained for my Private Pilot's Licence. My old instructor, Derek Johnson, and his wife Elsie were both at the clubhouse and it was great to spend some time in their company. An old friend, Mike John, walked into the room to say hello. I hadn't seen him since we had flown to Paris together in a Piper Arrow a couple of years before. He was no longer instructing but was now the chief pilot of Air Swift, who operated charter flights using a fleet of Piper Seneca aircraft. Mike asked me if I would be interested in flying charters for Air Swift. I explained that I'd have to check the situation with Dan-Air, but hopefully there wouldn't be any problem there and I could get back to him with positive news.

As it turned out, I didn't have to take him up on his offer because a few days later I got some great news from Dan-Air. My conversion course onto the Avro 748 was back on. I was to report to the training centre at Horsham, but this time it wasn't to work with the simulator engineers; this time I was going back to the classroom to learn all about the 748's systems. Following some weeks in the classroom, I would be sitting an exam at the CAA's building in Redhill as part of the process of getting my type rating. Then, I was to start training on the aircraft itself.

There were ten of us on the course. Some were just starting with the airline and would be trained as co-pilots. Others had been with the company for a while flying a different aircraft type as co-pilots and were now being promoted to captain. However, the purpose of the course was to get us all type rated on the Avro 748. This was a short haul airliner with two turboprop Rolls-Royce Dart engines, a pressurised cabin carrying 48 passengers and a crew of two pilots and two cabin attendants. It was an extremely rugged aircraft designed to fly multiple short sectors daily. Dan-Air had introduced it on their Link City scheduled services around the UK, in addition to scheduled services to the Channel Islands, France, Switzerland and Norway. The 748 was a well-designed, well built and thoroughly reliable aerial workhorse.

Over the weeks that followed, we learned about the aircraft's various systems. Our instructor would take us through each one in minute detail, displaying schematic diagrams onto a screen at the front of the classroom. He talked about the electrical system, the hydraulic system, the fuel system and the air conditioning and pressurisation systems. By the end of the classroom phase of our course, our heads were so crammed full of facts and figures that the data was practically pouring out of our ears. Before that happened, we rushed off to the Civil Aviation Authority to sit the written exam. We all passed, which goes to show that our instructor really was good at his job.

With my career back on track, Margaret and I got married. We now needed somewhere to live and, having been told I was going to be based at Gatwick, we looked for somewhere that was commuting distance. Margaret had been sharing a flat in Barnes with two other girls and had been working in a hotel in the city. There was no way we could afford to live in London, so we looked south of Gatwick. We found a newly refurbished flat in Hove and Maggie secured a job in one of the major hotels in Brighton. Things were looking up.

Having completed our ground school studies and passed the CAA examination for the type rating, the next stage was to do the base training in the aircraft itself, and this was to be done at Newcastle. We arrived in the early evening and then checked into the airport hotel. When the morning came, the weather was appalling. The sky was overcast with a very low cloud base. It was raining heavily, and the wind was blowing a gale. Not exactly perfect weather for our very first time at the controls doing 'touch and goes', the term used to describe a continuous series of take-offs and landings to refine a pilot's handling abilities.

We ate breakfast in the hotel restaurant while nervously looking out of the window at the torrential rain and the trees bending and straining in the howling wind. Captain John Ryder, the 748-fleet manager, was the man who was going to be putting us through our paces and the person who we were going to have to impress if we hoped to pass the base training phase. We spent time pouring over the latest weather reports showing the current conditions and the forecast conditions. Neither were good. The direction of the very strong wind at Newcastle airport was a real problem because it was blowing across the runway rather than along it. At times it was gusting well above the maximum crosswind limit for the aircraft. We then looked at the reports for Teeside, Manchester and Liverpool to see if things were more favourable elsewhere. They weren't. Eventually, to our immense relief, John declared the weather totally unsuitable for our first training day and told us we might as well return to the hotel because he was scrubbing everything for the rest of the day. He told us to come back at the same time the next day and we quickly scuttled away in case he changed his mind. The next morning the weather wasn't much better, but at least the wind wasn't quite as strong and was blowing more or less down the runway, so the crosswind component was acceptable for a couple of rookie pilots. Our base training was on.

With a maximum take-off weight of around 20 tonnes, the 748 was a giant of an aircraft compared to anything I had flown up to that time. The cockpit, although a snug fit, was comfortable enough once you were in your seat. There was an additional jump seat that could be swung into position so that a third person was seated centrally and slightly behind the two pilots. Nobody was ever going to pretend that the cockpit had been designed with ergonomic elegance in mind. Loads of switches, loads of dials and very little logic seems to have been the philosophy with regards to the layout. None of the systems were designed to work automatically, but instead had to be switched on, manually set and adjusted and thereafter frequently readjusted until switched off again.

Our ground school course had introduced us to these systems and their controls, but there was no simulator for the 748, so the first time you climbed into the pilot's seat was also the first time you got to see all the switches for real. Whenever lots of switches need to be selected in a particular order or sequence, then a checklist becomes your friend and saviour. When flying complex aircraft, it is vital that pilots become totally disciplined in the use of checklists. A pilot just starting on a particular aircraft type will work through a checklist—albeit slowly—and will ensure nothing gets overlooked. A pilot with plenty of time on an aircraft type should still use a checklist. The items will almost certainly be covered much quicker, but by using the checklist the pilot will ensure that nothing has been accidentally overlooked.

Base training was challenging but very rewarding. I found the flight controls of the 748 to be heavy, but effective. It needed large and prompt movement of the control wheel to counter any unwanted excursions in the rolling plane and with full flap extended, you could run out of elevator authority if you were slow to flare when the speed was close to minimum reference speed. This was particularly true once the throttles were closed because the resultant prop-wash over the tail plane was reduced. Once you were aware of these characteristics, the aircraft was a pleasure to fly. You could land it in a significant crosswind without too much difficulty and its greater mass and inertia ensured that it was far more stable and less affected by gusty winds than the lighter aircraft that I'd flown previously.

Now that I had demonstrated I could handle the aircraft well with both engines running, it was time to get more serious and explore the handling characteristics on just one engine. Again, as there was no flight simulator for the 748, this had to be done for real in the aircraft. As we accelerated down the runway for take-off, the training captain would simulate an engine failure by closing one of the throttles. I would then have to promptly apply rudder to prevent the nose of the aircraft from swinging to one side due to the loss of thrust from that engine. By carefully adjusting the pitch attitude and accurately controlling the speed, the aircraft would stagger into the air at a very much reduced rate of climb. I would then position it back onto final approach and start down towards the runway. Just when I was thinking that I had done a magnificent job and was seconds away from a successful landing and a hero's welcome, the captain would shout 'Go around! Go Around!' I would have to immediately discontinue the approach, apply full power to the one good engine and climb away again. This of course was to simulate a scenario where a landing was not possible because you were still

A Dan-Air Hawker Siddeley (Avro) HS 748

in cloud and unable to see the runway. Having climbed to a safe altitude, you were then expected to manoeuvre the aircraft back onto final approach and have another go at landing. Although it was hard work and very demanding, it was also really good fun. I felt that the Avro and I were going to be good friends.

Once a base check and instrument rating renewal flight had been completed with a flight examiner, I was signed off for the start of my line training. This meant that I was going to be operating revenue earning flights with fare paying passengers on board. Real people who had actually paid good money to be taken into the air by me! My line training began in May 1974 with a scheduled flight from Newcastle to Manchester and then to Birmingham and on to Bournemouth. The line training captain was a lovely guy by the name of Paul Ashpitel. Because it was the very start of my line training, we had an experienced 748 first officer 'riding shotgun' on the jump seat. This was standard practice for the first few flights of a new pilot's line training, because it wasn't unusual for them to become overwhelmed and in need of help from the safety pilot on the jump seat. I was no exception and most definitely did need help. My safety pilot was Owen Wright, who subtly stepped in and covered my shortfalls without fuss or attention. Quite frankly, I needed him to step in a lot. All three flights were a bit of a blur to be honest and I was more of a hindrance than a help to the operation. At the end of our flying duty, I was thoroughly demoralised and convinced that I wasn't up to the job. When we had taxied out for take-off at Newcastle, Lynn, the stewardess who was working at the front of the cabin, had brought me a cup of coffee. I'd placed it in the cup holder by my side. Now, here at Bournemouth, I noticed it for the first time. Cold and untouched. Paul pointed at it and joked 'when you have time to drink one of those on each sector, then I will know you are up to speed.' I laughed but felt even worse. Both Paul and Owen, who had seen it all before, were very supportive and did their best to assure me that everyone felt the same way at the end of their first day of line training. I went home full of doubt and hoping like hell that they were right.

My training continued at quite a pace over the following days and all of it was carried out by Captain Ashpitel. After a few more flights, he had announced that a safety pilot was no longer required and this was a great boost to my self-confidence, as it showed that he thought I was up to the job. He and I completed a total of twenty line training flights together and then he carried out my final line check. He passed me and I was finally cleared to fly as a 748 co-pilot.

Paul Ashpitel was a remarkable man. I consider myself very fortunate to have been teamed up with him because his relaxed style and lovely personality were just what I needed to set me off on the right course in my professional piloting career. Paul was a very gifted pilot. He had what is called in the profession a great pair of hands: a terrific feel for an aircraft and what it was doing at any given moment. He could 'hand fly' it so smoothly and accurately that it was a joy to watch. Flying an approach in gusty conditions that culminated in a landing right on the maximum crosswind limit was made to look easy when Paul was at the controls.

He had been a pilot in RAF Bomber Command in the Second World War, and as a sergeant pilot first flew a tour of combat operations on Vickers Wellington bombers. He then converted onto the Avro Lancaster and flew another tour of operations. He was very modest and self-deprecating with regards to his contribution throughout World War Two. We all knew that his modesty was misplaced, Paul was a war hero and someone that I really looked up to.

Having completed my conversion onto the 748, I was keen to get started and the crewing department assured me that they had a busy flying programme already mapped out for me. Unfortunately, they also had a surprise in the form of a 'slight change of plan' as they glibly called it. Despite having been told that I was to be based at London Gatwick airport, they now announced that my base had been changed to Ashford airport in Kent. This news didn't go down well. I had just signed a lease on a flat in Hove, which had been chosen because there was a regular train service from nearby Brighton to Gatwick airport. Also, the journey by car from Hove to Gatwick was perfectly acceptable from a commuting point of view. What was not acceptable was a car journey of two hours or more from Hove to Ashford! When I pointed this out, I received a shrug of the shoulders and the explanation that a pilot is obliged to operate from whichever base the company chooses. It was also gently pointed out that this fact was clearly stated in the terms of my contract. Once I realised that there was nothing I could do about it, I went to see my landlord to explain my dilemma. Fortunately, he was very understanding; he released me from all contractual obligations and wished Margaret and I the best for the future. We immediately drove to Folkestone in Kent and started working our way through the estate agents' offices in search for somewhere to live. Amazingly, we found a bungalow to rent that was available for immediate occupancy. It was in Cheriton, which was just a short drive from the airport and an ideal location. We had a roof over our heads once again.

I was now employed by the airline as a pilot on the Avro 748 fleet, with the rank of second officer. A second officer is at the bottom of the pecking order in terms of airline seniority. Next up the ranking order is a first officer, then a senior first officer and finally the captain. Up in the giddy heights of seniority are the training captains, who are instructors and examiners, then come the management pilots such as base managers and fleet managers. Finally, there is the chief pilot, who is so high up the seniority ladder that they will frequently suffer from nose bleeds.

In Dan-Air, a second officer was promoted to first officer after completing a minimum of twelve months service with the company and clocking up 1,000 flying hours. Both those requirements had to be satisfied before promotion. I was now earning considerably less money than when an engineer but didn't mind for two reasons. Firstly, I knew that each promotion I received would bring with it a significant rise in salary. Secondly, I was doing the job that I really wanted to do, and you couldn't put a price on that.

Lympne airport had been renamed Ashford after the expanding town that was located a few miles away. In 1971, Skyways Coach-Air was experiencing serious financial difficulties and a management buyout created Skyways International. This only managed to struggle on for another year and in 1972 Dan-Air bought the company which they briefly branded as Dan-Air Skyways. As part of the purchase, they got the 748 fleet of aircraft and scheduled service routes from Lympne to Beauvais, Clermont Ferrand and Montpellier. They also got Lympne airport. In May 1974, I walked into the small terminal building at Ashford ready to operate my first flight from that airport. It was going to be a busy day as I was about to do six flights. We were to fly from Ashford to Beauvais and back again, a total of three times. Each flight took on average about 45 minutes and we were aiming to turn the aircraft around at each end in approximately 25 minutes. I was really looking forward to the day and as I walked into the terminal

In 1971 Dan-Air took over the Skyways Coach-Air Service which operated from Lympne (later Ashford) Airport using HS 748s

building in my new uniform, I think I was feeling like some sort of Top Gun fighter ace.

I was proudly wearing my uniform and swinging my arms with the one lonely gold stripe boldly displayed for all to see. I was pretty sure that any women in the building who spotted me would instantly feel their heart flutter in excitement and all the men would naturally be wishing that they were me. However, one woman near the entrance didn't react in quite that way. She grabbed my arm and said, 'Ah good, a porter. Be a good chap and carry my bags to the check-in desk would you?' Suddenly, Top Gun, the steely eyed killer of the skies, had become a baggage handler. I meekly picked up her very heavy suitcase and staggered over to the check-in desks. I wondered, briefly, if she would give me a tip. She didn't.

A couple of minutes later I had partially regained my composure and met up with the rest of the crew. The captain was Geoff Davison who I would fly with many times over the coming months. Like Paul Ashpitel, Geoff Davison was a pilot whose stick and rudder skills were exceptional. When he flew the aircraft, he made it look easy. To the untrained eye, his subtle and perfectly co-ordinated movements on the controls appeared so effortless that it seemed he wasn't really doing much at all. However, a pilot watching could see that he was working in perfect harmony with the aircraft. He was anticipating the need for a control input before it became obvious to a less skilled person. A small correction on the controls at exactly the right time kept the aircraft perfectly balanced, in trim and with the correct power setting for the existing conditions. Rather than reacting to changes, he was anticipating what he needed to do to ensure those changes didn't happen. You could learn a lot from watching Geoff at work and watch him I did.

One day, we had both been rostered to travel by taxi from Ashford airport to Gatwick. Once there, we were to fly a scheduled service from Gatwick to Berne, the capital of Switzerland, and then back to Gatwick. We had noted that the weather forecast for our flight was not good, with a lot of thunderstorm activity in the vicinity of Berne itself, and a widespread and very active frontal system that lay directly across our track on the way there. About an hour and a half after taking off from Gatwick we were in the cruise and getting closer to the frontal system. The sky ahead was dark and menacing with towering cumulonimbus clouds extending way above our altitude. The front lay right across our track and extended for many miles to our left and right. There was no way we could fly around it and we certainly couldn't fly above it, so we were going to have to fly through it and Geoff was carefully studying the small monochrome screen that displayed the picture being painted by our weather radar. He was trying to find a gap in the angry looking wall of cloud so that we could avoid the worst of the turbulence and heavy rain. There didn't appear to be any gaps and the closer we got, the more solid and menacing it all looked. Geoff called the stewardess to the cockpit and told her to pack all catering equipment away and then strap in because things were going to get rough.

He spoke to the passengers on the public address system and told them to fasten their seat belts because there was some unavoidable turbulence up ahead. His voice was calm and reassuring, but he emphasised the need for everyone to get their seat belts on immediately. With another few moments spent studying the radar picture, he pointed to the screen and indicated an area to the left of our track that looked narrower than the others, then told me to advise air traffic control we were turning left twenty degrees to avoid weather ahead. I radioed the message and then returned to studying the radar. The sky looked so dark outside that it suddenly resembled the middle of the night. I could see lightning off to my right and then an intense flash appeared to our left. Geoff said, 'Tighten your seat belt, Bob, this is likely to be a rough ride.' He had already adjusted the engine power to get our speed nailed for turbulence penetration and then, moments later, all hell broke loose.

We hit an updraft that slammed us down into our seats and the needles on the altimeters started to rapidly spin clockwise. The vertical speed indicator showed a rate of climb that was off the scale. Geoff didn't seem to be doing anything about this altitude excursion and a second later I realised why. I was suddenly thrown upwards until I felt my shoulder straps bite into me. Now the altimeters started spinning rapidly anticlockwise with the vertical speed indicator showing a rate of descent that was off the scale. Suddenly, a deafening noise filled the cockpit. It took me a moment to realise what it was and looking up at my windscreen I could see hailstones the size of golf balls streaming towards us. As they smashed against the aluminium roof and fuselage, the sound was incredibly loud, but what concerned me was the sight of them hammering against the windscreen in front of me. I thought they would surely smash through.

Amidst the cacophony I thought I heard someone speaking. It was unintelligible so I wasn't sure if it was a call from air traffic control or Geoff saying something to me over the intercom. I glanced across for a clue. To my amazement, his face looked impassive and although he was clearly concentrating on his instruments, he appeared to be perfectly relaxed. His hands were on the controls, and he was repeatedly moving the control wheel to prevent the aircraft's gyrations from becoming too wild. One thing was clear though; he had the situation perfectly under control. A few long minutes later, we were spat out of the maelstrom into clear skies and bright sunlight. The noise that had previously been deafening us was suddenly gone and had been replaced by the steady drone of our engines. My heart rate started to return to normal. Geoff winked at me, smiled and said, 'that was an interesting few minutes, wasn't it?' I replied that the 'interesting moment' had cured my constipation.

Geoff gave a laugh and then spoke to the passengers on the public address system. I heard him jokingly tell them that some people pay good money at a fairground for a rollercoaster ride like we had just experienced, but that he hoped the turbulence hadn't been too uncomfortable for them. He updated them on our arrival time and then signed off. He had sounded so relaxed that I'm sure the passengers had been instantly reassured after their scary experience. The stewardesses resumed the cabin service and we continued to our destination.

The storm activity in the Berne area consisted of isolated cumulonimbus clouds that we were easily able to weave our way around and avoid. The airfield itself was in the clear when we came into land. After the flight, I told Geoff that was the worst turbulence that I had ever experienced, and I asked him if he had seen anything like it before. He told me that when he had been in the Fleet Air Arm, he had been assigned to a unit in America operating research aircraft which were deliberately flown into fully developed hurricanes. They penetrated the outer edge of the storm, then spent some time following the circular flow of the raging wind, while slowly nudging their way towards the centre of the hurricane. During this process, they would experience severe turbulence which could last for a long time. Eventually, they would pass into the eye of the storm, where the turbulence suddenly disappeared completely to be replaced by remarkably calm conditions. By maintaining a banked turn, they could stay within the calm funnel while some boffins in the specially equipped rear cabin recorded lots of data such as temperature and barometric pressure on an array of instruments they had at their disposal. Then, it was a case of carefully flying back into the screaming winds and turbulence of the outer weather band. After being tossed around for another extended period, they would once again be spat out into the calmer outer fringes. When they got back to base, a sign writer would add a twister symbol to the side of the fuselage, in much the same way that bomber crews would paint a bomb symbol on their aircraft after a successful mission. No wonder he had appeared totally unfazed during our 'interesting moment.'

The next Ashford based captain I flew with was Ken Mackie; a real gentleman. He was a softly spoken man who had gained the nickname 'Mother Mackie.' This hadn't been awarded in a cruel way but rather it referred to the fact that he was a caring man and was always fussing over his crew and checking to make sure they were alright. He treated all the stewardesses as though they were his daughters and he fussed over them like a concerned parent. He fussed over young co-pilots like me too. Always ready to answer questions and impart knowledge, Ken was also very encouraging when he thought you were doing a good job. He had a very relaxed manner and when the co-pilot was flying the aircraft, he would pull out his old pipe, fire it up and then puff away contentedly as he watched over his young 'captain in training' as he called his co-pilots. Ken had flown the American Martin B-26 Marauder medium bomber during the war, and I noticed that he wore the Distinguished Flying Cross ribbon on his uniform jacket. I asked him if that had been awarded following one particularly notable operation and he confirmed that it was. He was leading a squadron of B-26 bombers to a heavily defended target, and the squadron had been attacked again and again by German fighters. One by one, all the bombers in the squadron were destroyed except for one; Ken's aircraft alone made it back to England. 'That is why they gave me the DFC.'

Another Ashford captain was Jeff Henderson, who had flown Hawker Typhoon fighters during the war, and claimed to hold the title of 'shortest command in aviation history'. Years before, he had been a co-pilot with Skyways, flying the Douglas DC-3. He was promoted and—following his conversion training—set off for the first time as captain. Unfortunately, when he did the pre-flight walk around inspection, he failed to remove the external rudder lock. He managed to fly the aircraft around in a wide circuit with a combination of roll, using the ailerons, and yaw by partially throttling back one of the engines to give himself asymmetric thrust. He successfully landed back at the airfield—no mean feat in a taildragger with no rudder—and was immediately demoted to co-pilot again. Jeff would relate this tale and finally add 'So I was actually a captain for just five minutes in total.' The moral of his tale was: make sure you always do a careful pre-flight inspection and check for full and free movement of all the flight controls before take-off.

Another notable character who was based at Ashford was Captain Tom McEvoy. He was close to retirement age when I started flying with him and he was rather hard of hearing. He admitted to some high tone deafness, but we all suspected that his hearing loss was much more significant. Consequently, he used to have the aircraft radio turned up to maximum volume which was incredibly loud for a person with normal hearing. When I flew with him, I used to stuff cotton wool into my ears under my headset so that the noise of the radio didn't leave me with a headache.

In 1965 he was flying passengers on a C-47 from Beauvais to England. Lympne (Ashford) airport was closed due to the runway being waterlogged and the airport at Lydd was closed at that time of night, so the flight had been planned to London Gatwick. They had crossed the south coast of England, but the ground below them was completely obscured by solid cloud. Suddenly and without warning, they were plunged into complete darkness. The aircraft had suffered a freak total electrical failure. All the aircraft's radios were dead and all the navigation equipment. There was low cloud covering Gatwick, so Tom turned the aircraft around and when he estimated he was over the sea, began descending through the cloud. Eventually he caught sight of a lighthouse on the French coast. He then flew up and down the coastline trying to locate Le Touquet airport but was unable to pinpoint his position. With his fuel level down to a dangerously low level, he elected to ditch in the sea close to the shoreline. Dakota crews knew that if the propeller blades struck the water they could break off and penetrate the fuselage at a point in line with the pilot's seat. With this in mind, Tom instructed his co-pilot to leave the cockpit and secure himself back in the passenger cabin. Now on his own, Tom brought the aircraft down using the illumination from the lighthouse and the sight of the breaking surf to assist him. As he ditched the aircraft a propeller blade on the left-hand engine did detach and penetrate the fuselage, exactly as he had feared. Luckily, Tom was thrown forward at that moment, so the blade missed him and embedded itself into the back of his seat. All the passengers and crew were uninjured and waded ashore to safety. It was a truly remarkable story. What was even more remarkable, as far as I was concerned, was the fact that I had the pleasure of regularly flying with that very same captain.

There was another Dan-Air pilot who was a legend in their own lifetime, but I had to wait until September 1974 before I flew with Captain Yvonne Pope Sintes. I had been wanting to meet this remarkable lady for some time. She was Britain's first female air traffic controller and first female commercial airline captain, but her list of career achievements on the way to that title had been amazing. She was a lovely person and an excellent pilot, but it's important to remember just how unusual it was in the 1970s to see a female pilot on an airliner. Even forty years later, only about five percent of airline pilots are women, but in the seventies,

Yvonne Pope Sintes joined Dan-Air in 1969 and became Britain's first female commercial airline captain 'She was a lovely person and an excellent pilot'

they were as rare as hens' teeth. Thankfully, Dan-Air was enlightened with regards to employing women pilots and had more of them than any other airline during the seventies and eighties. Many airlines took a lot of persuading over the years to change their attitude and it was only Yvonne's stubborn determination, coupled with her obvious piloting skills that enabled her to clear all the hurdles that were placed in her way. She became an excellent role model for women and provided help and encouragement to them whenever she could. As part of that process, she co-founded the British Women Pilots' Association. It wasn't until 1987 that British Airways hired their first female pilot. Her name was Lynn Barton and, perhaps not surprisingly, she had formerly flown for Dan-Air.

I continued to have a busy flying programme at Ashford that summer. Most of the flights were the bread and butter run shuttling back and forth between Ashford and Beauvais, but there were also flights to Jersey, Ostend, Kassel, Brussels, Amsterdam and Frankfurt. Some days I flew as many as seven trips, so got plenty of handling practice. We would do 'leg and leg about' which meant that the captain would be the handling pilot and the co-pilot would be the monitoring pilot for one flight and then for the next flight, the roles would be reversed with the co-pilot being the handling pilot and the captain the monitoring pilot. We kept switching in this way throughout the day. It was all hand flying and it was carried out in good weather and bad. I was in my element and loved it.

Unfortunately, at the end of the summer, we received news that the Ashford base was to be closed. The scheduled service routes to Clermont Ferrand, Montpellier, Ostend and Jersey would be operated from Gatwick instead of Ashford. The population around the Gatwick area was, of course, far greater than on the Kent coast, so the passenger catchment opportunities were much wider. The scheduled services to Beauvais would continue but would go from nearby Lydd airport. Commercial operations from Lympne were to come to an end and the airport site would eventually become an industrial estate. I operated my last Ashford flights in October 1974. Ken Mackie and I did six flights back and forth to Beauvais—the end of an era.

Having been told that my base was to be closed, I briefly wondered if I might be reassigned to Gatwick. This, of course, would have been convenient, as my wife and I could stay in our bungalow at Cheriton—at least in the short term—until we found somewhere to live nearer to Gatwick. Sadly, it was not to be. I was told that I was going to be based at Leeds Bradford airport. So, on a cold, wet and windy day in late October, I found myself checking in to a rather scruffy bed and breakfast room above a pub a couple of miles from Leeds airport. I registered with the local estate agents so that they could let me know what rental properties were available in the area. Luckily it didn't take too long before we found a house to rent in Otley. On my next day off, my wife and I hired a large van, piled our possessions into it and then drove up from Kent to our new home.

The company had just one 748 based at Leeds and it operated scheduled services to Glasgow and Bournemouth.

Two Leeds based crews were required to cover each day's flying. The airport is perched on top of a plateau and with an elevation of 681 feet above mean sea level, it holds the title of being the highest commercial airport in England. When other airports are sitting below a low overcast of cloud, Leeds is often sitting in the clouds. Also, when the wind blows, it *really* blows. If you are a sadistic sort of person who is turned on by the sight of pilots desperately trying to wrestle their aircraft onto the ground amidst conditions of severe turbulence and wind shear, then I thoroughly recommend spending time watching aircraft land at Leeds.

In the winter of 1974, I got plenty of practice doing crosswind landings and dealing with turbulence and wind shear. The runway direction at Leeds is 14/32 and whenever the wind is really blowing, it is generally a howling south westerly: straight across, rather than down the runway. If you were lucky enough to break out of cloud before you got down to your decision height, the runway lights didn't appear in front of you, but in your side window due to the enormous crab angle you were forced to adopt to compensate for the crosswind. Often, the cloud base was so low that you never did see the runway and you had to pour on the power and carry out a go around. A second attempt probably resulted in another go around, whereupon you had to divert to Manchester. That airport is 424 feet lower than Leeds, consequently, the cloud base there wouldn't present a problem and you could land. The result was a plane load of disgruntled passengers because they now faced a journey by coach to Leeds. If it was the evening flight from Glasgow to Leeds that had failed to get in, then the crew generally stayed overnight in the airport hotel at Manchester. They would be tucked up in bed in the hotel before their passengers had arrived at Leeds airport.

I remember a very special day during my time at the Leeds base. My parents were going to travel up to stay with us for a few days. They planned to fly up from Bournemouth on the Dan-Air scheduled service. I fixed it so that when they got to Leeds, my wife would be there to meet the flight, greet my mother and take her home. Dad, however, would stay on board, because I was then taking over as first officer and flying him to Scotland and back. It really was a very special moment for both of us. He told me at the end of the flight that he felt very proud, and it was a proud moment for me too.

It would be fair to say that I didn't enjoy my time at the Leeds base. The house we were living in was shabby, the flying was repetitive, the weather was awful and, to make things worse, after we had been in Otley for about five months my wife became ill. She'd been working at a hotel near to the airport but had to have time off because she felt so unwell. This mystery illness continued for long enough to be very concerning and because she had been vomiting a lot, her GP sent her to the local hospital for X-rays. Once there, the radiologist studied Margaret's medical notes, asked a few questions and then said 'I don't think I'm going to do any X-rays on you. I think you might be pregnant.' Margaret was about to have twins! Being told that you are unexpectedly going to be a parent is a big deal. Being told that you are unexpectedly going to be a parent of twins is a *very* big deal. I was a second officer, earning little money and having to repay my training loan. My wife, who had been earning more than me at her job, was now going to have to give up work because she was experiencing a difficult pregnancy. In about seven months or so, we were going to have two extra mouths to feed.

Thankfully, help arrived almost immediately. First Officer Owen Wright who had been the safety pilot on my very first 748 line training flight had been offered a course on the BAC 1-11. Owen had been based at Bournemouth and consequently there was now going to be a vacancy at that base. As far as I was concerned, Bournemouth was the best base on the 748 fleet and so, as soon as I heard there was a vacancy coming up there, I put my name forward to bid for it. Shortly afterwards I was told that I had got it. We stayed with friends for a while, then found a house to rent in Ferndown, a short distance from Bournemouth Hurn airport.

I absolutely loved my time at the Bournemouth base. From a flying point of view, it was vastly better than Leeds. We had nine scheduled service destinations, including the Channel Islands—which meant I got duty free cigarettes to feed my nicotine habit—and we got frequent night stops in Newcastle which meant we got 'away from base' flight pay. The captains at the base were all nice guys and great to fly with. So too were the engineers and traffic officers. Ken Steele was the station manager, and he did a great job of ensuring it was a very happy base. We were also the nearest 748 crews to Gatwick, so occasionally were asked to operate flights from there. This usually meant passenger flights to Berne, or newspaper flights to Paris and Belfast. Varied flying, nice work colleagues, no night flights. What was not to like?

In November 1975, Margaret went into hospital and, when she came out, our family had doubled in size. Our twins, Paul and Nicole, had arrived, and I needed to earn some more money. We pilots were paid a basic annual salary, but in addition to this, we got 'flight pay.' You came on duty one hour before your scheduled departure time. You then carried out whatever flights you were rostered to do and, thirty minutes after your final flight had arrived, your duty period officially ended. Throughout that period, you were paid flight pay at an hourly rate. However, if at the end of your day's flying you wound up away from your home base and spent the night in a hotel, the hourly flight pay continued right through until thirty minutes after arriving back at your home base. Consequently, the more you flew and the more time you spent away from home, the more money you made. Good for the bank balance, but not good for home life.

North Sea oil exploration in the early seventies had revealed enormous potential. This soon resulted in a huge expansion in air traffic in Scotland, and Aberdeen in particular. Aberdeen was the ideal launching base for helicopter traffic to nearby oil rigs and for fixed wing aircraft to provide a link to the Shetland Islands. From the Shetlands, helicopters could reach the more distant oil rigs.

This 1993 painting by Edmund Miller GAvA celebrates the many aicraft types operated by Dan-Air in their four-decade history.

Dan-Air was quick to seize the opportunity and had the right aircraft for the job. The short runways at Sumburgh were limiting for many aircraft types, but not the 748. This put the company in a great position when it came to seeking contracts with the oil companies who needed to transfer their workers to and from their rigs. Dan-Air was able to offer the necessary air transport and in early 1974 won a contract with the oil company Conoco.

They initially based a single 748 at Aberdeen to fly Conoco employees back and forth between Aberdeen and Sumburgh, but as they won more contracts with the oil companies, they ended up with fourteen 748s based in Scotland. They carried out hundreds of flights, taking oil workers and equipment between Aberdeen, Glasgow and Sumburgh. Later, Scatsa airport was added to the list. Although I was based at Bournemouth, I spent a lot of time on Aberdeen detachments, during which time I was put up at the Skean Dhu airport hotel. It was very busy and a great social meeting place. However, I got so familiar with the meal choices in the restaurant, that I soon knew the menu by heart. When you were in the hotel, you could be excused for thinking you had arrived in Texas, because you frequently found yourself surrounded by tall Americans wearing cowboy boots, ten-gallon hats, smoking huge cigars and ordering Bourbon whiskeys.

Aberdeen had been a sleepy, under-utilised airport when I flew in and out of there during my qualifying cross-country flights for my commercial licence back in 1973. It certainly wasn't sleepy any more. Now it was incredibly busy and to witness the transformation was amazing. The expansion in both fixed wing and rotary wing air traffic was enormous. British Airways' and Bristows' helicopters appeared to be everywhere and, at one stage, Aberdeen handled more helicopter traffic than any airport in the world.

The crews flying out of Aberdeen were given a one-off payment to buy cold weather clothing and a quick trip to the local Army and Navy Stores satisfied all your needs. The payment was enough to buy a couple of pairs of long johns and thermal vests, a couple of pairs of thick thermal socks, a chunky NATO jumper, a pair of warm gloves and a quilted parka, complete with fur lined hood. Waddling around in that lot wasn't going to win us any prizes at a fashion show, but it kept us warm. Operating the first flight in the early morning was always the worst. You would make your way across to the Portacabin that served as a met office to get the weather forecast. The reports from Shetland and Orkney were always the same: No Information Available. Armed with those three helpful words, you left the 'No information Portacabin' and leaned into the wind as you headed for the Dan-Air cabin. Moving awkwardly in your multiple layers of bulky clothing, your boots crunching through the snow, and your body tensing against the gusting wind, you couldn't help feeling that the met office hadn't really needed to issue you with a strong wind warning because you could have worked that one out for yourself!

Having been parked overnight, the aircraft were

thoroughly 'cold soaked' and absolutely freezing inside. Groping around in the dark and working by torchlight, you would carry out an external inspection, before climbing aboard and making a start on bringing the aircraft to life. A ground power unit provided you with electrical power and the engineers would then fire up a fuel-burning cabin heater. The cockpit was separated from the passenger cabin by the forward baggage area, so the warm air never made it as far as the cockpit. Hunched in our seats, wearing parkas with fur lined hoods pulled over our heads, we didn't exactly fit the stereotypical image of airline pilots.

The drive to extract more oil was relentless and there was the feeling that money was no object as far as the big oil companies were concerned. I remember on one occasion being asked to operate an extra unexpected flight from Aberdeen to Sumburgh and back. We got the aircraft fuelled up and ready for departure. Shortly afterwards, a single figure walked out to the aircraft, climbed aboard and we were told to close the doors and go. It turned out that the guy was a specialist diver who had to be transported to one of the rigs as soon as possible. Oil extraction had been shut down on that rig and he was needed to sort out the problem. This lone figure sat on our forty-eight-seat aircraft, and we flew him up to Sumburgh. When we got there, a helicopter was waiting with its engine already running. He was quickly transferred onto the chopper and whisked away. We then turned around and flew back to Aberdeen empty.

On another occasion, a helicopter had developed a technical fault after landing on a rig's helipad. The pilot reported that he was not going to be able to fly off the rig until the fault was rectified. As there was no way to get anything to or from the rig until he was off the helipad, he was told that he had just three hours to get his aircraft away from there. They calmly added that if his helicopter was still there after the three hours, it would be pushed over the side into the sea. The helicopter company didn't wait to see if the oil company's threat was serious. Their technical problem was quickly sorted, and they flew out of there. The oil game is not for the faint hearted!

In late January 1977, I was told there was a BAC 1-11 conversion course coming up and I was going to be on it. This was terrific news. I was going to be flying my first jet. Not only was it a far more sophisticated type of aircraft, but it meant that I would be flying to loads of new and interesting destinations. It also meant I would be getting a significant pay rise. Win-win! On 11 February 1977, I operated my last flight on the Avro 748. I was crewed with Captain George Castellain and we flew G-ASPL from Bournemouth to Jersey, then to Guernsey and then back to Bournemouth. I was about to start a new chapter in my flying career.

Chapter Six

On 14 February 1977, just three days after I had flown the 748 to Bournemouth for the last time, I once again found myself sitting at a desk in the Dan-Air training centre at Horley. The BAC 1-11 was a revolutionary aircraft when it first arrived on the scene. It had been designed as a 'bus stop jet' which would operate lots of short flights each day and be turned around rapidly between each flight. To achieve that, it had to be as self-sufficient as possible. The cockpit and all the systems on the 1-11 were designed to be operated by just two pilots. It is difficult to emphasise just how controversial it was, at that time, to have only two pilots operating a jet. How could you do away with the valuable contribution of the flight engineer when that person's presence had always been considered vital on jet airliners?

Nevertheless, once the 1-11 entered airline service it quickly proved to be a fine aircraft and went on to become the most successful British jet in terms of worldwide sales. Eventually, 244 aircraft were built before production ceased. Back in 1977, the BAC 1-11 was a common sight at European airports and was being operated by numerous scheduled service and charter airlines. I was about to become a 1-11 pilot and could hardly wait to get started. Having completed the in-house ground school course at Dan-Air's training centre, I had then taken the 1-11 type rating exam at the CAA building at Redhill. After a nervous wait for the results, the news eventually came through that I had passed.

Dan-Air owned two simulators. One was a De Havilland Comet and the other was a Boeing 727. They did not have a BAC 1-11 simulator, but instead bought time in one at the Aer Lingus training centre at Dublin airport. This was where I was going to learn how to handle the BAC 1-11 before flying the actual aircraft. The training was carried out by one of the Dan-Air training captains and each session involved a pre-flight classroom briefing lasting about an hour. This outlined the plan for the simulated flight and detailed the way in which we were expected to execute the various handling exercises. There followed a question-and-answer session on some of the aircraft's systems to satisfy the instructor that you knew your stuff in those areas. Different systems would be covered each day, so by the end of your training you would have had to demonstrate your knowledge of the electrical system, the hydraulic system, the air conditioning and pressurisation system, the fuel system, the flight control systems, etc. After the pre-flight briefing in the classroom, we would climb into the simulator and begin the training session. This lasted for four hours, at the end of which you climbed out feeling exhausted. Then we received a debriefing in the classroom which lasted about thirty minutes. Following this, you headed off to the airport hotel for a well-earned beer and something to eat, knowing that—the next day—it would be more of the same.

The training captain and I enjoyed a couple of very welcome cold glasses of Guinness at the airport bar before checking in as passengers for an Aer Lingus flight back to Gatwick airport. The flight was—appropriately enough—on a BAC 1-11. As we climbed away from Dublin, the training captain turned to me and said 'Well done Bob, that's the simulator phase all completed. Next for you is the base training, so you'll be putting all that lot into practice in the real aircraft.' Now that was something I really *was* looking forward to.

Preflight checks and engine starting were all familiar enough, we had done it so many times in the simulator a few days before. We taxied out to the runway and ran through the before take-off checks. Again, all familiar stuff. Having lined up on the runway, the tower controller passed us the wind direction and speed and cleared us for take-off. I gripped the control wheel with my right hand and advanced the thrust levers with my left. We were flying the short-bodied variant of the BAC 1-11, which was sometimes referred to as the 'Pocket Rocket.' As we had no passengers aboard and a light fuel load, it really did feel like a rocket, and we were airborne and climbing away in no time at all. For the first few seconds, I felt as though I was hanging on for dear life and a voice in my head was probably shouting 'Bloody Hell, wait for me!' However, after a few prompts from the captain, my brain started to catch up with the aircraft. I levelled off at the circuit altitude and we turned downwind.

It was as rough as old boots and I had to work hard to keep correcting for the gusting wind. At circuit altitude, we were only just below the solid cloud base, but at least the horizontal visibility was okay. The captain told me to fly a normal visual approach, but added with a wink, that I didn't need to get worried about doing a landing because when we got down to a couple of hundred feet on short finals, he would call for me to go around, at which point we would carry out a missed approach. Because I knew that I wasn't going to be expected to try and land the damned thing, it did allow me to enjoy flying the approach and to remain relatively relaxed. I sorted out the required drift angle needed to keep us tracking down the approach centre line and concentrated on trying to keep us somewhere near the required approach speed. I received the prompt 'don't chase the speed too much. Allow momentary variations above and below the target and only make a correction if the variation remains constant.' That sounded like sound advice, so I did my best to achieve it. When we were about a mile short of the runway, the captain called for me to go around, which I did. As we climbed away again, I suddenly realised that I was enjoying myself. This was good fun!

We then left the circuit and carried out some work in the local area. Climbing, turning and descending and generally getting a good feel for the aircraft and how it handled. Then we flew back to the airfield and into the circuit for another approach. This time I continued all the way down for a landing and it wasn't too bad, thank goodness. We immediately took off again and I carried out two more landings. The wind was getting worse and had changed direction giving us more of a crosswind component. With lots of prompting and encouragement from the captain, my third landing was fine, but it had been very hard work and a bit of a wrestling match on the controls throughout the approach. As we cancelled reverse thrust and slowed to a walking pace on the runway, I breathed a sigh of relief. At the debriefing, Captain Richards was very complimentary and told me I had coped well in the windy conditions. I felt on top of the world as we headed back to the hotel.

The next day I completed my initial line check, and a couple of days later, Captain Fleming carried out my final base check. That concluded all my base training, so now I was to be let loose on normal passenger flights. For these I would initially be rostered to fly with line training captains. They would show me the ropes and tell me all I needed to know as I familiarised myself with normal operations. Once they were satisfied with my performance, I would undergo a line check flight under the watchful eye of an examiner. For my subsequent flights I could be rostered with any captain—those two days that I flew with Captain Richards were the only times that I did fly with him. Thanks to his style of instruction, I felt relaxed throughout the training flights and thoroughly enjoyed our two days together. Shortly afterwards, he was tragically killed on his motorbike in a road accident.

Dan-Air operated many different BAC 1-11 variants. There was the 207 series that was the original 'bus stop jet' and so had fuel tanks in the wings, but no centre tank. Its range capability was consequently less than the other variants and the operations department generally assigned it to domestic scheduled services, or to destinations that weren't too far away. Then there was the 301 series, that did have the additional centre fuel tank giving it a considerably better range. I got a particular kick out of flying those because they had previously been owned by British Eagle, my former employer when I was an apprentice engineer. Dan-Air also owned some 401 series aircraft that had originally been built for and operated by American Airlines. There was a single oddball aircraft designated a 414 series. This had been operated by the airline Bavaria but was badly damaged after an accident taking off from Gerona in 1970. The damaged airframe was taken to Bournemouth, rebuilt and then reincarnated as a 414 series. Whatever they did during that rebuild at Bournemouth, they certainly did it well, because the aircraft flew so well. With the aileron and rudder trims set to zero, it flew beautifully and used less fuel than any of the other 400 series aircraft. Consequently, whenever possible, it was assigned to the longer flights that would normally be challenging for the 1-11, such as Berlin to Rhodes.

As well as the short-bodied pocket rockets Dan-Air also had some 500 series aircraft. These were the stretched versions with a plug that added thirteen feet six inches to the fuselage length and a five-foot increase in wingspan. The 500 series aircraft could be further sub-divided into those with the old leading edge and those with the new leading edge. Those with the old leading edge, had awful take off and climb performance. Just as the short-bodied versions had the nickname pocket rocket, the stretched versions with the old leading edge were known as the 'lead sled.' Mind you, the versions with the new leading edge weren't much better!

One tremendous thing about flying the 1-11s was the variety of work and the amazing number of destinations that we flew to. If, as the old saying goes, variety is the spice of life, then we certainly had plenty. Consulting my logbooks, I see that I flew to 120 different airfields in that aircraft. Now that's what I call variety! Like most airlines, when we flew to an airport in another country, we didn't have any company engineers to greet us and help in the event of technical problems. All the Dan-Air pilots were trained to self-manage a turnaround away from base.

Consequently, we would carry out the inspection of the aircraft, check and, if necessary, top up the engine oil (we carried cans and an oil pump in the hold), top up the hydraulic fluid (again, we carried that in the hold), and set up and oversee the refuelling of the aircraft. As part of our initial conversion course, we had all been shown by the ground engineers how to do these things.

Most of the time, our turnarounds went without a hitch, but occasionally something unusual would crop up. If it needed to be sorted before we could consider taking to the air, then we were expected to track down any local engineers who were on site and willing to help (a wad of money usually encouraged willingness). If it was a serious technical problem—thankfully a rare event—then the company would have to get our own engineers out to us by the quickest means. That usually meant they would arrive by air with all their tools and whatever spares and components they had guesstimated they were going to need.

For my first summer flying the BAC 1-11, my family and I were still living in Ferndown near Bournemouth airport. However, I was now based at Gatwick airport and that meant I had a two-hour drive into work every day. Then, after flying all day long, the last thing I felt like doing was climbing back into my car for a two-hour drive home again. We really needed to move closer to Gatwick and had been checking out properties with the local estate agents for some time, but with no success. In the meantime, I just had to put up with the long commute.

Whenever there was a busy period such as a bank holiday weekend or during the school summer holidays, you could almost guarantee that ATC in France would take industrial action, either in the form of a go-slow or an all-out strike. The disruption to air traffic was inevitable and significant. As far as British air traffic was concerned, holidaymakers wishing to fly off to the sun had to head south into French airspace, on their way to their destination. Instead of being able to depart on schedule, they would be informed that because of industrial action in France, their flight would be significantly delayed. At the end of their holiday, they would probably be faced with the same depressing news. Of course, when a flight is delayed, there is an inevitable knock-on effect for any subsequent flights.

A short to medium haul airline based in Britain would typically plan to have an aircraft operating from its home base to a destination in Spain and back again. Then another rotation to Italy and back. Then it would fly to a Greek destination and back. All within a twenty-four-hour period. Now, if you imagine that due to French industrial action, the first rotation to Spain and back was delayed by two hours, when the crew arrive in Spain, they would do their very best to get the aircraft turned around as quickly as possible for the return flight to England. However, if they are now told that French ATC has imposed a restriction on when the aircraft can enter French airspace again, and that restriction means they have a further three-hour delay, the day really does start to fall apart. Consequently, the flight that it is supposed to operate from England to Italy is going to depart at least three hours late. If it picks up another ATC imposed delay, things go from bad to worse.

The legal aspects of a pilot's duties were something I was becoming increasingly familiar with, including the all too frequent use of captain's discretion or, alternatively, a split duty (the latter being a fudge that enabled a crew to come back on duty following a reduced rest period). With a summer of French discontent, my average duty day was very long indeed. A two-hour drive to the airport, followed by a thirteen-hour duty at work (because of ATC delays) followed by a two-hour drive home, resulted in a very tired me. Especially when I knew that I had to do the same again the next day. I remember one occasion when I got back to Gatwick after a horrendous day of delays and problems. We got back to the crew room and a first officer that I knew said 'You look knackered Bob. Bad day?' I told him that it wasn't really a case of a bad day, but the cumulative effect of far too many bad days. He then said that I really shouldn't even consider driving all the way back home, two hours away, but should rather crash out at his place which was only a fifteen-minute drive from the airport. It made a great deal of sense and I said so. The thought of a good night's sleep just fifteen minutes or so away was compelling. I arrived at Mick's house a short while later.

There was a wild party in session. This shouldn't have surprised me because Mick was a well-known party animal and his house had been the scene of many a legendary riot. As I walked in, I recognised several well-known reprobates, and we spent a few minutes talking. A short while later, I got the chance to speak to Mick (more of a shout above the loud music) and asked him where I would be sleeping. He momentarily looked sheepish and then admitted that my bed was the settee in the room we were standing in at the time. Three people were sitting on it and none of them looked like they were ready to quit the party any time soon. The revelries continued for many hours and when I eventually got to sleep on that very lumpy and uncomfortable settee, I couldn't help thinking that I probably would have been better off driving home to Bournemouth after all.

Thankfully, soon after this, we bought a house in Haywards Heath. Although Margaret and I had lived in several homes, this was the first one we had bought rather than rented. It was a small semi-detached property, but it ticked all the boxes for now and it was just a twenty-minute drive from Gatwick airport.

Our charters were generally to popular holiday destinations around Europe, but you could also find yourself operating a one-off charter to somewhere off the beaten track. We also found ourselves spending a lot of time in Berlin. Back in 1969, Dan-Air had opened their first overseas base at Tegel airport in West Berlin. At the time, only British, French and American Airlines were permitted to operate there. Dan-Air based Comets at Tegel operating charter flights on behalf of the West German tour company Neckermann und Reisen. Soon the Comets were replaced by Boeing 727s and BAC 1-11s. The German tour operators had insisted on greater seat pitch in the passenger cabin, so the Berlin-based aircraft had two complete seat rows removed. Most of the ground staff were locally recruited, including flight operations personnel and engineers. The stewardesses were also recruited locally, but the flight deck crews were based in England and were flown out to Berlin to operate a series of flights over consecutive days. We would then return to England until the next time. With five aircraft based there, there were a lot of crews in the hotel at any given moment. No matter what time of day you were flying, when you got back to the hotel at the end of it, there was always an off-duty crew around to hook up with.

Berlin is famously a city that never sleeps, and the choice of bars, restaurants and night clubs is vast. As we were all being paid an extra overseas allowance when we were away from our home base, we felt it was our duty to frequent as many of these establishments as possible. It is fair to say that we worked hard and played hard. Inevitably, this sometimes got out of hand and hotel room parties were the usual cause of our collective downfall. It's not just rock bands that get banned from hotels for rowdy behaviour. Airline crews are pretty good at it too and over the years we were barred from more than one hotel in Berlin.

On one memorable occasion, the hotel manager, who was a very unpleasant character with an undisguised hatred of aircrew, had furiously hammered on the door where a room party was in full swing. If I remember correctly, the pilot whose room it was had invited some of his colleagues to help him celebrate his birthday. The loud music, coupled with the shouted conversation and laughter, had prompted a phone call from the reception desk following noise complaints from some of the other hotel guests. This message was ignored. Eventually, the furious manager arrived at the room. He expected his angry protestations would result in everyone shuffling away with their tails between their legs. Instead, he was picked up by six of the party goers and carried—kicking and struggling—to the hotel swimming pool. Having thrown him in—amidst loud cheers and applause—everyone returned to the room party. Unsurprisingly, when the pilots came down to breakfast the next morning, their room keys were lined up on the reception desk along with a typed letter informing them that they were no longer welcome at the hotel. The good news was that the hotel we were moved to was better than the previous one. However, nobody was in any doubt that if we wished to remain there, it would be wise to keep a low profile for a while.

Flying in and out of Berlin was a very different experience because of the politically sensitive nature of the region. Tegel airport was in the French sector of Berlin. After take-off we had to fly at an altitude of less than 10,000 feet along the full length of the centre corridor, which took about 20 minutes. While in the corridor we were looked after by American military air traffic controllers. Beneath the corridor and spaced at regular intervals along it, were Russian military airfields with fighters parked ready to scramble and intercept any aircraft that strayed off the airway. Occasionally, a fighter would appear alongside and shadow us as we flew along. They would sit just outside the airway and follow us along its length playing a sort of cat and mouse game. It was somewhat unnerving to look out of your window and see a frontline fighter maintaining station alongside you.

Navigating along the corridors was achieved using VORs but those navigation aids sometimes proved very useful in another way. Occasionally, the Russians would jam our voice communication with the Air Traffic Controllers. At best, that action could be described as a bloody nuisance. A more sinister and accurate interpretation would be that they were deliberately compromising air safety by preventing us from sending or receiving messages. However, if the ATC frequency did become jammed and unusable, we would select 'Voice' on our VOR receivers—normally a radio navigation aid—this being the procedure we had been instructed to adopt. The American controllers would then start transmitting any vital instructions on the VOR frequencies. It was shocking to realise that the Russian authorities were prepared to interfere with safety in this way. Another unnerving thing we occasionally encountered when flying along the corridors in the hours of darkness, was the sight of tracer shells arcing up seemingly very close to the bottom limit of the airway. There were Russian military firing ranges and manoeuvring grounds beneath us and watching those tracers slowly arcing up towards us before dropping away tended to grab your attention.

On a lighter note, I met with one of the American military controllers for a couple of beers one night and he asked me if I was familiar with the Bigolo departure when using the centre corridor. When I said no, he explained that Pan Am's chief pilot in Berlin was Captain Bigolo. When leaving the centre corridor, he liked to cut the corner to save a bit of time and to wind up the Russian controllers. At a particular DME distance and VOR radial from the western end of the corridor he would carefully fly a track that he knew would take his aircraft right up to the very edge of the airway. The Russian air traffic controller sat right next to his American counterpart in the ATC centre. Apparently, he could be seen to visibly stiffen in his seat as he watched Bigolo's progress on the radar screen and he didn't relax until he realised that he wasn't going to have to scramble the fighters after all. I carefully noted the details of the appropriate radial and distance and on subsequent flights, I always asked ATC for approval to fly a Bigolo departure. The American controller would give a chuckle and then say, 'affirmative Sir, that's approved.' Many years later I ran into the legendary Captain Bigolo in a training centre at Miami airport.

Berlin started to feel like my second home. We would often do seven consecutive days there, working every day and then fly back to Gatwick for some time off. Sometimes, we would be rostered for a ten-day stint, in which case we would be assigned a single day off midway through the session. There was always plenty to do there during your free time and we could, for example, use the golf course which was next to Gatow airport in the British sector. Dan-Air had a locker in the clubhouse changing rooms with a set of golf clubs. Two of us could share these, playing with a half set each and then hack our way around the course. At the end of the game, we were able to use the club bar where the subsidised booze was impressively cheap. Alternatively, we could hire a dinghy from the Sailing club and spend the day on the Havel. The British military had a significant presence in Berlin and, as was typical at the time, they provided impressive leisure facilities for their personnel. Set in the very scenic woods and lakes to the southwest of Berlin, the British sector boasted a golf course, sail boats, tennis courts, swimming pools and an excellent restaurant and bar at the officer's club. As had been the case when my father was based in Berlin, the civilian airline employees were permitted to use all the extensive military leisure facilities.

During the summer months, the French, American and British military bases would each put on summer festivals. I believe the tradition was started as a way of extending a hand of friendship to the people of Berlin and trying to promote good relations between the civilians and the military. As public relations exercises go, it was successful, and the festivals were popular with everyone. There would be food stalls, fairground rides and attractions erected, and they were generally themed so that you would have New Orleans jazz bands playing and hot dogs sizzling at the American festival, while the French and British festivals would have their own themes. All in all, it wasn't too much of a hardship if you were rostered for a Berlin detachment.

Chapter Seven

We operated a great number of BAC 1-11 variants in Dan-Air, and they were dissimilar in many ways. They had different flap settings and a different flap retraction schedule between types. Some had water injection for the engines, some didn't. Some had automatic passenger oxygen drop down, some didn't. Consequently, some were cleared for a higher cruise altitude than others. Some had HF radios installed, others didn't. This was a source of embarrassment if you accepted ATC routing down the Tango tracks (which required position reports to be passed to Shannon via HF) only to discover that the aircraft you were flying today didn't have HF radios fitted! The basic cockpit layout was the same for all, but some switches had been installed in different locations by various previous operators, which resulted in the occasional mumbled question 'where have they put the damned switch on this one?' We took it in our stride but knew we needed to stay sharp to avoid getting caught out.

I remember one incident when the differences had a very serious consequence. The baby 1-11s (the short bodied 200/300/400 series) were inherently tail heavy, whereas the stretched 1-11s (the 500 series) were nose heavy. Consequently, to keep the aircraft nicely within its trim envelope, we had to devise a simple loading procedure for the hold baggage. Ideally, an aircraft should be loaded so that it has an aft centre of gravity in the cruise, as this results in improved fuel efficiency, but we had to keep it simple for multiple daily departures. The loaders were instructed to load the short-bodied aircraft with two thirds of the bags in the forward hold and the remaining third in the rear hold. The stretched aircraft were loaded in the opposite sense, two thirds in the rear one third forward. It was a system that worked well until—one day—it didn't.

A flight was scheduled for one of the short-bodied aircraft and the baggage handlers loaded the bags into the hold in the standard way. At start up, the aircraft developed a technical problem that was going to take time to rectify. The operations department knew that another BAC 1-11, parked nearby, wasn't due to fly until much later in the day, so the crew transferred to the second aircraft and prepared it for departure. The new aircraft, however, was a 500 series, but the baggage handlers had transferred the bags across from a 400 series and reloaded with two thirds of the bags in the forward hold. The load sheet was prepared assuming that standard loading had been carried out, so it was shown to be acceptably in trim for take-off.

A few minutes later, the aircraft roared down the runway and at the appropriate speed, the pilot pulled back on the control column to raise the aircraft's nose and lift off into the air. Nothing happened. He pulled back harder and still nothing happened. Finally, with the control column pulled back as far as it would go, the nose wheels were still glued to the runway. The aircraft had by now reached a very high speed, but the pilots had no option but to abandon the take-off. Fortunately, they managed to come to a halt before the end of the runway. A fine example of the validity of the phrase 'if something can go wrong, it will go wrong.'

Following this very serious incident, an instruction was given to the baggage handlers that all the BAC 1-11s, irrespective of type, should have the baggage loaded half and half, with an equal number of bags in the forward and rear holds. This was not an ideal solution for either the short or the stretched aircraft, but it would, at least, ensure that a seriously out of trim condition couldn't happen again.

The 500 series aircraft were often challenging from a

A BAC 1-11 301AG of Dan-Air, which originally belonged to my first employer, British Eagle

performance point of view, especially if operating from a shortish runway. We would frequently have to do a manual load sheet and use the very sharpest of pencils while juggling the numbers with regards to how many passengers we had, how many bags were going into the hold and how much fuel we could put on while keeping below the maximum allowable take-off weight in the prevailing runway and weather conditions. If we needed to, we could increase the maximum allowable take-off weight by using water injection to the engines. Water vapour, when heated, has a high coefficient of expansion, so by pumping demineralised water into the engines during the take-off you get more 'oomph' (the technical term used by pilots and other knowledgeable people).

However, as the weight of the water you uplifted had to be included in the zero-fuel weight of the aircraft, it was important to calculate the minimum amount of water needed to maintain wet power from the start of the take-off roll until the aircraft reached an altitude of 1,500 feet. The water was stored in fifty-gallon drums that had been prepositioned at airfields where it was expected they would be needed. As part of the turnaround, you would have to manhandle these heavy drums into position alongside the demineralised-water servicing panel. Then, having connected a wobble pump you would furiously pump away by hand. This was a very physical and sweaty process in the summer heat. When it was finally time to take-off, you would select the appropriate switches for water injection and then advance the thrust levers. Unfortunately, once you were roaring down the runway and committed to taking off, it wasn't unknown for the water to stop pumping into one engine or the other. This resulted in a partial loss of thrust from that engine, but by this time you couldn't stop. The resultant climb away was painfully shallow!

The Rolls-Royce Spey engines were very robust and reliable. Although people complained they were very noisy, at least you knew that while they were making all that noise they were working. During the five years that I flew the BAC 1-11, I had to shut down an engine in flight on two occasions. On both occasions it was because we had received a high engine vibration warning. Ironically, Rolls-Royce eventually concluded that the vibration transducers were starting to give lots of false warnings and that there was, in fact, nothing wrong with the engines when they examined them after the flight. Their solution was a novel one: they disabled the vibration transducers by pulling the circuit breakers and told us to leave them pulled! They reassured us that if the engine was really vibrating, we should be able to feel it through the thrust levers, or the HP fuel cock. Or the seat of our pants maybe? Oh well, if that's what the manufacturer says ...

Although the Spey was a robust and reliable engine, there was one memorable occasion when I had one fail on me during a take-off. We had flown from Gatwick to Minorca and were preparing to make the return flight. We were operating a 500 series aircraft with a full load of 119 passengers, and every one of them had checked in suitcases to go in the hold. Although late in the evening, the surface temperature was still very high, the barometric pressure was quite low and the surface wind calm. None of these things were helpful to us as they had a detrimental effect on the aircraft's performance and restricted the maximum weight at which we could take-off. Even with the absolute minimum of fuel required for the trip, we were going to be right up to that limit. At times like this, we carefully checked to see how many of the passengers were female, because we were permitted to use a lower assumed weight for female adults when calculating the overall passenger weight. Also, any children included in the figures were factored in using a lower assumed weight. Finally, having carefully taken all these details into consideration, we calculated that we were just a few kilograms below the absolute maximum allowable weight. With everything completed, we taxied out to the runway.

On the 500 series aircraft, the fourth stewardess sat on the flight deck jump seat for take-off and landing as there were only three crew seats in the main cabin. After take-off, the fourth girl would leave us and join her colleagues until shortly before landing. On this occasion the fourth girl had joined the airline recently and, having completed her training a few days before, was on her first flight. Consequently, she was very excited and acting like a kid in a sweet shop; fascinated by everything that we were doing and everything that was going on around her. She chatted away merrily until we started to taxi and then watched wide-eyed as I steered the aircraft onto the runway. I carefully manoeuvred the aircraft up to the very end to give us the maximum possible take-off run. Once the tower controller had given us clearance, I held the brakes on and took the engines up to maximum power. Satisfied that both engines were developing full thrust, I released the brakes, and we began to roll. We knew that there wasn't going to be much tarmac left by the time we got up to flying speed and, as we continued to accelerate, the end the runway seemed to be mighty close when the captain finally called out 'V1', the speed at which it was no longer possible to stop on the runway. Almost immediately, there was a mighty bang and I saw, out of the corner of my eye, all the number one engine instruments winding anti-clockwise. Simultaneously, the nose of the aircraft began to yaw to the left and I immediately applied right rudder to stop the movement. I rotated to the required initial pitch attitude and then, on achieving V2 speed, fine-tuned the pitch to hold it there. The captain called 'positive rate of climb' which I confirmed before calling for him to retract the landing gear. Once the gear was up, he made a terse but accurate comment. 'Okay Bob, keep the ball in the middle and nail that bloody speed. Then we just might see this thing actually gain some altitude!'

We did gain altitude, but my goodness it took a long time. The needle on the rate of climb indicator didn't seem to want to move very far above the zero mark at all. Although it was pitch dark and we couldn't see a thing outside, at least I knew the area ahead of us was flat and we would soon cross the coast and head out over the Mediterranean. There followed some heated exchanges on the radio, because the tower controller—who was unaware of our plight—told us to change radio frequency and added 'goodbye, have a nice flight.' The captain's response had been to tell him that we had a problem and would remain on frequency until we had time to call him back. This seemed beyond the controller's limited knowledge of English, so he told us again to 'change frequency and have a nice flight', but he got the message in the end. Everything went well and I can confirm that landing the aircraft on one engine with 119 passengers and 6 crew aboard most definitely concentrated my mind. The touchdown was like a cat peeing on velvet, even though I say so myself.

The engine strip down report from Rolls-Royce, some weeks later, concluded that a couple of compressor blades had sheared off and rattled back through the engine breaking off several turbine blades on their way through. Even the bullet-proof Spey couldn't keep running in that state! Incidentally, it didn't put our new stewardess off flying. In fact, she said she had found it all very exciting. I only hope she didn't find her subsequent flights boring by comparison.

I wanted to upgrade my Commercial Pilot's Licence (CPL) to an Air Transport Pilot's Licence (ATPL). After a pilot had built up a couple of thousand flying hours using their CPL, they were able to upgrade to an ATPL. You had to sit written exams in all the subjects that you had previously been tested on for your CPL but going into greater depth and covering some additional subject matter. Once your flying records had been checked to confirm you had gained the necessary experience in terms of flying hours, your CPL was swapped for an ATPL. Nowadays, you sit all your written exams to the ATPL standard at the very beginning and you are then awarded a 'frozen' ATPL. This means you can exercise all the privileges of a CPL until such time as you complete the required number of flying hours, at which point your ATPL is unfrozen and issued. This is a far more sensible way of doing things of course, but it just wasn't an option at the time.

Now I had to pass all the theory exams a second time, I needed to do an intensive period of studying to refresh my memory. Recognising this need, Dan-Air gave their first officers three weeks unpaid ATPL leave to enable them to study and then sit the exams. I paid to enrol on a course being run at the City of London Polytechnic that was specifically designed to bring you back up to speed ready to sit the ATPL exams. There were about twenty of us on the course, including two other Dan-Air first officers.

Each day I would catch a train at 6:30 from Haywards Heath to London Victoria. I then took the underground to Tower bridge from where it was a short walk to the Polytechnic. I would be in a classroom with various instructors for the whole day until it was time to journey back to Haywards Heath again. My wife would pick me up from the station and drive me home and after an evening meal I would hit the books again until around midnight. With only five hours sleep, I was up again and heading for the train station for more of the same. It was relentless and I basically shut myself off from everything else that was going on in the world and just concentrated 100% on my studies. At the end of the course, my head was so stuffed full of aviation related data that it was practically dribbling out of my ears. I sat the exams over a period of two days and to my immense relief, received the news from the CAA that I had passed with flying colours.

The reason for getting the ATPL, of course, was in preparation for promotion to captain. With a CPL, a person can only fly as pilot in command of aircraft with a maximum all up weight of 5,700 kgs. To be captain of a heavier aircraft you need an ATPL. Dan-Air had a further requirement that you needed a minimum of 4,000 hours flying experience before you could even be considered for promotion to captain on jet fleets. I still had some way to go, so it was back to work for me to clock up those additional flying hours.

In 1978, several Dan-Air directors felt the airline needed to modernise the fleet. Alan Snudden, the managing director, had been instrumental in getting the Comet into the airline some years before. He had negotiated a terrific deal for the company, not only in the purchase of the aircraft themselves, but also for an aircraft spares and crew training package as part of the overall deal. Since that time, he had also seen the introduction of the BAC 1-11, Boeing 707 and Boeing 727. Now, however, he saw the need for the airline to expand its European charter network with more fuel-efficient aircraft.

The company's director of flight operations, Errol Cossey, agreed with Snudden and the two of them attempted to persuade Fred Newman (the company Chairman) that this was vital if Dan-Air wished to remain one of the leading charter airlines in Europe. The new Boeing 737-200 Advanced was generally accepted as being the ideal aircraft in terms of performance, flexibility, and fuel efficiency. Martin O'Regan was Dan-Air's finance director and, in collaboration with Snudden and Cossey, he tried to convince Fred Newman that leasing brand-new fuel-efficient aircraft made better commercial sense than buying and owning older fuel thirsty types.

Newman remained unconvinced and elected to stick with what had worked well for the company up to that time. This decision had enormous implications. The three directors resigned from the company and their expertise was a sad loss for Dan-Air. It proved to be a blessing for Monarch Airlines, however, because Alan Snudden became their Managing Director. At the same time, Errol Cossey and Martin O'Regan helped to create a brand-new airline called Air Europe financed by Harry Goodman, the founder of Intasun Leisure.

Air Europe operated brand-new Boeing 737-200 Advanced aircraft that were coming straight off the production line at Seattle. They were directly linked (vertically integrated) with Intasun, who were a successful, very visible and expanding holiday company. They were also offering better pay and conditions to pilots. It's fair to say that they got everyone's attention and the idea of applying for a job with Air Europe did cross my mind more than once. It was a brand-new start up with fresh ideas and a very modern image. They were operating shiny new Boeing aircraft that were reliable, fuel efficient and proving to be ideal for the European charter market. The company was paying its aircrew a good salary and there were excellent prospects for rapid promotion for young first officers based on the airline's well publicised and ambitious expansion plans.

As for the negatives? Well, Dan-Air was a well-established airline and had already been operating for 26 years. Would this new upstart be successful in breaking into the charter market? Did they have the financial resources to back up their bold expansion plans? These were just a few of the unknowns at the time. Also, if I did join them, I would be forfeiting five years of seniority that I had earned with Dan-Air and, when I resigned, I was contractually obliged to immediately pay off my outstanding training loan in full. I decided to play it safe, stick where I was and see how events unfolded.

That said, the fact that three of Dan-Air's senior managers had decided to move on, left us feeling more than a little nervous. Did they know something that we mortals were unaware of? Were we clinging to a sinking ship? What was particularly worrying was the fact that those same managers had all felt it was vital that the company re-equipped with more modern fuel-efficient aircraft, but they had failed to convince the Chairman. We very much hoped that Mr Newman would change his mind sooner rather than later. Life continued much as before through the remainder of 1979, and I flew a total of 643 hours in 10 months. I took the whole of November off for annual leave so that my wife and I could take the kids to Australia to see their relatives. Apart from enjoying everyone's company down under, it was great to enjoy a few weeks of lovely summer weather during a month that normally guaranteed anything but lovely weather in Britain.

1980 was a busy year for me, and I continued to build on my flying experience. In the winter months—especially January and February at the start of the year, and November and December at the end—the weather was problematic. In the UK it often meant fog and in places like Norway—we had regular scheduled services to Kristiansand, Stavanger and Bergen—it was snow. Whatever the challenge, life never became dull. I was rostered to do a full Certificate of Airworthiness air test on one of our 400 series aircraft. The aircraft had undergone a major check at our Lasham maintenance base and had to have the air test prior to being returned to passenger service. As previously mentioned, C of A air tests are very thorough and require the pilots to take the aircraft to the very limits of its capabilities. This includes exploring the full speed range, from maximum to minimum. Needless to say, following the crashes during the BAC 1-11's early test programme, pilots were very wary of the bottom end of the speed envelope. Nevertheless, it had to be examined as part of the air test.

The stalling characteristics of the BAC 1-11 were such that if an excessively high angle of attack was adopted, instead of a natural pitch down occurring in response to the loss of lift, a pitch up could occur which would quickly lead to a deep stall from which recovery wasn't possible. Because the angle of attack was so critical during low speed, the engineers would remove a window from either side of the passenger cabin and replace them with blanking plates that had very sensitive vanes on the outside. The angle that they adopted was displayed on a large gauge in the cockpit and the cables from the vanes were rather crudely taped to the floor of the passenger cabin and routed forward to the flight deck. The large angle of attack display was temporarily mounted on top of the glare shield between the two pilots using more of the trusty tape. It all looked like a poor DIY job but, in fact, was perfectly adequate for our needs.

During the air test, the handling pilot smoothly increased the nose up attitude of the aircraft, causing the speed to decay at a steady rate. While that was happening, the monitoring pilot would be keeping a watchful eye on the angle of attack indicator mounted on the glare shield. The instrument had a red sector marked on it and if the needle entered that red zone, we knew that recovery was probably not possible. When it came to this portion of the air test programme, we were concentrating very hard on the job in hand. That said, I've always enjoyed doing air tests over the years. It reinforces your total confidence in the aircraft when you take it beyond the limits that are set for normal in-service passenger flights. Simply put, air tests are good fun.

In December 1980, my father retired. As the managing director of Dan-Air Engineering, he had steered the company through some enormous changes from his arrival in 1956. The engineering company had been steadily enlarged, not only to keep pace with Dan-Air's ever-expanding fleet, but also to accommodate third party airlines that rightly respected the engineering company's reputation for excellence. I remember feeling very proud on my father's behalf when I spoke to a senior Boeing official at the Farnborough Air Show in the late seventies. He told me that Boeing held Dan-Air Engineering in very high regard; one of a very few aviation engineering organisations they truly admired. That was certainly good to hear.

What many people (including a lot of his colleagues) didn't realise in 1980, was that Dad wasn't retiring because he'd had enough; it was because he was seriously ill. He was very much of the generation that 'didn't make a fuss' and so had kept his illness to himself, but the fact was, he was a walking time bomb in serious need of heart surgery. Eventually he admitted defeat and took early retirement to undergo open heart surgery: a quadruple bypass. The operation was conducted at Brompton hospital and my mother and I were at George Sutton's house when the operation was carried out. George was the fleet manager of Dan-Air's Boeing 707 fleet at the time and he and his family were close friends of my parents. I remember phoning Brompton from George's house to see how the operation had gone and being so relieved that they were happy with the outcome. I drove to London later that evening and spent time at Dad's bedside in the intensive care unit. The outcome was quite incredible: it was as though the surgeons had 'wound his clock back' because not only did he bounce back, but he seemed to have the energy and enthusiasm of a teenager. That crisis certainly ended very well.

As we began the busy summer season in 1981, there was still no sign of our chairman changing his mind about introducing Boeing 737s. Britannia Airways and Air Europe were two British airlines that were already utilising the Boeing 737 very successfully. Many of us in Dan-Air wished that we too could start operating the aircraft. I was kept busy as usual through the summer months, but as we approached the end of the season, we were told that the winter programme was looking much quieter than usual and offered the chance of taking winter off on half our normal salary. As it happened, my wife and I had recently put our house up for sale with the intention of upsizing. Now we considered the idea of selling our house and then heading off to Australia for the whole of the winter. With no mortgage to pay, we could easily survive on the half salary being offered by Dan-Air. We could spend time with Margaret's family and enjoy some nice weather in the Australian summer months. I could also explore the possibility of getting a flying job down under. Almost immediately, someone put in an offer on our house, so that made up our minds for us. At the end of August 1981, I operated my last flight, and the Williams family boarded a flight to Australia.

We arrived in Melbourne and were met by Margaret's parents who drove us to their home in Benalla in Northeast Victoria. We stayed there for a couple of weeks and then found a flat to rent in the South Yarra district of Melbourne. I bought a car, we enrolled the kids at the local school and I made an appointment at the Department of Civil Aviation's main office in Melbourne. Being married to an Aussie, gave me the right to reside and work in the country, so I needed to find out what was required to get an Australian senior commercial licence. The syllabus for the Aussie licence was based closely on that of the British ATPL, so I was advised that I needed to sit exams in senior commercial air law and airways operating procedures, followed by a flight test with a DCA flight examiner.

I had no idea what the airways operating procedures exam entailed as there was no equivalent in the UK, so I contacted a flying instructor who informed me that it was an 'open book' exam, and you took the Australian equivalent of our Air Pilot into the examination room with you. That reference book is very weighty indeed. The format of the questions would assume you were operating a charter flight from one airfield to another. You were then given questions covering pre-flight planning: route, fuel requirements, weather considerations, etc. A few 'curved balls' were then introduced to simulate unexpected changes to your original plan once the flight had begun. These might be in the form of changing weather conditions or altered requests from your passengers and so on.

It was a very practical and sensible exam that explored your knowledge over a wide range of subjects. All the answers were, of course, contained somewhere in the enormous reference manual, a book that was made up of hundreds of pages sub divided into various categories and sections. There was, naturally, a time limit for completing the exam once you had started the questionnaire, so you really had to know your way around the reference manual beforehand. From memory, I believe the minimum percentage mark for a pass was seventy percent, so I knew I had some hard work to do. I went to a flying club, explained my dilemma, and told them I needed access to the reference manual so that I could fully familiarise myself with it and then run some 'dummy questionnaires' to get up to speed for the exam. They kindly allowed me to borrow their manual and I locked myself away for some serious studying. Three weeks later, I got my Aussie licence. All I needed now was a flying job.

At the time, I was a member of the British Airline Pilots' Association (BALPA), so I called into the office of the Australian Federation of Air Pilots (AFAP) to find out what exactly was out there. Although Australia is a vast country and very dependent upon air travel, it had relatively few aircraft when compared to European countries. The total population of Australia was approximately the same as the population of Greater London at the time so, unsurprisingly, with fewer people to shift around, fewer aircraft were needed to do it. The AFAP representative that I met was brutally frank and honest but very helpful. He said that as long there were any unemployed Australian pilots, they would remain his priority. Once they were all gainfully employed, he would consider helping foreigners with an Australian pilot's licence.

Just to twist the knife that he had plunged between my shoulder blades, he showed me the salary scales for pilots in Australia. They earned considerably more than their counterparts in Britain and were flying far fewer hours judging by the average annual totals that he showed me. He might as well have said 'Here is what our pilots enjoy. Too bad you won't get to experience it personally.' I honestly believe that the average Australian airline pilot didn't realise how well off they were at that time in terms of salary, lifestyle and terms and conditions. Unfortunately for them, it all came to a messy end a few years later (1989) in a very bitter industrial dispute. It was the most expensive dispute in Australia's history and came to a head when AFAP pushed for a mind-boggling twenty-nine percent pay increase for their pilots. It backfired on them when the Government refused to give in, and both sides decided to dig in for a battle.

When a government official was quoted as saying the pilots had a distorted view of their own importance and that they had no more responsibility than a bus driver, the pilots responded by stating that they were now only prepared to work office hours: 9 am to 5 pm. The resultant travel chaos turned pretty much everyone against them and made the government even more determined to wipe out AFAP.

The government then brought in the Royal Australian Air Force and chartered several foreign airlines and crews to operate domestic air services. This was followed by the airlines threatening to take the pilots to court for breach of contract, which resulted in the mass resignation of 1,600 pilots, who quit to avoid litigation. The government was now even more determined to smash the Australian Federation of Air Pilots and open the way for deregulation of the aviation industry in Australia. New individual pilot contracts were drawn up that were far less favourable than before. The airlines began recruiting pilots under the terms of those new contracts, including many foreign pilots who had their visas fast tracked by the Australian government to assist with their speedy arrival. Air services finally began to get back to normal levels, but it has been estimated that as many as eighty percent of the pilots that had resigned during the dispute never returned to fly in Australia. I was to meet many of them in various parts of the world in the years ahead and not surprisingly, they were still bitter about the whole debacle.

Chapter Eight

All that was still to come, but in the meantime, there were no airline jobs to be had for me. Despite that, I sent off letters and CVs to anyone and everyone who was operating an aircraft commercially in Australia. AFAP had at least provided me with a list of all those operators along with their contact details. There followed a depressing stream of letters in my mailbox, all saying the same thing. 'Thank you for your interest, but unfortunately …'

To keep myself sane, I got a job as a delivery driver with Safeway supermarkets. I also worked as a barman in a pub in Melbourne. I now realised that a flying job wasn't going to happen. It was time to move on and do some sightseeing instead. The kids had just broken up from school for their summer vacation, so the time had come for us all to start enjoying ourselves. We loaded up the car with our stuff, filled the tank with fuel and hit the road. We had a ball. We drove back up to Benalla and stayed with my in-laws for a couple of days. Then we went up to Deniliquin in the Riverina region of New South Wales. We had some friends who lived there, who we hadn't seen since they had attended our wedding. After a couple of days staying with them, we drove on up to Canberra and stayed in motels for a couple of days. From there, we went to Swansea, a town at the entrance to Lake Macquarie.

Julie and Des were a lovely couple and Julie had been the bridesmaid at our wedding. They had a very laid-back lifestyle and lived in a comfortable home with a garden (back yard in their parlance) that literally ran down to the lake shore. Des had a boat and took me out onto Lake Macquarie to show me the area and share a beer or two. As we gently made our way across the water, a shadow briefly passed over our boat and I looked up to see a de Havilland Twin Otter fly overhead. It was so low, that I jokingly said to Des 'Either there is an airport around here, or that guy is in serious trouble.' Des laughed and confirmed that the aircraft was operated by Aero Pelican, an outfit based at nearby Newcastle airport who flew scheduled services between Newcastle and Sydney. He saw that my interest was aroused and added that he knew the chief pilot, who was often to be found cruising around the lake on his boat. Sure enough, we later ran into the guy, but when I asked him if he had any pilot jobs going, he replied that most of his captains were ex Qantas or Ansett who had taken early retirement from the big airlines, and he would have to use dynamite to get them out of the company. They usually flew a couple of round trips between Newcastle and Sydney and then got back to the serious business of fishing off the deck of their boat on the lake! I could well see the need for dynamite to extract them from that sort of lifestyle and I tried very hard not to look green with envy.

After staying with Julie and Des, we continued up to the city of Sydney for a while, then on to Townsville and Cairns. We rode on the amazing and beautiful Kuranda scenic railway over the Great Dividing Range to the Atherton tableland. We went out to Green Island and went snorkelling on the Great Barrier Reef. We did everything and yet, there was still more that we could and wanted to do. I well and truly fell in love with Australia.

My six-month extended leave from Dan-Air was due to end in February 1982 but, long before then, I was seriously thinking of settling in Australia for good. I still felt that I would be able to secure a flying job eventually and, in the meantime, I could find casual work to keep the wolf from the door. We were in love with the country, its laid-back lifestyle, the wide-open spaces, the lack of crowds, the barbecues, the beaches, and the lovely weather. Why leave?

The answer came in February of 1982 when we heard that Laker Airways had gone bust. I felt desperately sorry for all the Laker employees but—from a purely selfish point of view—my immediate thought was that Laker had been operating a fleet of BAC 1-11 aircraft, as well as his DC-10s and Airbuses. That meant there would be plenty of 1-11 rated pilots looking for jobs. I reckoned I'd better get back home before Dan-Air forgot that I existed! Once again, our family was on the move.

We arrived back in England in late February 1982 and a few days later I found myself standing in the Dan-Air operations building at Bournemouth airport. I was back with George Forman, the 1-11 chief training captain, and we were there to get me 'back in the saddle' after my six-month absence. Three fast and furious circuits of Bournemouth airport followed. We took off, flew around the circuit, made an approach and a touch and go. We then flew another circuit and another touch and go. On the climb out from the second touch and go, George failed an engine on me. I climbed to circuit altitude, flew around the circuit and came in for a single-engine landing. As we taxied in, George turned to me and said 'Welcome home Bob. It's good to have you back.' Having not flown an aircraft for six months, those three circuits had been a heck of a reawakening, but it felt really good to be back at the controls again.

Four days later, I operated a flight from Gatwick to Frankfurt and back. The next day, to Majorca and back and the day after that, to Turin and back. That was in March 1982, and it turned out to be my last flight on the BAC 1-11. I got a phone call telling me there was to be a Boeing 737 course starting in eight days' time and I was on it.

I had clocked up 2,466 flying hours on the 1-11 and carried out 1,259 take offs and landings during that time. In spite of a few incidents, my abiding memory of flying the BAC 1-11 is of a reliable aircraft that was built like a tank. Apart from unimpressive take-off performance, it was a very nice aircraft to fly. Most of my problem flights were actually weather related. Although it coped well with

A Boeing 737-2L9 (Advanced) of Dan-Air

turbulence and crosswinds, being a CAT 1 aircraft, we had a decision height of 200 feet and a minimum horizontal visibility of 550 metres when making an ILS approach. Consequently, in very foggy conditions, we could find ourselves having to divert to our alternate airport but, of course, that would have been true of any CAT 1 aircraft.

Now it was time for me to go back to school again. This time, to learn all about the Boeing 737-200 Advanced. It was the latest variant to come rolling off the production line at Seattle and I could hardly wait to start flying it. After the BAC 1-11, the Boeing 737 seemed like a hot rod. The take-off and climb performance was especially impressive in comparison. We used to joke that when the 737 was flying with one engine shut down, its rate of climb was better than the BAC 1-11 could manage on two engines. Because of its excellent runway performance, the 737 was also able to take-off and land using the very short runways to be found on some of the popular Greek holiday islands. Previously, those runways could only be used by propellor driven commuter aircraft, but now holiday makers could fly there direct from the UK.

After a flight to Greece, we would only have a light fuel

load remaining, so were able to land on a short runway. However, at airfields with a very short runway, such as Skiathos, we had to take a limited amount of fuel for the flight home if we had a full passenger load. Consequently, we would have to land somewhere on the way back for a refuelling stop. From Skiathos, for example, we usually flew to Thessaloniki on the Greek mainland. That airport had a long runway, so we could quickly fill up with fuel and take-off again for the flight back to the UK. We normally aimed to be in and out of there in about twenty minutes. The passengers remained on board throughout the process, while the crew ran around like maniacs trying to get everything done as quickly as possible. Maybe we weren't as slick as the pit crews in a Formula One motor race, but it was well choreographed, nonetheless.

The aircraft's versatility enabled us to use pretty much any airfield and with built-in airstairs at the forward passenger door and an auxiliary power unit (APU) for engine starting and air conditioning, we had no need for any fancy ground equipment to be put in place at those more 'basic' destinations. The 737's despatch reliability also proved to be excellent, and the airline was able to achieve very high utilisation. Each aircraft flew thousands of hours per year and the crews were kept extremely busy.

In March 1984, I received some very welcome news. The company was getting more Boeing 737s and, consequently, needed more captains to fly them. Following my simulator check flights every six months and regular line checks over the years, the training department had recommended me for promotion to captain while I was still flying the BAC 1-11, but there hadn't been any command vacancies for some time, so I had been patiently waiting. Once a pilot had been assessed as being suitable for command promotion then they were given the rank of senior first officer (denoted by a third stripe on their uniform sleeves.) Now they just had to wait for a command vacancy to come up. The standard joke was that a captain should be very wary if a senior first officer stood to one side when at the top of a flight of stairs and invited the captain to descend ahead of them. A firm push in the back, would instantly create that long awaited vacancy! Anyway, it now seemed that I wasn't going to have to resort to such dirty tricks.

I started my command conversation course in March 1984. That was followed by four days in the simulator, sixteen hours in total, and then base training at Newcastle airport including six approaches, four of them with one engine shut down. Finally, there would be ten sectors of line training, including a final line check. My logbook confirms that my final line check took place on 24 April with Captain Malcolm Grant, our 737 Fleet Manager. The first officer for the trip was an Australian pilot by the name of John Byrnes and the flight was from Gatwick to Tenerife and back. I was now a Boeing 737 captain. It felt pretty damned good, and it also felt very comfortable. I knew that I was taking on more responsibility, but I was fine with that.

In the past, if something unusual occurred, or an on-the-spot decision had to be made, I had always had the luxury of turning my head to the left and looking to the captain for confirmation. Now, if I looked to the left, all I saw was my own reflection in the side window. The buck stopped with me from now on and that was just fine.

They were busy days, and I was soon averaging over 700 flying hours a year and spending a lot of time away from home base. We would be despatched to Birmingham, Stansted, Manchester and Newcastle any time there was a shortage of crews at those bases due to sickness or annual holidays or whatever, because the company tended to keep the outstations slightly under crewed. The Berlin base, however, was entirely dependent on (mainly) Gatwick based pilots to cover their flying programme. We would spend up to ten days at a time in Berlin, before returning to the UK for a few days off and then we'd be off again for a spell somewhere else. One year, I only flew from Gatwick seven times throughout the whole year, despite the fact it was supposed to be my home base. All my other flights that year had originated from one of the company's outstations.

In terms of flights that were slightly out of the ordinary during that period, I did certificate of airworthiness test flights on two aircraft belonging to Bahamasair. Their chief pilot rode on the flight deck jump seat as an observer on the first flight and he was going to fly that aircraft back to Nassau the next day. The aircraft's galley had been removed during the maintenance check to be completely refurbished in the workshop. We decided to do the test flight first and then the guys could refit the galley into the aircraft when we got back.

The weather that day was not good, with a relatively low overcast of cloud and quite strong winds, however, the skies above the cloud layer were clear and suitable for us to do our air test. The flight went to plan, and the aircraft was performing well as we carried out the required manoeuvres and ticked off the many items on the test programme. We had been airborne for a couple of hours and only had a few more items to complete when we requested an update on the weather situation. The news wasn't good; the weather had deteriorated, and the cloud base was even lower than before. Worse still, the wind had really picked up and was now very strong with frequent gusts.

There were no radio navigation aids at Lasham and we normally located the airfield by flying a radial from the nearby Midhurst VOR. At a certain DME distance along the radial, we knew we were overhead the airfield. However, with the weather that Lasham had described, I calculated that we were going to need them to give us a radar talkdown for the approach. Then they came back with the bad news that they would not be able to give us radar assistance today, because the wind was too strong; the very ancient radar at Lasham could only work in relatively light winds, above which the radar scanner was literally unable to rotate.

Under normal circumstances, we would have merely shrugged our shoulders and diverted to Gatwick, as it was only about fifteen minutes flying time away. However, these weren't normal circumstances because the aircraft's galley was sitting in a workshop at Lasham airfield. What to do? I suddenly remembered a trick that I employed a couple of times back when I flew light aircraft from nearby

The Dan-Air engineering base at Lasham (above) and a Boeing 737-2K5 (Advanced) of Bahamasair (below)

Blackbushe airfield. I called Farnborough radar and asked if they could put us onto the extended centre line for Lasham's runway. They readily agreed and began giving us headings to steer towards the airfield. As they counted the miles down, we descended into the thick cloud. It was dark, raining heavily and the windscreen wipers were sweeping back and forth across the blurred screens. Fortunately, I caught sight of Lasham's dim runway lights moments before a missed approach would have been necessary. They were very basic battery powered runway edge lights but had been good enough for our needs on this occasion. Farnborough radar had saved the day, and the Bahamasair pilot on the jump seat let out a sigh of relief. The engineers could get on with the job of refitting the galley into his aircraft and he could fly off tomorrow towards much nicer weather awaiting him in the Bahamas. Funnily enough, when I did the air test on the second Bahamasair 737, the weather was bad again at Lasham and we ended up having to divert to Gatwick on that occasion.

I once had an unusual problem when nearing the end of a flight into Gatwick. We had started the day by flying from Manchester to Malta. Having dropped off passengers there, we set off for our return to London Gatwick. The flight had been unremarkable until we were descending towards our destination. As we passed 10,000 feet, the cabin pressurisation suddenly went berserk. The cabin altitude had been descending nicely at about 300 feet per minute, but now it suddenly started climbing at 4,000 feet a minute. With my ears popping, I called for the first officer to switch the pressurisation controller from auto to standby. This appeared to be unserviceable as well, so he selected manual DC, which was the primary way to manually open or close the outflow valve. Amazingly, this was having no effect either. The only remaining option was to select manual AC, which was a courser (and faster) way of opening the outflow valve. This didn't work either! Thoroughly confused and with the cabin altitude refusing to come down, I advised air traffic control that we were temporarily unable to depressurise the aircraft and wanted to take up the holding pattern at Mayfield, to the southeast of Gatwick airport, to try and sort it out.

Needless to say, we had been getting reports from the cabin crew that the passengers were complaining about their ears hurting because of the cabin pressure changes. I spoke to the passengers on the public address system to confirm what they had already guessed—that we had a pressurisation problem—and to apologise for their discomfort. I told them we were working on it and would be landing soon. I then spoke to our engineers on our company's dedicated radio frequency. Having outlined the problem and explained that we had lost four separate control systems; automatic, standby and two manual systems, I left them scratching their heads trying to work out what had happened. We continued to fly around the holding pattern at 3,000 feet and kept trying to open the outflow valve using the two manual systems. For some time, the outflow valve refused to move, but then, after about fifteen minutes, with a sudden whoosh of air, the valve opened, and the cabin altitude came down at around 2,000 feet per minute. With our ears popping, we finally got the aircraft depressurised and came in to land.

After the passengers had all disembarked, I hung around with the engineers as they started to investigate the cause of our problems. It didn't take long, and we soon got the full story. When on the ground at Malta, the ground service personnel had replenished the domestic water tank and serviced the toilets. Unknown to me, when they filled the water tank the automatic high level cut off had failed to operate, resulting in them temporarily flooding the rear galley floor area. They quickly mopped up the water from the floor area and had it looking fine again. Unfortunately, a good deal of water had seeped below the floor and soaked into a large insulating blanket that was attached below floor level. The insulation had become so water soaked and heavy that it became detached and dropped a couple of feet, draping itself across the drive mechanism for the pressurisation outflow valve. After we took off for our flight to Gatwick, the outflow valve had closed normally, but the blanket became tangled around the drive mechanism in the process. When we climbed to cruise altitude, the temperature dropped dramatically, and the water-soaked insulating blanket froze solid. That prevented the movement of the outflow valve until we had spent some time at low altitude, and it had all started to thaw out again. That was certainly a very unusual incident, and one that resulted in the publication of an engineering bulletin, highlighting the need to modify the method of securing those insulation blankets. The new fasteners would ensure that it couldn't drop onto the outflow valve motor. Another modification in response to another incident. Future problems avoided.

Airfields are categorised A, B or C by the airlines. Cat A airfields are 'no problem' places. They will have good air traffic control facilities, will be in areas where there are no terrain issues—in other words, no dirty great mountains nearby—and there will be precision navigation and approach aids in the form of VOR, DME, ILS, approach radar, etc. They will have a nice long runway, or multiple runways, that are more than adequate for a pilot's needs. There will also be full fire and rescue services available on site to deal with any emergencies.

Next is the Cat B airfield. These will have at least one feature that crews need to be made aware of. It could be, for example, that when the surface wind is blowing from a certain direction the local terrain, or a large building or structure, can cause rotor turbulence that affects aircraft on final approach. It could be that the air traffic controllers only have a basic knowledge of English because it is not their native language. Whatever the noteworthy feature is, crews should be aware of it and keep it in mind. This is normally achieved in the form of a specific written brief on that airfield. The pilots should read and familiarise themselves with the brief before operating in or out of there, forewarned being forearmed.

Last is the Cat C airfield. This is deemed to be demanding in some way and needs unique procedures or precautions to safely operate there. A pilot may need special training in a flight simulator to practice those procedures, and they will then have to be checked into the airfield under the supervision of a training captain who is fully familiar with the place. Only then will they be allowed to operate in and out of there without further restriction. Dan-Air used to operate into quite a few Cat C airfields and I had been cleared to fly into all of them.

The runway at Funchal, Madeira (above) and Skiathos, Greece (below)

At that time, the runway at Funchal, Madeira, was short, with a vertical drop into the sea at either end of it. They have since made the runway significantly longer by building an extension on an impressive array of pillars or stilts. However, the windshear, and the drop into the sea off either end of the runway, are problems that remain.

Skiathos was Cat C and had some novel features. You would arrive overhead and then fly a lazy orbit before letting down over the sea and manoeuvring onto the approach for the runway. They didn't have a fire engine at the airfield, the only fire engine on the island was based in the town, and when they saw your aircraft flying overhead, the firemen would leap aboard their truck and race the short distance to the airfield. By the time you had manoeuvred your aircraft onto final approach the guy in the control tower—who was not a licensed air traffic controller—would advise you that 'The Fire engine is here and ready for you.' We could then continue our approach and land. Once they saw that you hadn't crashed, they would stand down again. It made me smile every time.

One evening, I received a phone call from Alan Howard, the head of training on the 737 fleet. I was rostered to fly to Zakinthos the next day and he wanted to tell me that a Boeing instructor pilot would be coming along on the flight. Apparently, it had come to Boeing's attention that we were routinely flying into some demanding airfields with short runways. In fact, some of them were shorter than the airfield that Boeing used in America to demonstrate the short landing capability of their 737 to potential customers. Alan said the guy wanted to sit on the flight deck jump seat and observe me going into Zakinthos the next day just to get a feel for our operating procedures and how we dealt with the trickier aspects of flying into Cat C airfields. I must admit that I was a little unnerved at the thought of having an ace Boeing instructor pilot looking over my shoulder for the flight, but thought that it would, at the very least, be interesting to meet him.

The next day in the flight planning office at Gatwick, my first officer and I met up with Boeing Captain Ed Hoit. He was a very pleasant guy and we hit it off straight away. The flight down to Greece was uneventful and I had shown Ed the Cat C briefing in our operations manual. I then gave him and the first officer a thorough approach briefing. I explained to Ed that Athens air traffic control would be looking after us until we got to our top of descent point. Athens ATC didn't have radar in those days, so any requests for descent clearance were invariably followed by the instruction 'Standby, I'll call you back.' Of course, all the time you were 'standing by' and waiting for his call back, you were getting closer to your destination at the rate of seven miles a minute. A further request for descent usually elicited another 'Standby' response. A third, by now more urgent request, would be followed by the controller asking another aircraft what their distance was from a particular DME station. After a delay, that aircraft would respond with his distance. Then the controller would ask you what your DME distance was from the same station, and you would tell him, but nothing would happen. Quite a few 'seven miles a minutes' passed by and by now you were a lot closer to your destination. Finally, you would be given descent clearance to a lower level. You then closed the thrust levers all the way back to idle thrust, lowered the nose of the aircraft, extended the speed brake and started plummeting down like a streamlined crowbar. Before you got down to your cleared level, you would tell the controller that you had Zakinthos in sight, which was, of course, a blatant lie. You did have the island of Zante in sight, but not Zakinthos airfield itself. The controller would ask you to confirm that you had visual contact with Zakinthos and you lied once again. This was exactly what the Athens controller wanted to hear as he could now get rid of you. He would sign off with the words 'You are cleared to leave controlled airspace by descent. Your IFR flight plan is cancelled. Maintain VFR and contact Zakinthos Tower. Good day.'

While all this was going on, the first officer would be on the second radio talking to a nearby Greek Air Force airfield, to try and find out if there was any military traffic in the area. More often than not, his calls went unanswered, so we kept our heads on a swivel in an attempt to spot any conflicting traffic. The Greek fighters used UHF radio frequencies which we didn't have, and they were unlikely to be monitoring our VHF frequency. The person in the control tower at Zakinthos was not a licensed controller and could only give you the QNH (altimeter setting) and surface wind direction and speed. Based on that, you told him in which direction you were going to land. There were no navigation or landing aids on the island so, if it was cloudy, we would find the airfield by tuning a couple of distant VORs and dialling up the appropriate radials for a position fix. The approach was purely visual and there were no VASIS or PAPIS for approach slope guidance. The runway was much narrower than the 150 foot industry standard—just 90 feet wide—so the visual picture was unusual, and you had to beware of the impression that you were too high on the approach. The runway was also very short back then (it has since been extended), so autobrake and full reverse thrust was needed on touchdown. In later years they lengthened the runway, installed a VOR with a break-cloud procedural let down and installed Precision Approach Path Indicators (PAPI). In other words, they took all the fun out of it!

As we came to a halt on the small parking apron and I shut down the engines, Ed said 'If you know how much fuel you need for the return flight Bob, I'll jump out and set up the fuel panel for you.' I thanked him and gave him the fuel figure. As he turned to leave the flight deck, I suddenly remembered something. The guy who drove the fuel truck at Zakinthos was a very cheerful character and he always enjoyed talking and joking with the pilots and, of course, chatting up our stewardesses. The last time I had seen him, he had asked if I could bring him a bunch of bananas—they were expensive on the island—and I'd brought a bunch in my flight bag. I called to Ed, held out the bananas and said, 'Please give these to the refuelling guy.' Ed stared at them for a moment and said 'I've paid for fuel using credit cards, local currency, US Dollars, but never bananas! Will that bunch be right for the fuel we need, or are you expecting some change?' I enjoyed flying with Ed.

Chapter Nine

It is an unfortunate fact that there is a high divorce rate among aircrew. This applies to flight deck crews mainly, as the majority of cabin crew are young and single. In fact, in Dan-Air for many years, if a stewardess got married, she was required to immediately resign from the company, as per the terms of her contract. Anyway, in October 1985 I added to the broken marriage statistics when I moved out of the 'former matrimonial home' as solicitors like to call it. Things had not been right with our marriage for a long time, and I then started a relationship with one of our Birmingham based stewardesses. My marriage was well and truly over and—when the breakup finally came—it was a relief but, at the same time, deeply upsetting. There is never a 'good' time for a couple to separate and with Paul and Nicole just coming up to their tenth birthday, that statement never rang truer. My coping mechanism was to throw myself into my work and, as far as I was concerned, the busier I was, the better.

I went to see my fleet manager, Captain Malcolm Grant. I really liked Malcolm and had always enjoyed flying with him when I was a first officer. I told him that my wife and I had split up and he asked me if I wanted to take some compassionate leave. I explained that I really wanted to be kept busy and also wanted a transfer to the Birmingham base. Up to that time, all the cabin crew who flew out of Birmingham were based there, but the pilots were from Gatwick and came to Birmingham for a few days at a time. The company had now decided that they were going to assign pilots to the Birmingham base on a permanent basis. Once I explained to Malcolm the reason I wanted to be based there, he realised that it would be to everyone's benefit and authorised it.

The Dan-Air Birmingham base was small but friendly. The crews based there were a great bunch and we worked and socialised well together. If we had needed a motto, it would have been 'Work hard, but don't forget to play hard.' and we did our very best to follow that doctrine. Initially, there was a single Boeing 737 based there, but it was later joined by a BAC 1-11. The 737 (G-BKNH) was fitted with the more powerful JT8D-17 engines. The commercial department had sold a gruelling and incredibly busy flight programme from Birmingham and our 737 quickly proved to be a shining example of just what utilisation could be achieved from a well-maintained Boeing. A crew would operate an early morning departure to 'A' and back. They would be replaced by another crew who took the aircraft to 'B' and back again. In the evening, a third crew would take the aircraft to 'C' and back. This would get the aircraft into position and ready to repeat the same process all over again the following day. The aircraft was clocking up around sixteen hours of flight time per day and a total of approximately 4,600 flight hours per year. We had excellent engineering back up and we knew 'our' aircraft. November Hotel was our baby, and we understood every one of her quirks and peculiarities.

In 1986, we were unexpectedly short of captains at Birmingham (someone who was due to transfer to the base failed his command conversion course and another person left the company) so those of us who were already based there found ourselves working very hard indeed. That year I clocked up 818 flying hours and, if I wasn't busy enough doing that, my girlfriend Sara and I bought a house in Solihull that was in serious need of tender loving care. I built and fitted a whole new kitchen and Sara and I redecorated every single room in the house. It was a very busy time indeed, but also very satisfying from both a professional and personal point of view.

In 1988, Sara and I got married and took a short honeymoon in Sri Lanka, before getting back to work again. Not long afterwards, Dan-Air had an unpleasant surprise for us; they were going to close the Birmingham base. In the mid to late eighties, the inclusive tour market in Europe had been going through a lot of changes with several tour companies and airlines becoming vertically integrated. The tour company Intasun, and the airline Air Europe, were a good example and their expansion had been impressive. To our disappointment, there appeared to be no sign of Dan-Air either buying an existing tour company or creating one of their own. They were relying on selling seats to tour companies that hadn't set up their own airline. Inclusive tour charter flying has always tended to be seasonal in nature, with inevitable 'peaks and troughs.' Most charter airlines rely on having made enough money in the frantic summer months to see them through the lean winter months. Scheduled service flying on the other hand, generates revenue all year around with little difference in traffic between summer and winter. Dan-Air had begun to expand their scheduled service network by this time, with some routes doing well, but the company had no scheduled routes from Birmingham and competition for the charter work was getting keener all the time. Like it or not, our base was closing, and we were all going to have to relocate.

I was offered a transfer to either Gatwick or Manchester. I opted for Manchester which, unknown to me at the time, would have a profound effect on my career four years further down the line. However, for now I was back to having to commute quite a distance to work every day. If there were no traffic problems, it took me around an hour and a half to drive from our home in Solihull to Manchester airport, but it could take a lot longer, so I had to allow extra travel time. This meant I was back to doing very long working days and clocking up a lot of mileage in my car. There was no getting away from it, we needed to move house again!

Many weeks passed as we searched for our next home.

Sara would do the rounds of all the estate agents in the Manchester area. She would pick up details on any houses that looked to be of interest, make appointments to view them and then, when I finished work, we would check them out together. The housing market was very buoyant at the time and prices were rising fast. We had put our home on the market and had received several offers almost immediately. It was crazy because people were bidding against one another and offering us more than our asking price!

They say that moving house is one of the most stressful things you can do. Although I had done it many times since becoming an airline pilot, it certainly didn't get any easier. Anyway, after some more stress and disappointment, we finally did manage to buy a place in Wilmslow, and we moved into our new home in February 1989. Sara was now living close to her parents and her brother and sister, and I had a very short drive to work at Manchester airport. Perfect. Unfortunately, this idyllic state of affairs would only last for just over three years, but at this stage we weren't to know that.

In April 1989 I was flying from Manchester to Las Palmas and because of ATC problems (the French air traffic controllers were playing silly buggers again) we had refiled our flight planned route out to one of the 'Tango airways' in the Atlantic that kept us clear of French airspace. We were feeling quite pleased with ourselves for having minimised our delay in this way and beating the French ATC industrial action. Suddenly, the flight deck door opened, and the 'number one' (senior cabin crew member) came in and said 'Just to let you know Bob, I've got a passenger who is showing all the symptoms of a heart attack. Too early to say for sure yet and I will of course update you, but I just wanted to give you a heads up that we might need to divert.' With that, she closed the door and disappeared.

The first officer and I looked at each other for a moment. I had a lot of respect for this particular 'number one.' She was a no-nonsense girl who was very good at her job and wasn't prone to overreacting. Cabin crew frequently have to put up with an awful lot. Disruptive, rude or drunken passengers are an all too frequent occurrence. Disruptive, rude and perfectly sober passengers are all too common as well. Some people seem to think that cabin crew are nothing more than airborne waiters and waitresses, but in fact they are primarily there for their passenger's safety. I knew from previous experience that she calmly dealt with all that was thrown at her during a flight. Consequently, if she was now concerned about a passenger's health, I knew that I should be too.

I told the first officer to get the latest weather report for Lisbon, as that was the nearest suitable airport from our current position. I extracted the approach and landing charts for Lisbon from our 'ship's library' of Jeppesen charts. Moments later, he gave me the latest Lisbon weather conditions, including the current runway in use and altimeter pressure setting. Armed with that information, I told him 'You have control. I'm going to nip back into the cabin and see how they are getting on with that passenger they were worried about.'

I climbed out of my seat, stepped out into the forward galley area and stopped dead in my tracks. On the floor in front of me was a man lying on his back. The senior stewardess was kneeling beside him and giving him mouth to mouth resuscitation, followed by chest compressions. The passengers who were in the first row of seats and in full view of the proceedings were staring, wide eyed and horrified. I watched for another couple of seconds before retreating to the flight deck. I immediately radioed Lisbon air traffic control, declared a medical emergency and requested clearance for a diversion direct to Lisbon airport. The response was excellent, and I was immediately cleared to turn towards Lisbon and begin my descent when ready. The controller then issued lots of instructions to other aircraft to get out of our way and he followed that up with the information that I was cleared for an unrestricted descent to make an approach onto the runway of my choosing at Lisbon. I kept up maximum possible speed as we descended and told the first officer to advise the passengers that everybody needed to get strapped in for an immediate landing. I told the tower controller at Lisbon that we needed paramedics to meet the aircraft on arrival and that our aircraft had airstairs so they could immediately board our aircraft via the forward passenger door.

We landed a few minutes later and shortly after clearing the runway, we were told to stop on the taxiway. The ambulance pulled up alongside us and the paramedics came aboard moments later. The senior stewardess was still kneeling alongside her patient as the medics came aboard and—once they had transferred him onto a stretcher—soon had him on his way to hospital. It was all very impressive, and we got a loud round of applause from our passengers. The cabin crew were the ones who had earned it, but the first officer and I soaked it up too.

When we finally got to Las Palmas, our passengers disembarked, and we got the aircraft refuelled, re-catered and the cabin cleaned before our next passengers boarded. The senior stewardess told me, with a smile, that quite a few of the joining passengers moaned as they got on because we were running forty-five minutes late. She hadn't bothered to tell them it was because she had been busy saving someone's life, so I made a point of telling them when I made my 'welcome aboard' announcement. We heard later that the passenger spent some time in hospital in Lisbon and, when he had fully recovered, was flown home to Manchester.

In November 1989, Dan-Air received some devastating news. Harry Goodman's International Leisure Group—which had been giving Dan-Air a great deal of work through their subsidiary, Intasun—transferred all the contracts to their in-house airline, Air Europe. At the same time, they took their maintenance work away from Dan-Air Engineering. This instantly created a cash flow problem for the company. In response, they began talks with Michael Bishop, the head of British Midland Airways, but the negotiations came to nothing. To make matters worse, Goodman called press conferences in which he made disparaging remarks about Dan-Air and—while staying on the safe side of libel—hinted that Dan-Air was ailing financially and might be best avoided if you were making holiday travel plans. He obviously wanted Dan-Air removed from the scene to leave the way clear for Air Europe. Baring Brothers—Dan-Air's financial advisors—were nervous about the company's predicament and recommended to the board that they should call in David James, a 'Company Doctor' who had successfully turned around several ailing companies. In October 1990, he was asked if he would take over as chairman of Dan-Air, but he refused.

The company desperately needed a cash injection, but when talks between Fred Newman and the banks broke down, James was again asked for help. This time he agreed to take over Dan-Air's negotiations and managed to secure a £70 million bank guarantee following which he was appointed Dan-Air's chairman, replacing Fred Newman. It seemed that the company's survival was secure, at least for the time being.

In November 1990, I was put on a course for the Boeing 737-300 and 400 series aircraft. It followed the usual classroom and flight simulator format, and I was soon cleared to line on the new types. The glass cockpit certainly increased a pilot's situational awareness and, with me being an old school stick and rudder man, my healthy dose of suspicion regarding all the whistles, bells and gizmos ensured there was no likelihood of over-reliance on automation (a trait that would become apparent among some pilots in later years). The 400s didn't handle quite as nicely as the 200s (particularly the rate of roll) but they were superior in pretty much every other way. I was thoroughly enjoying flying them and I also enjoyed playing with all the boys' toys on the flight deck. Perhaps because I was determined not to turn into a pushbutton pilot, I often liked to hand fly the aircraft from lift off up to the top of climb. I would then engage the autopilot and fly it that way until we reached the top of descent point.

Having disengaged the autopilot, I would then hand fly the aircraft all the way down to the runway. My aim was always to achieve a continuous descent at idle thrust until on final approach.

At the end of 1990, we received more shocking news. Dan-Air's board of directors had invited tenders for the sale of Dan-Air Engineering Limited. The company was trying to raise more cash, but this felt like a desperate measure—it was obvious that our survival was still in the balance. The Danish owned FLS Aerospace won the bidding at a price of £27.5 Million and in February 1991, ownership of the company was transferred to them, along with 1,800 employees.

In January 1991, I flew a 737-400 to Istanbul. I had just got out of the shower when the phone by my bed rang. The person on the other end of the line checked to see if he was talking to Captain Williams of Dan-Air. When I confirmed that was indeed me, he told me that we would not be flying from Istanbul to Goa the next day, as planned, but would be taking the aircraft back to Gatwick. When I asked why, he said it was because the Gulf War was starting! My initial reaction was that it was a wind up and the person on the other end of the phone line was really my first officer impersonating a military official. I said something rude and told him to stop mucking about and to get around to my room with a couple of beers and a bottle opener. There was a stunned silence before the person went on to explain that it was a genuine call. The Gulf War did, of course, have a profound effect on air travel and on Dan-Air's fortunes.

In 1991 Air Europe went bust. Their demise was sudden and spectacular. Staff members turned up for work at the airport to scenes of chaos. Huge queues had formed at the passenger check in desks. The flight information boards in the terminal building showed the word 'Cancelled' alongside every single Air Europe flight. Uniformed staff members at the check in desks, on the ramp and in the crew room were in a state of shock and many of them were crying. They were finding out at the same time as the travelling public, that the airline had collapsed. Many refused to believe it until news reports started coming through on the radio and television confirming the shocking news. Angry scenes began at the check in desks with some passengers demanding to know what they were supposed to do now their flight had been cancelled. Nobody in authority had told the staff what was going on and many of them broke down in tears.

Because of the Gulf War and several other factors, there were a lot of changes taking place within Dan-Air and some of them made me feel uncomfortable. Decisions were being made and then, five minutes later, were being unmade again. One example was that we weren't going to have any 300 or 400 series Boeing 737s based at Manchester after all, so in April, less than five months after my conversion course onto the 400 series aircraft, I was converted back onto the 200 series. With an understandable feeling of *deja vu*, I once again took to the air in the clockwork 737.

In a series of newsletters to staff, David James made it clear that his business plan called for Dan-Air to maintain a strong presence in the charter world but reduce the size of the charter fleet, while developing our scheduled services network and rebranding the airline in the eyes of the public. Instead of thinking of it as a holiday airline, they should now identify Dan-Air as a scheduled business carrier. The introduction of a 'Class Elite' business section in the passenger cabin was proving to be very popular and was considered superior to the equivalent product being offered by rival airlines. The interiors of the existing aircraft had been refurbished and the whole image of the airline enhanced. New 737 aircraft continued to arrive from the Boeing factory in Seattle and the idea seemed to be that the Boeing 737 and BAe 146 fleets would be continuously expanded to serve the scheduled service side of the business. Unfortunately, what could not have been foreseen was the Gulf War with its negative effect on air travel, especially for business. We all crossed our fingers and hoped that things would pick up again sooner rather than later.

My logbook records another 'interesting' flight in

September 1991. We took off from Berlin Tegel for Turkey. Initially everything was going to plan, and we were well established in the climb towards our initial cruising altitude. As we passed 20,000 feet, the flight deck was suddenly filled with the unmistakable sound of a fire warning. The red master warning indicator in front of me was illuminated and, glancing down at the console beside me I saw that the fire handle for number one engine was also illuminated. We had a fire in our number one (left side) engine. The first officer was flying the aircraft, so I told him to level off at our present altitude. We then carried out the emergency drill for 'Engine Fire, severe damage or separation'. We fired a shot from the fire extinguisher into the engine and I broadcast a mayday message. I explained that we were carrying out our fire drill and would call them back with my further intentions as soon as we could. At the end of thirty seconds, we still had a fire warning indicated so I fired off the second shot. Shortly afterwards, to our relief, the fire warning light went out. I called up ATC and advised them that we wanted clearance for an immediate return to our departure airfield and needed descent clearance. Looking out of the side windows on the flight deck, you can see the outer portion of the wing, but it isn't possible to see the engines. I called the Number One (senior stewardess) to the flight deck and quickly briefed her on the situation. I told her that we were turning back to Berlin and asked her to go back into the passenger cabin and look out of the passenger windows alongside the port side engine. I needed her to check and see if there was anything unusual in what she saw, such as damage or signs of scorching to the engine cowling. No sooner had she left the flight deck, than the fire warning in number one engine started again. However, the warning was very intermittent and would cease for several seconds before flashing on and off again for a few more seconds. The nature of the warning led me to suspect that it was some kind of short circuit or similar fault that was now giving us these false indications, but it was a great relief when the stewardess came back and reported that she could see nothing unusual out of the windows.

The cabin crew in Dan-Air were well trained in emergency procedures. They immediately carried out their assigned duties while I spoke to the passengers on the public address system. With all our emergency checks, normal checks, and preparations complete, I took control from the first officer and gave him an approach briefing. We were flying on one engine and were still very heavy, having burned little of our trip fuel. When on one engine, the procedure was to land using an intermediate flap setting rather than the high drag full flap setting. This resulted in a significantly higher approach and touchdown speed. Add to that, we were still very heavy with lots of fuel on board which further increased our approach speed. The very high touchdown speed would add a great deal to our required landing distance, but we had carefully checked our graphs and charts and concluded that the runway at Berlin was long enough with an acceptable margin to spare. Even so, as it was my name in the technical log as aircraft commander and everything was ultimately my responsibility, I had elected to be the pilot at the controls for our landing. Air traffic control was extremely helpful and gave us top priority for an expeditious arrival and, as we turned onto final approach for the runway, they instructed us to change frequency to Tegel tower and wished us good luck. When we tuned into the tower frequency, someone was already talking. It was a British Airways aircraft who had obviously been instructed to hold clear of the runway and wait for an inbound aircraft. The conversation went something like this:

BA: 'I have been sitting at the holding point for five minutes now. How much longer are you going to keep me waiting?'

Tower: 'We are waiting for an aircraft that is coming in with an emergency.'

Me: 'Aha, I do believe you are talking about me. Good morning, it's the Dan-Air mayday traffic.'

Tower: 'Good morning, Dan-Air. Be advised the emergency services are standing by. The surface wind is calm, you are cleared to land.'

There is nothing like a good overweight engine-out landing to concentrate the mind and the resultant touchdown was nice and smooth. We stopped long before the end of the runway without any need for harsh braking. We then heard a round of applause from the passenger cabin and the British Airways captain even apologised over the radio for his impatience, saying that he hadn't realised the nature of the problem. After we parked the aircraft and shutdown the engine, the first officer and I even got a kiss on the cheek from our grateful senior stewardess.

I briefly considered suggesting that a kiss should be incorporated into the after-landing checklist on the 737 fleet, but then I remembered that we now had some male cabin crew in the company, so I decided to ditch that idea. One vital ingredient in an emergency is to have a well-trained crew who can work together as a team. We were lucky in Dan-Air, we had plenty of those.

Two more developments now occurred within the Dan-Air group. In October 1991, we disposed of the ship-broking arm of Davies and Newman. On a positive note, an equity issue had raised an additional £53.75 million by issuing new ordinary shares. Also, the application for new scheduled service routes to Athens, Barcelona, Oslo, Rome and Stockholm had been approved. The airline now had scheduled services to nine UK destinations and twenty-one European destinations.

Chapter Ten

In July 1992, I decided that it was time to revalidate my certificate of test for Group A aircraft. It had been a long time since I had flown a puddle jumper and I wanted to reacquaint myself. I phoned the licensing department of the Civil Aviation Authority to find out what I needed to do to revalidate my license. I knew I had to do a check flight with an instructor, but wondered if there was any other requirement. A young man at the licensing office answered my phone call. I explained what I wanted to do and waited for his reply:

'When was your last cross-country flight?'

'Two days ago.'

'Where did you fly to?'

'Manchester to Alicante and back.'

(After a long pause) 'That won't count I'm afraid.'

'Why not?'

(With a suspicious hint of smugness in his voice) 'It has to be over a triangular course.'

'You are bloody kidding, right?'

'Nope.'

Two days later, I booked myself a flight test with an examiner at Liverpool airport. I explained the need for me to fly a cross country over a triangular course, and I was delighted when the examiner also said, 'You are bloody kidding, right?' When I assured him that I wasn't kidding and that I had been told it was indeed required of me, we planned the shortest possible route we could come up with. I did the flight test with him in a Cessna 172, and during the test we flew from Liverpool to Woodvale and landed. A few minutes later we took off again and flew to Sleap. After landing there and grabbing a cup of coffee, we took off again and flew back to Liverpool. Job done and revalidated on Group A aircraft.

A few days later, I did a very rash thing. I jumped out of a perfectly serviceable aircraft from an altitude of 12,000 feet. Fortunately, I was wearing a parachute at the time, and I was strapped to a guy who knew how to use it. The first couple of seconds were mental overload and totally overwhelming. Then we were in a stable free fall and my brain caught up with events. It was without doubt one of the most exhilarating things I have ever done. We floated in towards the cameraman (or did he float in towards us?) and I waved at him while grinning like a Cheshire cat. There wasn't really a feeling of falling at that moment—just flying alongside another mental human being—it was fantastic. The chute opened after thirty seconds of free fall and the silence was amazing. I had already spotted our landing site on Cark airfield and was impressed at how manoeuvrable the parachute appeared to be. I was allowed to briefly pull on the grab handles to alter the steering lines and change direction. Far too soon it was over as we landed right in the middle of the target touchdown area. I walked around with a grin on my face for a week. I also prompted several people to say, 'Yes Bob, you have told us about your damned parachute jump. Twice!'

The skydiving centre was run by a nice guy named Lynn George. He confirmed that they could use the services of a pilot and he and I went up in his club's Cessna 182. He made sure that I knew what I was doing and then let me get on with it. Over a period of approximately four months, I completed 113 flights dropping parachutists over Tilstock airfield. It was good fun and I enjoyed the relaxed, no nonsense, no red tape, no flight plans, no bullshit flying, surrounded by a nice bunch of people who were all there for just one reason. To have fun. It was a fine tonic and a welcome distraction from the woes of the airline industry.

By the end of the summer season of 1992, it had become

obvious to Dan-Air's directors that the airline wasn't going to be able to survive the winter alone and they began looking for an airline partner with whom they could form an alliance. In September, they met with Richard Branson and engaged in talks. He was keen to save the airline and his plan was for an interlining agreement, with Dan-Air acting as a feeder for his long-haul operations. Richard would invest £10 Million and in exchange would hold approximately 15% of the company which was to be named Virgin European. It would benefit from totally co-ordinated marketing and sales and from the impressively strong Virgin brand name. Sadly, Branson's financial people and management team didn't share his enthusiasm for the idea and in October, he announced that he had been unable to carry a consensus of his management. I spoke to Richard about this years later (I was working for him at the time), and he was clearly still of the opinion that it would have been a successful venture and he regretted that he had been unable to sway his management team.

British Airways was delighted because they now knew that they could pick up the company for a song. What is more, the government had indicated that if BA took over Dan-Air, it would not be referred to the monopolies and mergers commission. Lord King, the British Airways chairman, offered to buy Dan-Air Services Limited for one pound sterling. They would settle all Dan-Air's liabilities and the company would become a wholly owned subsidiary of British Airways. All charter operations would immediately cease, and Dan-Air's scheduled service destinations would be reduced from twenty-eight down to just twelve. Of the thirty-eight aircraft Dan-Air were operating at the time, all would be disposed of apart from twelve Boeing 737-400s. There would be major redundancies and the staff who were to retain their jobs, would be offered lower terms and conditions. We were left reeling from the news, but for some of us there was worse to come.

Dan-Air had never made a pilot redundant in its entire thirty-nine-year history, but traditionally a company's redundancies are carried out on a 'last in, first out' basis. As

I had been with the company for just two months short of 19 years, I thought I would be safe. Also, with the news that BA was only keeping the Boeing 737-400s, I felt relieved that I had been type rated on that particular aircraft. My relief didn't last long. BA announced that they would only be offering jobs to Gatwick based Boeing 737-400 pilots irrespective of their date of joining. All the 737 pilots based at Manchester and Newcastle were to be made redundant.

I initially thought that I would receive one month's salary for every full year of service, so my 18 years and 10 months with the airline should earn me 18 months' salary which would at least ensure that the mortgage could be paid while I attempted to get another flying job. However, dear Lord King had another surprise for me. Because Dan-Air hadn't put a redundancy agreement into our terms of contract (they had never made a pilot redundant) British Airways were only prepared to pay statutory minimum redundancy to the pilots. That amounted to a paltry £205 for every full year of service. In my case, a total of £3,690. The need to find another job suddenly got very urgent indeed!

The last few flights I did with Dan-Air were tough. It takes a great deal of effort and self-control to stay focused on the job when you know that you will be unemployed in a few days' time. I was so impressed with how professional my colleagues were throughout those sad days. They put on a brave face for the travelling public and provided the best possible service as always.

Out of sight of the passengers, tears were being shed by crew members who had completed their last flight. One evening, the Manchester airport authority offered one of the event rooms in the terminal building for a 'Farewell to Dan-Air' party. Not so much a party really, more a gathering of people who were in a state of shock. It felt strange to look around that packed room and realise that everybody there had just lost their job.

My last flight with Dan-Air took place on the 30 October 1992. First Officer Ross Waddams and I flew from Manchester to Rome and back. I had completed a total of 5,418 flights for Dan-Air, and 10,695 flying hours in their aircraft. At the end of my last flight, I handed in my uniform and airport security pass and left the Dan-Air offices for the last time.

My wife Sara received another important piece of news that October. She was pregnant. We were absolutely delighted, but at the same time, the need to get myself a job now became more urgent than ever. Sara had been working for the airline Loganair since our move to Manchester, but now, of course, she was going to have to quit flying. Consequently, there would be no income coming into the household at all. I had already been to the unemployment office and signed on as being out of work. The very nice gentleman I had seen there had noted down all my details and then, after a careful search through some files, announced that they didn't currently have anything in my 'field of expertise.' No surprises there then.

I had also had an interview at the Citizen's Advice Bureau, where they had told me that they couldn't really help while I still had some money in my bank account. Apparently, only once Sara and I were both completely broke, would they be able to take steps to help us. Armed with this depressing information, I was frantically trying to find a job, but it soon became obvious that there were no flying jobs to be had in Britain—I had to look overseas.

Late in November, I heard that representatives from Malaysian Airlines were conducting interviews in London. They were planning to offer temporary contracts to successful applicants, flying their Boeing 737s in Malaysia. I immediately got myself down to London and was interviewed by Captain Ooi who was a senior management pilot in the company. He told me that they were only looking for Boeing 737-400 pilots and, although he acknowledged that I had experience on that type, he pointed out that I was now current on the 737-200. Sensing that any job offer looked to be slipping away from me, I suggested that I could arrange to get someone to conduct an instrument renewal test on me in a 400 series. He liked that idea and said that if I came back to him with a revalidated instrument rating on the 737-400 stamped in my license, he would give me a job. But, he added, I had just two days to get it done. After that, my time was up. I frantically made several phone calls.

I needed to find a slot on a Boeing 737-400 simulator. Dan-Air had used one at the Aer Lingus training centre in Dublin. I phoned Dublin to see if they had any vacant space on the simulator and they confirmed that I could buy some time in the very early morning the next day. They knew I was unemployed, so they assured me that they would keep the cost as low as possible. Grateful for their offer, I booked the simulator and assured them I would get back to them as soon as I could get hold of an examiner to conduct the test.

I tried to contact a friend who had been a Type Rating Examiner (TRE) with Dan-Air, but he was away flying. Next, I phoned another TRE, and explained my dilemma. After a brief pause, he said 'Can you get to East Midlands airport tonight?' I said yes, and he explained that he was already carrying out a simulator check on two pilots in the 737 simulator there. He would ask the guys to step up the pace and skip their half-time coffee break to allow time at the end for me to undergo my check flight. Late that evening he signed up my licence and handed it back to me. I reached for my wallet and asked him how much I owed him. He smiled and said 'British Airways has already paid for this four-hour simulator session. They don't know that you have been here for the latter part of it, and I'm certainly not going to charge you for my services. I think in view of the way that you have been treated by BA, it's only fair that they pay for your rating renewal' I will always be grateful to him for that.

I contacted Captain Ooi first thing the next morning and confirmed that I had done a check ride in the Boeing 737-400 simulator as he had requested. He said that if I could get myself over to Dublin, one of his airline's TREs was already there and would carry out a Malaysian Instrument rating check flight on me in the simulator. Provided that I passed that to his satisfaction, then I would be offered a job with Malaysian Airlines. More frantic phone calls secured a flight from Manchester to Dublin and a night in the Dublin airport hotel.

Captain Alwi Hashim put me through my paces in the Aer Lingus simulator, at the end of which he shook my hand and said, 'Congratulations captain and welcome to Malaysian Airlines.' He then said that the offer was subject to me agreeing to travel on Malaysian's scheduled service from Heathrow to Kuala Lumpur in just eight days' time! When I said that I had a thousand and one arrangements to make before leaving the country, he apologised but confirmed that it was a take it or leave it offer. I took it.

I immediately flew home to Manchester and started on the thousand and one arrangements, including giving my wife power of attorney for pretty much everything and getting our house rented out through a local estate agent. Sara packed up everything that wasn't staying in the house, so that it could all be placed in storage, while she moved in with her Mum for a while.

I asked my brother-in-law to try and sell my car—the money was going to be much needed—and forward it to me in Malaysia. The plan was that as soon as I had managed to find us somewhere to live in Kuala Lumpur, Sara would fly out and join me there. All this crazy rushing around took place over the next six days and then on the seventh day I said my farewells to friends and family, and Sara and I drove down to Heathrow to check into a hotel for our last night together. The next day was tough. Sara took me to the airport, and we said our emotional goodbyes before I went through to the departure gates.

There were nine ex-Dan-Air Boeing 737 Captains aboard that flight to Kuala Lumpur. Some were travelling with their wives, while some, like me, had been forced to leave theirs behind. There were some other British captains aboard who had been flying for different companies and had also been recruited by Malaysian Airlines. It seemed that Captain Ooi and his colleagues had been very busy.

When we arrived in KL (that's how everyone referred to Kuala Lumpur) we stepped out of the airport terminal building and were immediately surprised by the overwhelming heat and humidity. Close to the equator, the country doesn't experience seasons like the UK and every day is the same. A daytime temperature of around 32 degrees Centigrade and humidity of around 85%. Bearing in mind we had left winter weather in England about fourteen hours earlier, this was very different!

Malaysian Airlines were paying for us to stay in a hotel in the city for a week until we 'found our feet,' after which we were to pay our own way. In addition to our basic salary, we were to be paid a monthly accommodation allowance. During our interviews in London, we had been left with the impression that this allowance would fully cover the costs of acceptable accommodation in KL. However, it soon became apparent that the word 'acceptable' was subjective. An estate agent who was recommended by the airline arrived at the hotel the next day and met up with us and arranged viewings. In addition to this, I teamed up with a friend and his wife and set off in a taxi to drive around the various suburbs and regions of the city to decide where we might want to set up home. It was a daunting and exhausting process, but obviously very necessary. When we weren't trying to find somewhere to live, we were at the airline's offices ploughing our way through a seemingly endless series of forms to get ourselves 'absorbed' into the system. There were forms to set up a bank account, forms for monthly salary transfers, private health insurance, registration of dependent family members, personal details to obtain an airport security pass and very importantly, for work permit applications. We also had to sit a written examination in Malaysian air law, following which applications were submitted to the Aviation authorities to have a Malaysian Air Transport Pilot's Licence (ATPL) issued in recognition of our British ATPL.

I found a bungalow to rent that was owned by a pleasant couple. He was British and had originally come to work in Malaysia for the British Oxygen Company in the 1960s. He had married a Chinese Malaysian woman and had

A Boeing 737 400 of Malaysia Airlines

been there ever since. The bungalow was in a district called Petaling Jaya and a couple of friends would be living nearby. I was keeping my fingers crossed that my choice of home would meet with my wife's approval when she eventually flew out to join me.

Captain Ooi, who had interviewed us back in London, gathered us together in a large room at the airport and gave us an overview of what to expect. He pointed out that we had specifically been chosen because of our previous extensive experience of airline operations. He added that they were relying on us to impart that experience and knowledge to the junior pilots who were being introduced into the airline. He emphasised that we would be working in an air traffic environment that—with very few exceptions—had no radar coverage. He went on to point out that many of the airfields we would be flying into had extremely basic facilities and few, if any, navigation aids. I couldn't help thinking 'Well Bob, you always said that you like a challenge.'

In some areas, the airline was very well organised. For example, all aircrew—pilots and cabin crew—were entitled to free company transport to and from their home to the airport. A minibus picked you up from your home but then proceeded to visit the homes of several other employees as it meandered its way back to the airport. Eventually, the vehicle would arrive at the airport and disgorge its bum-sore passengers who, by that time, had already wondered if the journey was ever going to end. Likewise, when you had finished a long flying duty, the last thing you wanted to do was to sit in a crowded and stuffy room waiting for your name to be called once the controllers had eventually rustled up a van load of aircrew who were waiting for a lift to the same district.

In other areas the airline was less proficient, notably with getting us work permits. To be fair, it wasn't really the fault of the airline, but rather the amount of red tape that was thrown at them by the government. Eventually it was all resolved, and we were let loose on the unsuspecting travelling public of Southeast Asia.

If any of us had been expecting to be held by the hand and gently shown the ropes by our new employer, then they would have been quickly disappointed. I had heard people say that it was, 'Teach Yourself Airlines', but that was unfair. They had taken on experienced pilots from many different parts of the world, and they reasonably expected that these people would integrate and adapt to their new environment without too much help.

My first day operating with Malaysian Airlines was in January 1993. It was a 400 series aircraft, and I was being supervised by Captain Lam, who sat on the jump seat and barely uttered a word all day. We flew from KL to Saigon, then back to KL and from there to Singapore. At Singapore, we checked into a hotel for the night. There had been no invitation from the others to meet up or to go somewhere for a bite to eat and this felt very different to what I was used to. I sat in my room feeling like a fish out of water. Eventually, I wandered down to the hotel bar, ordered a beer and then sat at a table by myself drinking it. I had flown the aircraft well throughout the day, but I had felt absolutely no connection with my crew members. I hadn't got a clue what the training captain was thinking or feeling. The first officer had been, apparently, too nervous to speak to me or anyone else and we had ended the day by heading off to our hotel rooms without any intention of getting to know one another. This was most definitely not what I was used to, and it made me feel like I really was a very long way from home. I desperately missed Sara and the music that was playing through the nearby speaker didn't help either. It was Eric Clapton's song *Tears in Heaven*. Sorry Eric, much as I like the song, I really didn't need it at that exact moment.

I went on to complete more flights under the supervision of various training captains without any comment or input from any of them. I was to undergo a final line check flight with a gentleman I had not met before and he was rather aloof and uncommunicative when I finally did so. We operated from Johor Bahru to Kuala Lumpur and then to Langkawi. From there we flew to Penang and then back to Langkawi. Having done four flights up to this point, I had done all the flying, but now my uncommunicative co-pilot/check captain, announced that he was going to be the handling pilot for the next leg back to Kuala Lumpur. We completed all the appropriate checklists, and then began our take-off. The communications between us went as follows:

Me: '80 knots' (as we accelerated through 80 knots).

Him: (Unintelligible mumble).

Me: 'V1' (as we accelerate past the speed at which we can no longer abandon the take-off).

Me: 'Rotate' (as we reach the speed where we should rotate the aircraft into the lift off attitude).

Me: 'V2' (as we reach the engine-out safety speed).

Me: 'Positive rate of climb' (I see clear indications that we are now climbing).

Him: (Unintelligible mumble).

Me: 'Positive rate of climb!'

Him: ……

Me: 'I have control.'

Having glanced across to my non-communicative co-pilot, I could see that he was staring straight ahead with a vacant expression on his face. To be perfectly honest, as far as I was concerned, this was the way this guy always looked. However, I gave him the benefit of the doubt and said, 'If you really have clocked out and can't hear what I'm saying, I'm about to broadcast a Mayday.'

Him: 'Okay, no need for the Mayday. I'm back with you.'

A short while later, after we had climbed to a safe altitude and I had asked him what the hell he thought he was doing, he smiled and then replied, 'Now you know what it's like to fly with a Malaysian cadet pilot.' His little game was wrong on many levels. The Malaysian cadet pilots were generally of a high standard when they came out of their respective pilot training schools. It was very wrong of him to be so rude about their abilities. More importantly, you don't play silly buggers pretending you have turned into a zombie when you are the pilot of an aircraft that is full of fare-paying passengers. He then signed me off as being fully competent and cleared to fly as an unsupervised captain. I promised myself that if an airline made me a check captain, I would not pull a 'zombie pilot' stunt on a passenger-carrying flight.

My first Christmas in Malaysia hadn't been a joyful affair because Sara and I were still thousands of miles apart. I spent the day with friends, but when I phoned Sara that night (KL being seven hours ahead of Manchester) neither of us could manage to keep up any pretence of feeling very festive. It wasn't helped by the fact that I had to make the call from a public phone on a noisy street corner. Getting a landline installed into a home in KL was a very painful process and although airline pilots were supposedly categorised as key workers and as such were on a high priority list for getting a phone, it was expected to take two or three months. Consequently, I bought a second-hand mobile phone. It was a Motorola and was the size and weight of a house brick. You had to extend a long telescopic aerial if you hoped to get any kind of a signal and, after holding the thing up to your ear for a few moments, your arm started to ache with the effort. Also, you couldn't help noticing that your ear was becoming very hot. I suspect that it was doing a great job of frying my brain. After not many minutes of use, the battery would die and needed recharging. Overall, it was better than nothing, but only just.

Next, I bought a Proton car from one of the engineers at the airport. Protons were marketed as a Malaysian product, but it was really a Japanese car assembled in Malaysia. The Proton people said you could choose from a range of colours for your car, but if you chose anything other than white, it would cost considerably more. As a result, nearly everybody's Proton was white. This posed a problem if you returned to a large car park where you had left your vehicle some time before, only to be faced with row upon row of identical white Protons. Crucially, it had powerful air-conditioning. Nobody asked, 'what's the acceleration or the fuel economy like?' Instead, they would ask 'what's the aircon like?'

The day finally came when Sara flew out from England, and I met her at the airport. We drove back to the bungalow so she could see her new home, but soon after we got there, she said she was keen to explore KL. We took a cab into the city and wandered around the bustling streets for a while. Sara's positive mood suddenly took a nosedive when she felt something pressing down onto her foot. When she looked down, a large brown rat had decided to curl up on the top of her sandal. It rather spoiled the afternoon but gave the other expats a good laugh when they heard about it.

With Sara being pregnant, we were keen to get her registered with a good gynaecologist and after a couple of unsuccessful choices, we then found Doctor Choong. He had trained in England and was married to a Scottish midwife. Now located at the impressive Pantai hospital, he was very reassuring, and we felt relieved to be under his care. All was well for the expected birth in June.

The flying in Malaysia was enjoyable, with a good variety of destinations. The airline had a large fleet of Boeing 737-400s and some 737-300 freighters. As I discovered one day, they also had a 737-500. As I walked out to our assigned aircraft with the young first officer, I said to him 'that aircraft looks weird, it looks shorter than usual.'

He smiled and said, 'that's because it's a 500 series aircraft.' I told him that I didn't even know that Malaysian Airlines had a 500. After we climbed aboard, out of curiosity I looked at my Malaysian pilot's licence and saw that it stated I was licensed to fly the Boeing 737-300 and 400 series aircraft. No mention of a 500. I pointed this out to the flight dispatcher and told him I needed someone from the flight operations department to clarify the situation. A short while later, the Boeing fleet manager arrived and asked to see my license. After studying the type ratings page for a moment, he said 'Hmm, you are quite right, there is currently no mention of a 500 series on here.' He then borrowed a pen, carefully wrote B737-500 onto the page, and handed the license back to me.

I asked if there were any differences I should be aware of and he replied that there were a few, but they were outlined on a placard in the cockpit. I smiled and said 'Fair enough. Sounds good to me,' and headed into the flight deck. That's the sort of no-bull approach that I like. The placard kept me out of trouble that day, but I can't say that I particularly liked the way that the 500 handled with a sort of constant fishtail waggle in the cruise as though the yaw damper was overactive and working overtime. However, when all was said and done, it was just another 737. Interestingly enough, a few days later, I was given a replacement page to insert into my license. This one now showed that I was rated to fly as pilot in command of Boeing 737-300, 400 and 500 series aircraft. It had an official DCA stamp alongside the entry and looked a lot more official than the page with the handwritten entry.

I can't say that we worked particularly hard, and the airline could have got a lot more productivity out of their pilots. Needless to say, I wasn't about to point that out to them, nor was I going to complain about the time off. We night stopped at most of the destinations and the airline always put us up in the best hotels. What I wasn't impressed by was the definite 'us and them' discrimination between flight deck and cabin crew. The flight deck always stayed at the best available hotel, whereas the cabin crew were usually assigned to a cheaper one. The flight deck would be transported to and from their hotel in a limousine, while the cabin crew were taken to theirs by minibus. The senior cabin crew supervisor was always male and at the start of the day he would enter the flight deck and ask if I was ready to 'receive my crew?' If I said yes, then one by one the female cabin crew would come into the flight deck, place their hands together as if praying and solemnly bow. They said 'Good morning captain. My name is Sue Lee and it is an honour to fly with you.' After another bow, they would back out of the door, to be replaced by the next girl who repeated the process. At the end of your day's flying, they would again come into the flight deck one at a time and this time would say 'Thank you for a safe flight captain.' This was a process that I never got used to, but it was strictly adhered to in accordance with company procedures. You must bear in mind that I previously flew with Dan-Air where a greeting from the cabin crew was likely to be something along the lines of 'Hiya Bob. How are you doing?'

Occasionally I would have a stark reminder that I was living in a third World country with some very different values and attitudes. On one such occasion, I was flying from Kuching to Kuala Lumpur. I had been told that one of our passengers was a man who was travelling with his baby son. The child was very poorly, and his parents had been told that he needed an operation which could only be performed in KL. The man was travelling alone with his son because the family couldn't afford to accompany him. I was surprised there was no doctor or nurse because the baby's condition was so obviously serious. The supervisor shrugged and said that the family couldn't afford to buy a ticket for anyone else. I told him to keep a close eye on the man and his baby throughout the flight and to let me know if there was any change in the baby's condition. I realised that even if there was a sudden deterioration, we couldn't do much about it because we were already heading for the only place that could provide suitable medical assistance, with the possible exception of Singapore. I put Singapore airport into the aircraft's flight management computer so that I had a readout of the 'direct to' distance throughout the flight.

When we were approximately forty minutes from our destination the supervisor came into the flight deck looking visibly upset: the child had died and they were unable to revive him. He wasn't sure exactly when it had happened, but when he saw that the father had tears running down his cheeks, he checked the baby's condition. He told me that the poor man was now cradling his son and wouldn't let him go. Having established that there was nobody else sitting next to him, I suggested that he should be left alone with his son and not bothered unless he specifically asked for assistance. I radioed ahead to our company operations requesting that they meet the aircraft with someone who could take the father and child into their care and was told this would be done.

After arrival, the first officer and I were rather subdued as we completed the post flight duties. Once the passengers were all off the aircraft, I left the flight deck and was surprised to see the father was still sitting in his seat cradling his dead son. Nobody was with him, and the cabin crew were keeping a respectful distance. I asked our cabin supervisor where the ground staff were, and he told me that they had left with the passengers but hadn't returned. The grieving Father spoke no English, so when I realised that nobody was coming to assist him, I asked the supervisor to tell him that I wanted to take him and his son somewhere quiet and I would then find some people to help him. We left the aircraft and started to walk side by side along the long corridor towards the main terminal. The man continued to gently cradle his son as I walked alongside him. It was a fairly long walk, but that night it felt like a marathon. Eventually I was able to find two members of the airline's ground staff and hand him over to them, by which time I had a lump in my throat the size of a cricket ball. My wife was shortly due to give birth, so the tragic scene that night was all the more poignant.

On another flight, shortly before our departure from Penang to KL, the dispatcher told me that one of the passengers was a woman who would be travelling with her very sick baby. The child needed a heart operation and the only hospital equipped for this was in KL. Therapeutic oxygen would be needed throughout the flight and arrangements were being made to provide this. The woman was with her baby and a nurse in the departure lounge, so I told him to board them first and, once they were settled, to bring out the other passengers. The mother was clearly in a state of shock and was generally overwhelmed by everything that was going on around her. She had never flown before, so with that, and her baby's serious condition, her apprehension was understandable. I said 'Well, tell her not to worry because the nurse will look after the oxygen situation.' There was a pause and then the dispatcher told me that the nurse would not be accompanying her on the flight. I said that was ridiculous and that I wasn't prepared to take the lady and her baby without the nurse in attendance. After a conversation between them in Chinese Malay, during which the mother started to cry, the dispatcher told me that the nurse would need a ticket and the mother couldn't afford to buy one. I told him to just write out a ticket and not even think about charging her for it, but he replied that he didn't have the authority to do such a thing without approval from the station manager. The station manager was called to the aircraft, and I told him that as captain of the flight I was authorising him to issue the ticket, but he started muttering that only head office in KL could make such a decision. In Dan-Air, the captains had been issued with blank passenger tickets that we could fill out ourselves for situations like this, but not here. I took out my wallet, asked how much the fare was from Penang to KL and then paid him. After a pause he said the nurse would also need a return ticket. I pressed the money for the return ticket into the manager's hand instead of ramming it where I really wanted to put it. The two tickets were then issued, and we finally set off for Kuala Lumpur. I couldn't believe the callous inflexibility of the people I'd been dealing with in Penang, so I later wrote a letter of complaint to the company and told them that they needed to immediately inform station managers at all our outstations that in cases such as this, they did have the authority to act on their own initiative. As far as I'm aware, no such instruction was sent.

Every day the temperature rose to thirty something degrees, every day the humidity was high. There was one other vital and highly impressive ingredient to the weather. As the sun beat down throughout the morning, the temperature and humidity increased, and cumulonimbus clouds started to rear up to impressive heights. Eventually and inevitably, by mid-afternoon they would release torrential rain, the likes of which we never witness in Europe. This rain was accompanied by thunder and lightning and if you were caught up in it when on the ground, it felt like you were standing under a cold power shower. In a matter of minutes, the deep storm drains that lined either side of the roads were filled to overflowing and the roads themselves looked more like rivers. If it was impressive to someone standing on the ground, then it was even more impressive when encountered in the air. Obviously, we tried our very best to avoid these thunderstorms, and by careful use of our onboard weather radar, we could skirt around the more intense storm cells. However, we would occasionally have to grit our teeth as we tried to squeeze between the cells while torrential rain hammered on the windscreens and forward fuselage. The flight deck would be illuminated by lightning flashes all around and Saint Elmo's fire—a build-up and discharge of static electricity—would appear like bright blue cobwebs dancing across our windscreens. It is a sight that is always quite mesmerising.

I remember one flight to Kuching when I was with a brand-new first officer who had just completed his pilot training in the USA. We nicknamed these guys 'Space Cadets' and they were incredibly keen and enthusiastic individuals but, inevitably, very inexperienced. That said, they were quick learners and soaked up every snippet of information that you fed them. There was a great deal of storm activity in the Kuching area, and I had been doing a fair bit of 'weaving and wandering' to avoid the worst of it. We eventually turned onto final approach and started to descend towards the runway. Just as the tower controller told us that we were cleared to land, I noticed that our radar was showing some very worrying looking weather returns close to the runway itself. We then flew into a veritable wall of water. The rain was unbelievably intense, and the conditions became very turbulent. I decided to abandon the approach and go around. I pushed the thrust levers forward and raised the aircraft's nose while asking the first officer to retract the flaps to 15 degrees. With a positive rate of climb indicated, I called for the landing gear to be retracted, but I had to repeat both instructions because the first officer looked scared to death and seemed to have frozen in his seat. While he was temporarily out of the picture, I advised ATC that we were going around and would be taking up a holding pattern close to the airfield but well clear of the thunderstorm. We were uncomfortably close to a very active storm cell and as I banked the aircraft away from it, I suddenly detected a distinctive smell coming through the air conditioning vents.

Me: 'Oh oh! Can you smell that?'

First officer: 'Yes. What is it?'

Me: 'It's ozone. When you smell that, it usually means that you are about to be ...' There was a sudden very loud bang and a blinding flash of light '... struck by lightning!'

The first officer really did look scared now, but I was soon able to reassure him. I defused the situation by looking through my side window and glancing back at the wing. I turned to him and said 'I've still got a wing on my side. How about you?' At first, he couldn't stop himself from turning to look out of his side window. When he slowly turned back to face me, he had a sheepish grin on his face as he replied 'Yes, I've got one too.'

Provided an aircraft has been electrically bonded

properly, a lightning strike is not as dramatic as you might think. Damage to the airframe is usually negligible and, in our case, after we eventually landed, an external inspection revealed that the lightning had struck the nose of the aircraft just below the windscreen on my side. This had resulted in a scorch mark at the entry point. The lightning had then exited the airframe via the static wicks on the trailing edge of the starboard wing. Two of the wicks had been blasted off and were now missing. A quick repair and clean up at the entry point and the fitting of two replacement static wicks had the aircraft fully serviceable again. In the meantime, we had finished our flying duties for the day, so we checked into our hotel for a couple of well-earned cold beers. My Space Cadet had just added to his flying experience.

In June 1993, I had just completed a busy day's flying and checked into a hotel in Singapore, when the phone rang. 'Bob? Hi, it's Chris here (it was my good friend Chris Olsson), 'Just to let you know, Sara has gone into labour, so Sue and I are getting her into the car and will be setting off for the Pantai hospital in a few minutes.' There followed a couple of seconds of stunned silence from me, followed by an expletive. 'Thanks Chris. Tell her I'll be there as soon as I can.'

Having made a quick phone call to our airline's operations department, they told me they would get another captain to Singapore straight away. I then rushed back to Singapore airport and jumped on the next available flight to Kuala Lumpur. When I walked into Sara's hospital room, I was relieved to see that the big event still hadn't taken place. She said that I looked like I was falling asleep on my feet, so suggested that I lay down on her bed for a while. She wasn't using it because she was pacing the room in her discomfort from the labour pains. I'm ashamed to admit that not only did I lay on her bed but was quickly fast asleep and snoring loudly.

A few hours later, things became rather tense. We already knew that our baby was playing hard to get because he had positioned himself upside down in the womb. Doctor

Choong had been hopeful that a normal delivery was going to be possible anyway, but all was not going well, and the baby was becoming distressed. A caesarean delivery was needed right away.

At that time, the hospitals in Malaysia preferred it if the father was not present in the delivery room during birth. However, they knew that we strange Europeans often did want to be present. If the Doctor overseeing the delivery had no objection to the father being there, then a formal letter had to be sent to the hospital authorities applying for permission. This was given on the understanding that if anything other than a normal delivery was necessary, the father would be kicked out.

Luckily, Doctor Choong had a trick up his sleeve. He took me into a changing room and told me to gown up in surgeon's scrubs. Then he took me into the delivery room and introduced me to the medical staff as a doctor with whom he had trained in England. He went on to explain that I had asked to supervise the breech birth out of professional curiosity. Choong told me that if I kept quiet behind my surgical mask, nobody would be any the wiser. So, thanks to Doctor Choong, I was present for the appearance of Joe Williams. Just thirty days later, he took his first flight in an aircraft.

Expatriate pilots with Malaysian Airlines and their family members were entitled to a free business class round trip to their 'home country' each year, provided it was on the network. Some pilots recorded a different 'home country' in their personnel files every year. Our next-door neighbour in KL was an Australian captain, and he and his wife had taken vacations in Australia, New Zealand, USA and the UK by nominating each of those countries as their 'home' every time they made a travel application.

Sara and I planned to do the same, but obviously our first vacation would be to the UK, so that we could show off our recently arrived son. When we checked in for the flight at KL, Sara and I were concerned that Joe's first ever flight was to be the non-stop 13-hour journey to London. Clearly a case of learning to swim by being thrown in at the deep end. The business class section was very comfortable and soon after take-off, the cabin crew set up a sleeping bassinet for Joe. He promptly fell asleep and stayed that way until his mother took him out of his little bed when the aircraft started its final approach into Heathrow. It seemed clear that Joe, just like his dad, was happy up at 37,000 feet.

Chapter Eleven

In January1994 I contacted Alan Dix, having heard he was setting up a new charter airline in the UK. I had flown with Alan when he was a captain on the BAC 1-11 with Dan-Air, but he later resigned to join the Rothmans Aerobatic Team. Once he had got that out of his system, he joined Air Europe and was fleet manager of their Fokker F-28 fleet until the airline collapsed. I lost track of his movements after that, until I heard about this new airline venture.

I had been told that the new airline was going to be operating Boeing 737s, but when I got in touch, I discovered that, in fact, they were going to be operating Airbus A320s. As I was not rated on the Airbus, I assumed that would exclude me. However, Alan told me that with every A320 they took from the manufacturer, Airbus would train and type rate 5 captains and 5 first officers as part of the deal. He offered me a job as a captain but explained that it would only be for a summer season and the aircraft would then go off to Canada for the winter, to be flown by Canadian crews. Operations would then return to Europe for the following summer season, and we would be employed once again. The Airline was to be named Air World and for the first summer season, they would have one aircraft based at Manchester and another at Cardiff.

Although six months on and six months off was far from ideal, I jumped at his offer. Everything happened pretty fast after that. My temporary contract with Malaysian had been for a three-year period, but now, having completed

16 months with them, I handed in my notice. We parted amicably and Captain Ooi wished me well for the future. On my last day with the airline, I flew from Singapore to Penang and then onwards to Kuala Lumpur. At the time, I thought it was my last flight operating a Boeing 737, but things turned out differently.

There followed a mad scramble to pack up everything for our return to the UK. As part of our contract, the airline would air freight items up to a generous weight allowance when their pilots were finally leaving and being repatriated to their home country. This was free, but on a 'space available' basis on their scheduled flights, so in our case it would be flown to London Heathrow on the first flight with freight space available. It was then up to us to collect the stuff as soon as possible before the Heathrow airport authority started charging us for holding it there. It was surprising just how much stuff, including furniture, we had managed to accumulate over such a short period of time, but we soon got it all packed up and transported to the freight terminal at KL.

I then had to pay all the tax that I owed the Malaysian government and that involved a frustrating day going from one Government department to the next and wading through a sea of paperwork and red tape. Finally, I was armed with all the necessary paperwork to confirm that I had paid all my dues. Now the immigration officials at the airport would allow me to leave the country. As if my day hadn't been frustrating enough already, I got done for speeding on my way back home from the tax office. We flew out two days later.

A couple of days after arriving in England, I boarded a Virgin Atlantic Boeing 747 and headed off to Miami. Air World had enrolled four of us at the Airbus training centre at Miami airport, while the other Air World guys would be training at the Airbus centre in Toulouse. We had each been given some money to cover our expenses for the duration of the course and it was left up to us to sort out our accommodation. I was pleased to discover that I had been teamed up with Dave Rodgers who was a first officer I had flown with many times when we both worked for Dan-Air. At the training centre we were introduced to a couple of the instructors who turned out to be ex-Pan Am guys.

During our tour of the training centre, I was introduced to Captain Bigolo who had once been Pan Am's chief pilot in Berlin. I made him laugh when I told him that I had used his famous 'Bigolo departure' when exiting the centre corridor from Berlin. Each crew—captain and first officer—was assigned a hire car to share between them for the duration of the course. This was great news and meant that we didn't have to find accommodation in the immediate vicinity of the training centre. By this time, we had met up with the other two Air World pilots who were on the training course with us. We all knocked off early that afternoon and drove north along the coast road in our two hire cars. Each time we came to a likely looking hotel, we went in and asked how much they would charge for a thirty-eight day stay. The further north we went (away from the city) the cheaper the quoted figure was and eventually, we settled on some slightly scruffy but perfectly acceptable self-catering apartments. A quick visit to a nearby supermarket saw our fridges filled with some essentials—mostly beer—and we now had somewhere to call home for the next five weeks.

Our course started with several days of mind-numbing Video and Audio Computer Based Instruction (VACBI). We spent hours listening to a narrator with the most soporific voice imaginable. It was completely devoid of any emotion or intonation and could induce a severe case of drooping eyelids within minutes. Unfortunately, the voice, along with the accompanying videos and diagrams was describing how all the various systems and components worked on the Airbus A320, so falling asleep was not an option. Every now and then, a quiz would pop up on the screen, presumably to check if we had managed to stay awake. We would be asked several questions about the system that had just been discussed and if you got the answers right, you were able to move on to the next section of the syllabus. After several days of the dreaded VACBI, we had covered all the various aircraft systems and we moved onto the far more interesting part of the course: flying the simulator. It was a cutting edge, state of the art, all singing, all dancing device and we were certainly going to get to know it very well.

Dave and I clocked up a mind-boggling total of sixty-five hours 'flight time'. Unfortunately, in my opinion, a good deal of that time was unnecessary and repetitive. Simulating non-normal scenarios by introducing system failures makes a lot more sense and kept us interested. As ex-Boeing pilots, Dave and I immediately noticed that the Airbus training philosophy placed a huge amount of emphasis on automation and much less on physically hand-flying the aircraft. There were several simulator exercises that were clearly designed to demonstrate to the trainee that the Airbus was a brilliant piece of kit and that its designers had built in all the necessary safeguards to ensure that stupid human pilots wouldn't endanger the aircraft in any way. Indeed, if those same stupid pilots did try to carry out an unsafe manoeuvre, or to place the aircraft into an unnatural attitude, the aircraft would damned well prevent them from doing so. In my opinion, this philosophy can lead to an over dependence on automation.

Clever computers made symbols and target bugs appear on the airspeed indicator of the Boeing that I used to fly. The same was true on the Airbus, but the difference was that the Boeing training philosophy had always been to keep a ballpark figure in your mind and then see if the computer-generated figure validated what you were expecting. The Airbus training syllabus seemed to be based on the idea that the aircraft was so clever that it would never get you into trouble. It was as if you didn't really need to know how fast you were supposed to be flying in your current configuration. You just needed to fly at the 'target bug' that the computer had created on your airspeed indicator.

The problem with that theory is that if you put rubbish data into a computer, you'll get rubbish data out. If a pilot types in the wrong zero fuel weight for the aircraft, or the fuel summation unit gives an erroneous figure for the current fuel on board, then the ideal speeds that the computer tells you to fly will be wrong. If you blindly follow its guidance without having any approximate ballpark figure in the back of your mind, you won't pick up the error. I also noticed the amount of emphasis that was placed on the aircraft's stall protection wizardry. Some exercises that were flown in the simulator were designed specifically to demonstrate that it was impossible to stall the aircraft. We were instructed to deliberately ignore the speed prompts and to continue to decelerate the aircraft in an attempt to stall it. Sure enough, just before it appeared inevitable that you were going to fall out of the sky, the aircraft's protection system would kick in and make all the necessary adjustments to prevent the aircraft from actually stalling. It would even override the pilot's control inputs if they continued to mishandle the situation. It was a very impressive demonstration and it certainly helped to bolster your confidence in the protection systems. They then got you to repeat the same low speed exercise, but this time with a fault simulated in the system so that it had automatically downgraded from normal flight law to alternate flight law or direct flight law. Under those conditions, the stall protections were removed, and it was possible to stall the aircraft. Ironically, I found that demonstration somehow reassuring, because the aircraft now behaved in a way that aircraft were supposed to behave when mishandled by the pilot. However, by the end of the low-speed handling exercises, the overriding impression you were left with was that you just couldn't stall an Airbus even if you tried. I'm sure that for many pilots coming through the training system, this subconsciously added to their over-reliance on automation.

In the years since my Airbus training course, an over-reliance on automation is a trait that has been identified by many training organisations and aviation authorities. Coupled with it, there has been a measurable deterioration in the average pilot's manual flying skills. Both these trends have resulted in aviation incidents and sadly, some have resulted in fatal accidents. A turning point came following a tragic accident involving an Air France Airbus A330 that crashed into the southern Atlantic Ocean with the loss of all on board. The aircraft was flying at high altitude at night, and because of weather related factors, the airspeed indications being displayed to the pilots became inaccurate and contradictory. As a result of this, the autopilot disconnected, and the flight control systems downgraded automatically from normal law. Responding to the erroneous airspeed indications, the first officer mishandled the controls when attempting to manually correct the situation. The aircraft went into a stall from which it didn't recover. It was established that neither pilot understood the situation or realised that the aircraft had actually stalled. The last thing the first officer was heard to say on the cockpit voice recorder was 'I can't understand it. I've been pulling hard back on the side stick all the time.' Of course, that is entirely the wrong action to take in an aircraft that has stalled. It was, however, exactly the action you were encouraged to take when demonstrating low speed flight in the simulator. With the aircraft in normal flight control law, the stall protection system will save you, but when the flight control law has downgraded (as happened in this case) it is up to the pilot to initiate stall recovery action. The pilot's first action should then be to start moving the side stick forward.

Following this tragic accident, Airbus industries revised their training syllabus and introduced more manual handling exercises into the simulator phase of their courses. Various aviation authorities and individual airlines around the world highlighted the dangers of over-reliance on automation. They also introduced training to demonstrate how to recover from unusual aircraft attitudes.

Having completed the conversion course, we hopped onto a Virgin Atlantic B.747 for the flight back to the UK. A couple of days later, we flew down to the Airbus training centre at Toulouse and climbed into a simulator for our 1179 flight test on the A320. The examiner was Jacques Vermont who was an Airbus instructor pilot

An Airbus A320 of Air World

and, somehow, we fooled him into thinking that we knew what we were doing. Consequently, he signed up all our paperwork and sent us on our way. Two days later, I made my way to Cardiff airport to fly a real Airbus A320 for the first time. Four of us did our instrument rating renewal tests shuttling between Cardiff and Liverpool airports. Over a period of six days, I carried out line training flights to Malaga, Ibiza, Skiathos, Dalaman, Gatwick, Manchester, Leeds and Cardiff. Alan Dix carried out my final line check from Cardiff to Dalaman and back and that was me checked out on the A320.

If I thought that I'd had a busy time getting my Airbus rating, then it was nothing compared to what was to come in the following months. Airline pilots are allowed to clock up a maximum of 100 flying hours per month. However, as I soon discovered, in Air World that wasn't a limit, it was a target! The Summer of 1994 was, without doubt, the busiest and most intensive period of flying that I had undertaken in my career up to that time.

In June, I was rostered to fly with a first officer whom I did not know. He was a quiet but very personable guy and I immediately felt sure that I was going to enjoy our day's flying together. His name was Martin Withers and I suddenly realised that he was the Martin Withers who, on 30 April 1982, during the Falklands war, had flown his Avro Vulcan XM607 from Ascension Island to the Falklands and dropped bombs on Stanley airfield. This was, at the time, the longest bombing raid ever undertaken. It was achieved by means of a complicated relay of tanker aircraft providing air to air refuelling for Martin. At one stage, it was feared that it would not be possible to provide sufficient aircraft in the relay to enable the Vulcan to get back to Ascension. This effectively turned it into a suicide mission because even if the crew succeeded in safely baling out somewhere over the southern Atlantic Ocean, there was no way they could be rescued. Despite being told this, Martin decided not to abort the operation. To cut a long story short, by the time they made the rendezvous with the last tanker aircraft in the chain, they were flying 'on fumes' in their own aircraft. Martin was awarded the Distinguished Flying Cross in recognition of his bravery. I had the pleasure of flying with him several times in Air World and a more modest and pleasant person you would struggle to find. Fortunately, our paths would again cross some years later when we found ourselves both flying for another airline.

We were all anxious at the end of the summer season. We hoped that there would be at least some winter work for us to keep the wolf from the door but, in fact, we were to be laid off throughout the winter months and then welcomed back to the fold for the following summer season. Needless to say, we would not be getting paid while laid off and, with a substantial mortgage on my house, I really had to find myself another job. A new airline was due to start scheduled services from Heathrow to the Middle East and it was rumoured that they would be operating the Airbus A320. Bob Seed was going to be the director of flight operations and I phoned him straight away. Bob invited me down to his home and, following a long chat and a very pleasant lunch served by his wife in the garden, he offered

An Airbus A320 of British Mediterranean

me a job with the new airline which was to be called British Mediterranean.

My first passenger flight was to be from Heathrow to Beirut in just five days' time. My uniform was not yet ready, and Bob asked me if I had any suitable clothing to wear. I told him that I had a couple of white uniform shirts from my time at Malaysia Airlines, along with some gold epaulettes. He then asked if I had a pair of black trousers, and I told him that I had a dark grey pair. 'That will do fine. Just wear what you've got'. Only one thing seemed certain; it should be an interesting inaugural flight.

When I and the rest of the crew checked in for our flight, we were all wearing different uniforms and must have looked an odd bunch to the security staff. One of them said, 'I've just seen your passenger list. It certainly is an impressive read.' He handed me the list to see for myself. There were several Lords and Ladies, including Lord Hesketh, the former minister of state in the department of trade and industry, who was now chairman of British Mediterranean. We had senior trade officials and managers from the travel industry on board, as well as some travel reporters. I noticed that we even had the famous travel reporter Alan Whicker travelling with us. Over the years I had thoroughly enjoyed watching his television series *Whicker's World*.

With a flight time just short of five hours, we arrived at Beirut airport right on schedule. We were the first British airline to operate scheduled services into the city since the start of the Lebanese civil war in 1975. There was a brass band and reception committee awaiting us and I had to carefully position the aircraft so that we stopped with the forward passenger door lined up perfectly with the red carpet that had been laid out for our arrival. A television crew interviewed us at the bottom of the aircraft steps after our passengers had disembarked. A lavish banquet had been laid on at a hotel in town for later that evening and we were all entertained by musicians and a belly dancer as we ate our meal. It was quite an arrival and the Lebanese people seemed genuinely delighted that a British airline had resumed scheduled services into Beirut after such a long absence.

The following day, we flew a group of people who were all connected to the travel industry from Beirut to Cyprus where we landed and checked into a hotel for a few hours. Bob Seed announced that the first officer and I were now cleared for unsupervised line operations and that once we had flown back to Beirut, we would be left there while he and another pilot flew the aircraft back to London the following day. The next time the aircraft returned to Beirut, we would climb aboard and fly it back to Heathrow. B-Med's scheduled service between London and Beirut had officially begun.

I had not been to Lebanon prior to operating that first flight into Beirut. However, it was a place I would be seeing a lot more of in the months ahead. The extent of the damage and destruction caused by years of war in the region was immediately and shockingly apparent. Many buildings in the city had been reduced to rubble, particularly along the so called 'green line' which was the demarcation line that ran along Damascus Street and divided the predominantly Christian area to the East of the city from the predominantly Muslim area to the West.

Our crews stayed at the Coral Beach hotel, which was owned by one of the Lebanese investors in our airline. It was to become my second home, and, at times, it seemed that I spent more time there than I did at my home in Wilmslow. Because the airline was operating just one aircraft at this stage, the crews were a very small and tight team. They were a great bunch of people and we all got on very well together, which is just as well because we were destined to spend a lot of time in each other's company. Boozy room parties and wild nights spent in the city's restaurants and clubs ensured that our presence in Beirut didn't go unnoticed.

On the 23rd of December, I was on my way home for Christmas. The flight from Beirut proceeded normally until we were a couple of hundred miles out from London Heathrow. By now we were picking up weather reports over the radio and the Heathrow weather was not good. When ATC asked us what minima we required I replied that we needed CAT1. They responded with the bombshell statement: 'Sorry, we are only accepting aircraft into our area with CAT2 or better. You will have to divert.'

The First Officer and I had both received training in CAT3 operations and we had both carried out landings in CAT3 weather conditions when flying with our previous airlines. However, because British Mediterranean was a new airline, they hadn't yet obtained the necessary approvals from the authorities to conduct CAT3 operations. So, reluctantly, I had to set course for London Gatwick, where the weather conditions—although not great—were well above CAT1 minima.

After landing, my problems really started because the airport was being swamped with unexpected arrivals like ours. As you can imagine, with so many diverted flights and stranded passengers, just about every bus operator in the south of England was being contacted to try and secure transport to Heathrow. To cut a long story short, our passengers did eventually set off on the final part of their disrupted journey. I then sent all the cabin crew home, but the first officer and I stayed with the aircraft. The hope was that there would be an improvement in the Heathrow weather before we finally ran out of duty hours, and we could position the aircraft across. It was scheduled to operate the Heathrow to Beirut service later in the afternoon, but as the time dragged by, the Heathrow fog stubbornly refused to lift. Just as we ran out of hours, the captain who was rostered to operate the afternoon service to Beirut got word to me that his passengers were going to be brought by bus from Heathrow to Gatwick and the flight would be leaving from there. His crew would of course be spending their Christmas in Beirut, so I sincerely hoped that things would improve for them after this bad start. We were now free to leave, so after securing the aircraft, we headed for the terminal building.

The first officer was going to be staying in the south of England for his Christmas, but I had to try and get back to Manchester. I went to see if I could buy a ticket on the last British Airways flight to Manchester, but the flight was full. As I was wearing my uniform, I was able to use my airport ID pass and make my way to the departure gate. Once there, I asked if there was any chance of bumming a ride on the flight deck jump seat. The agent on the desk looked at me and said—probably because I looked like a very weary man who had clearly had a bad day and was desperately trying to get home for Christmas, 'I'll go and ask the captain, but I'm almost certain that he'll say no because they only take BA staff members on the jump seat.' Just as he turned to go to the aircraft, I looked through the window and noticed the registration of the aircraft. It was an ex-Dan-Air Boeing 737-400 series, G-BNNL. I suddenly had an idea and asked the agent to wait a moment. I quickly wrote a note on a piece of paper and asked the agent to give it to the captain: 'The last time I was on the flight deck of November Lima it was painted in Dan-Air colours prior to BA taking it over. I'd really appreciate seeing that flight deck again and getting home for Christmas.'

I'm delighted to say that it worked, but my worries

nearly didn't end there because I could see that fog was rapidly forming outside. By the time all the passengers were on, and we had pushed back from the stand, it had suddenly got very thick indeed. We had to taxi very slowly because the forward visibility was so bad, and we listened as the controller kept broadcasting the latest runway visual range (RVR) figures. By the time we eventually turned onto the runway, the RVR had dropped down to the absolute minimum allowed for a take-off. I've never been more relieved to get out of Gatwick. Christmas 1994 was destined to be a good one, after all.

In 1995 I took my Dad with me on a trip to Beirut. He had last been there in the late 1960s on a working trip for Dan-Air. He had fond memories of his last visit to Beirut and remembered it as a very beautiful city. I told him that much of the old city had sadly been ruined during the war, but that he should come and check it out for himself. When the first officer and I were running through our pre-flight checks, the dispatcher brought Dad onto the flight deck, and we got him settled into the jump seat. There was a lovely moment when we found ourselves passing the old British Eagle hangars where I had worked as an apprentice when I first started in the airline industry. I pointed them out to the first officer and told him of their significance to me. I glanced back at Dad and his smile and wink told me that the moment meant a lot to him too. Dad stayed up front until we got to the top of climb and then one of the stewardesses came to take him back into the passenger cabin. He had a seat waiting for him in first class, along with a large Scotch. The cabin crew fussed over him and made sure that he wanted for nothing during the flight and then he re-joined us on the flight deck for the landing at Beirut.

We checked into the Coral Beach Hotel and the next day, my friend Fuad Saab met up with us and drove Dad and I up into the Chouf mountains for a tour around. We had a great couple of days in Beirut and then when we flew back to Heathrow. One of our stewardesses, Alison Morgan, kindly offered to drive Dad back home to South Wales as she lived not many miles from his home. It was a great way to finish off his trip and he thoroughly enjoyed himself.

As if G-MEDA wasn't already flying hard enough, we also started to operate flights to Kyrgyzstan. In October 1995, I was flying from Bishkek to London with first officer Paul Davies. We did everything we could to save time and fuel by flying economically and cutting out dog legs on the airway to reduce track miles. At one stage, I asked the Russian controller 'Do you have radar?' to which he replied 'No.' I then asked if we could proceed directly from our present position to a reporting point some considerable distance away. This requested routing would cut out a dog leg and reduce our mileage by a useful amount. The reply came back a stern 'No.' I asked if there was any other traffic in the area and the reply was, 'No traffic.' A few moments later, I said to Paul 'Well, he said he hasn't got radar, so let's see.' I started to cut the corner on the airway. Moments later, the Russian controller said 'You are approaching the left side edge of the airway. Turn right immediately and return to the airway centreline.' I said to him 'I thought you said that you didn't have radar?' he replied 'That is correct. I have no radar.' Like hell he didn't!

I had been running some fuel calculations for a while and I said to Paul, 'I reckon if the wind component doesn't change significantly, we can make it from here to Heathrow without having to stop off in Berlin.' I showed him my calculations and he agreed. I then said that if things started to go against us, we could always lob into Amsterdam and pick up fuel there, so that was our plan B. He agreed, so I called ATC and told them that we wanted to change our flight plan and nominate Heathrow as our intended destination. Eight hours and fifteen minutes after taking off from Bishkek, we landed at Heathrow. We shut down the engines with just over the legally required thirty minutes of holding fuel in the tanks. Shortly afterwards, I received word that Airbus had officially recorded that as the longest ever passenger carrying flight in an Airbus A320. It wasn't a record that I had any intention of trying to break any time soon.

The very high daily utilisation we were achieving with our aircraft hadn't escaped the notice of the people at Airbus. In fact, rumour had it that they would cite it to potential customers as an example of just what could be achieved with their wonderful product. Delta Alpha certainly was reliable and a fine advert for the Airbus company. We used British Airways engineering at Heathrow but didn't have any engineering cover at any of our down-route destinations. As with all commercial aircraft, we carried a minimum equipment list (MEL) that we had to refer to if any item became unserviceable. It was perfectly acceptable to depart with certain unserviceable items and fly to a destination where engineering work could be carried out. The MEL listed exactly which items could be dispensed with and which items had to be serviceable for further flight. Obviously, some systems had a lot of built in redundancy and because of their back up or alternative components, you were allowed to bring the aircraft home to get the unserviceable item replaced. For example, each engine was fitted with an engine-driven electrical generator. Under normal circumstances you would depart with two generators working, safe in the knowledge that if one generator failed in flight, the remaining generator was perfectly capable of supplying all the essential electrical systems. However, if prior to departure you discover that one of the engine-driven generators has failed, can you take-off and fly home? When you check the MEL, you discover that if you keep the Auxiliary Power Unit (APU) running throughout the flight, you can use its generator in place of the unserviceable one. The APU is normally shut down after starting the engines because it is no longer required, but in this scenario, it would be kept running. It uses a certain amount of fuel so you would make an allowance for that if embarking on a long flight. So, for example, if it uses 150 kilograms of fuel per hour and you are embarking on a five-hour flight, you will uplift an extra 750 kilograms of fuel. Job done—problem solved—you are on your way home.

The amount of time I was spending away from home

was really getting me down. I think Sara had started to feel like she was a single parent as she was bringing up our son Joe on her own. I was supposed to get eight days off a month and that's all I was getting. In fact, on more than one occasion, I was credited with having had a 'day off' in Beirut to make up the eight and to make my work roster legal on paper. During 1995, I had 141 overnight stops in Beirut alone. In addition to that I had overnights in Dalaman, Amman and Bishkek. Any more nights away and I would be needing a map to find my way home. I might also need to send updated photographs of myself to Sara to ensure that she recognised me when I walked through the door.

Another worry with regards to my job at British Mediterranean was the fact that the Middle East continued to be a volatile area and if trouble flared up in Syria, Lebanon or Jordan, the airline would instantly be adversely affected. Moving around Beirut and other parts of Lebanon, we were well used to encountering armed Syrian soldiers at checkpoints and roadblocks around the place. We were also very aware that the Hezbollah were active in the south of Lebanon.

I was due to fly out to Beirut when news channels started to report an escalation in Israeli military action in southern Lebanon. Israeli helicopter gunships had carried out rocket attacks on Hezbollah targets in the area, and ground forces and armoured divisions were amassing along the border. A short while later, we were on the aircraft getting ready for the flight ahead. The passengers had just started boarding and one of the cabin crew came onto the flight deck to tell me that they had recognised several television news reporters amongst the passengers. Unfortunately, they were the same familiar faces that you always saw on your television screen when they were reporting from a war zone! It seemed that this might turn out to be an interesting trip.

While close to Cyprus, the Nicosia controller came back with some worrying news: his radar was showing traffic in the immediate vicinity of Beirut airport believed to be

Israeli helicopter gunships. When I asked him if he knew what was going on, he replied that he didn't and that his efforts to phone the air traffic controller at Beirut airport had gone unanswered. I got the First Officer to start monitoring Nicosia on one radio, while I tried to raise Beirut on the other. There was no response, and I was now thinking that we were going to have to divert to Cyprus.

Suddenly, a voice came through on the Beirut ATC frequency. The message was abnormal to say the least. He called us by our call sign and flight number as usual, but then said slowly and clearly 'You are an Airbus A320 on a scheduled passenger service from London to Beirut. Be advised that the military helicopter traffic will be withdrawing from the immediate vicinity of the airfield. They will maintain their position out to sea in order to allow you to land.' As we didn't need him to tell us that we were an A320 carrying passengers on a scheduled service into Beirut, I assumed that his message was intended to stop any trigger-happy Israeli pilot from taking a pop at us.

I mentally thanked him for coming up with that idea and we reverted to more normal radio transmissions as we continued towards our destination. About fifteen minutes later, we taxied to our parking stand and shut down the engines. As the passenger door opened and our passengers started to disembark, I looked out of the window and spotted some of the news reporters among them. I had worked on the principle that they were used to ducking and dodging bullets in a war zone so, if things really kicked off, we should follow their lead. We met up with many of them in the hotel bar, and they really were a great bunch. They spent a lot of their time travelling from one war zone or volatile hot spot to another. They are intelligent people, with a great deal of knowledge about the political situation in various countries around the world. They have a tremendous network of useful contacts and local interpreters and although the reporters were all working for different networks and news companies, they all found themselves popping up in the same locations again and again. Consequently, despite the rivalry to get a great news story, there seemed to be a 'band of brothers' feeling when they were together. As you might expect, they had some great stories to tell, most of which involved a healthy dose of dark humour. Kate Adie was in the hotel, although she seemed to keep to herself most of the time. We thoroughly enjoyed the company of the BBC correspondent Jeremy Bowen, and ITV's correspondent Terry Lloyd. Tragically Lloyd was killed in 2003 by American forces in a dreadful 'friendly fire' incident while he was reporting on the Iraq War.

We were effectively trapped in Beirut; our aircraft had flown back to London and there were no more flights in or out of Beirut because the airport had been closed. We could hear heavy artillery fire at times to the south of Beirut and reports of concentrated rocket attacks by Hezbollah kept coming through to us. Our plan, if a hasty evacuation became necessary, was to make our way to the port at Jounieh and try and get a ferry to Cyprus. In the meantime, we stayed put in the hotel. The press guys had set up an assortment of satellite dishes and equipment on the roof, and it also made a good backdrop for the reporters when they sent a broadcast back to the UK. Speaking directly to camera, with a view of the city behind them, it gave the television viewers an impression of actually being there. I remember an amusing moment when I was talking to Jeremy Bowen, and then, suddenly, as I looked over his shoulder, I saw his face appear on the television that was at the end of the room. We watched the news report he had done up on the roof a few minutes earlier and then turned to one another and carried on our conversation. An example of the wonders of modern-day news reporting.

A couple of days later, reports came through that the Israelis had hit a United Nations compound containing civilian refugees and many of them had been killed and wounded. The camp was to the south and now there were further reports of plenty of 'action' in the area. Some reporters planned on heading there to take a look and one of them told me that the sea road heading towards the southern border, had been given the nickname 'Sniper Alley.' Dark humour in action again!

I later watched as a couple of them attached duct tape to the roof of their car. The tape spelled out the word PRESS in letters that covered the whole roof. We suggested to them that bullet proof Kevlar might make a more suitable covering. Clearly, the press reporter's dark humour was starting to rub off on us now, and the guys responded in the time-honoured fashion with a two fingered gesture. Shortly afterwards, they set off towards the border between Lebanon and Israel. My crew and I decided that setting off to the hotel bar was a much better idea.

One morning, an Israeli Air Force fighter flew at high speed, very low over the hotel, rattling the windows and putting the wind up everyone in the process. I was amused to hear the rattle of a heavy machine gun a couple of seconds later. Presumably, the Hezbollah had fired it into the air in the hope of bagging an Israeli F-16. With the speed the aircraft had been travelling, the fighter would have been overhead Tel Aviv before the first bullet had got halfway out of the machine gun's barrel. We remained stranded in Beirut for a few days, but eventually things died down sufficiently for the airport to reopen to civilian traffic. The reappearance of the B-Med Airbus was a very welcome sight. It had certainly been an interesting trip.

During 1996 our services to Beirut, Damascus, Amman and Bishkek continued but there were worrying rumours that some of the airline's investors were getting cold feet. Then came news of a possible franchise agreement with British Airways. This made a lot of sense because BA also operated scheduled services to the Middle East, but British Mediterranean, with their much lower operating cost, could do it more profitably. I, however, had already applied to Virgin Atlantic for a job, and had been offered an interview.

The interview was at the Virgin Flight Centre. However, when I got there, I realised that I knew it by another name. It had formerly been Newman House, after Fred Newman, the chairman of Dan-Air. I'd been in the building many times and it felt strange to be back under these circumstances. I found the Spanish inquisition style interview rather nerve wracking. I was seated in front of four people who were seated in a line opposite me. They immediately started quizzing me on a variety of subjects, some personal, some technical, some predictable and some unexpected. It was quite a workout. I had been asked to bring along my logbooks and they had clearly studied those in some detail. I was asked about various individual flights or periods in my career that interested them, and this process continued for some time. The fleet manager of Virgin's Boeing 747 fleet was one of the four interviewers, and he commented that I had a great deal of flying experience and noted that I had been a captain for more than twelve years. As I was applying for the position of first officer on the Airbus A340 fleet, he felt he should point out that there were several young captains on that fleet who had far less flying experience than me. After a pause, he gave me a serious look and asked how I felt about that and whether I would find it difficult to accept taking orders from them. Fortunately, this was a question that I had been expecting and one to which I had given a good deal of thought. I was able to honestly say that I was perfectly comfortable with the prospect and hoped that my twelve years in command would enable me to provide useful backup to those young captains. In case he thought I was just being a creep, I added that I hoped it would stand me in good stead for when my time came for promotion in Virgin. My response seemed to satisfy him, and a few days later, they offered me the position.

I would soon be flying for another airline which meant yet another training course. I told British Mediterranean that I was going to be leaving and began working my notice period with them. If a surgeon or senior consultant decided to leave the hospital where they had been working for some years, they wouldn't expect to have to start their new job as a junior doctor at the next hospital. Similarly, if a headteacher left to go to another school, they wouldn't expect to start again as an assistant teacher. However, if an airline captain leaves his or her current employer to start at another airline, they have to go back to being a first officer. To avoid any favouritism, nepotism or personality disputes adversely affecting a pilot's career prospects, the rule is that when a pilot first joins an airline, they always come in as a first officer, irrespective of their previous rank or experience level. The only exception to this rule would be if the airline had an immediate need for an additional captain, but none of their first officers were currently sufficiently experienced for the job. I would be a senior first officer until such time as my number came up for promotion.

In November 1996, I found myself back in Miami at the Airbus training centre for the Cross Crew Qualification Course that was to reveal the differences between the Airbus A320 that I was already rated to fly and the A340 that I was going to fly. In just 10 very intensive days, we had completed the course and three weeks later, I was in Shannon to do my circuit training: the fun part of the whole conversion course.

By consulting my flying logbook, I see that my first scheduled flight on the A340 was on 6 January 1997, from London Heathrow to Washington. After an overnight stop, we flew back to London the next evening. It's funny what you get used to, because it didn't take long before I considered flights to the east coast of America as 'quickies.' Compared to the other destinations we served on the A340 fleet they were, indeed, short.

On the long flights, we carried an extra pilot and for Hong Kong and Narita, two extra pilots. This enabled us to get some rest during the cruise, before returning to the flight deck for the final part of the flight. Going into Hong Kong Kai Tak was good fun because it involved flying the notorious chequerboard approach to runway 13. Because of high terrain in the vicinity of the airfield it was not possible to fly a straight-in approach to the runway. Instead, you initially flew down the IGS (Instrument Guidance System) which was like an ILS in terms of the cockpit presentation for the pilots. However, instead of the beam guiding you towards a runway, it was actually guiding you towards a hill. Before you got to the hill, it was necessary to establish visual contact with the ground, using the good old mark one eyeball—in other words—by looking out of your window. You stared ahead, searching for a large chequerboard that had been erected on the side of a small hill. Shortly before reaching it you turned through about forty-five degrees towards the runway, descending as you did so, and rolling the wings level again mere seconds before reaching the runway. Throughout the turn you were skimming over the rooftops of the high-rise apartment buildings in the vicinity of the airfield. The runway itself jutted out into Hong Kong harbour and was surrounded by water on three sides. It was a spectacular and unique approach and, in typhoon season, reduced visibility in torrential rain and gusty winds could make it extremely challenging.

There was a local gentleman who owned a camera shop in Kowloon, and he would always have an employee located in position at the chequerboard. They would photograph every single aircraft that made an approach and landing at Kai Tak. You could go to his shop the day after you landed, give him the flight number of your inbound flight and he would pull out the shots of your arrival. You could then choose the photo that you wanted, the size of the print, what type of frame to mount it in and he would have it all done within minutes. Also, if you asked him nicely, he would show you the 'rogue's gallery' which was a collection of the most hair-raising approaches and landings that had been recorded over the years. He also sold a terrific range of cameras at very reasonable prices and gave a good discount to aircrew. Consequently, it was a place we all simply had to visit when in Kowloon.

While the landings at Kai Tak could be challenging in certain weather conditions, the take-offs could also get your pulse racing. We always came out of there with the aircraft right up to its absolute maximum take-off weight for the prevailing conditions. The A340 had a huge capacity in the cargo holds below the floor of the passenger cabin. Carrying cargo out of Hong Kong was very lucrative for the airline and, at that time, they were charging five pounds

An Airbus A340 of Virgin Atlantic

sterling for every kilo carried. Because it was so lucrative, the dispatcher wanted to know our exact maximum take-off mass (MTOM) under the current weather conditions. Initially they would load cargo pallets into the holds until they were close to the permitted weight. Then they would open a pallet and put individual boxes and packages on to take the weight right up to the maximum. Now with the aircraft at its absolute maximum permitted mass, we were ready to go.

With the engines at full thrust, you'd start accelerating down the runway. Your eyes glanced down at the airspeed indicator and then straight ahead through the windscreen. Back to the airspeed, back to the windscreen. The runway centreline lights would be streaming past at a terrific rate emphasising just how bloody fast you were going. The end of the runway was clearly in sight and getting frighteningly close. Your colleague called out 'V1.' Then he called 'rotate.' You eased back the side stick and raised the aircraft's nose to the initial take-off attitude. As soon as you did so, you immediately lost sight of the runway and all you could see ahead was the inky black sky. You knew the nose wheels were airborne but the wheels of the main gear way behind you were still glued to the ground. You felt sure that you had now passed the end of the runway and then your colleague called out 'positive rate of climb.'

With the dark water of Kowloon Bay lapping at the end of the runway, your colleague's comment 'I reckon we washed the tyres that time Bob', made you chuckle, but probably wasn't too far from the truth. The aircraft's initial rate of climb was poor and the maximum altitude you could achieve was only about 28,000 feet. Later, once you had burned off a few tonnes of fuel, you could request a step climb to a higher level which should keep you above most of the cumulonimbus clouds that had been forecast. In the meantime, you kept one eye on the weather radar for any sign of trouble ahead and you settled down for the thirteen-and-a-half-hour flight.

On 23 February 1997, I landed at Heathrow at the end of a flight from Hong Kong. An hour after landing, I climbed into my car in the staff car park and began the three-hour drive home to Wilmslow. I knew that by the time I got home, I would have been on the go for about twenty hours, but there was a very good reason for me to get back as soon as possible. My wife Sara was due to give birth any day with our second child and I had booked some annual leave to ensure that I would be around for the big event. It turned out that our timing was excellent, because on 25 February our daughter Phoebe made her appearance. I wasn't due back at work for another three weeks, so we all made the most of that time getting to know the new addition to the Williams tribe.

There is plenty of medical evidence to show that constantly crossing time zones has an adverse effect on a person's long-term health. The more zones crossed, the greater the time difference and the more pronounced the resultant effect on the crews. Virgin had destinations as far west as the Californian coast in America and as far east as Japan. The time difference between those places is fifteen hours. If a crew operates a flight from London to Los Angeles, they will spend two nights in a place where the local time is eight hours behind London time. Then they fly back to London and spend a brief time there. Now, if they operate a flight to Narita, they will spend two nights in a place where the local time is seven hours ahead of London. Then it's back to London with another seven-hour time difference to adjust to. Believe me when I say that is very debilitating and leaves you feeling punchy. The flight crew rostering department at Virgin recognised that allocating a flight series like that would have an adverse effect on a crew member. Consequently, they tried to avoid rostering such a combination where possible. One solution after rostering a round trip to Los Angeles would be to follow it up with a round trip to Johannesburg where the time difference is only one hour.

We were all acutely aware that the limited amount of manual flying we were doing resulted in a significant reduction in our stick and rudder handling skills. Although there was little we could do about it in terms of our airline flying, there was one solution that several of us employed. We reacquainted ourselves with flying light aircraft. I decided that it was time to get an instructor's rating and to teach people how to fly single-engine aircraft. At the same time, it would hopefully remind me how to fly an aircraft myself!

In March 1998, I started a flight instructor's course at a local flying school called Ravenair. At the time, they were based on the north side of Manchester airport, a short drive from my home. The company was owned by Jeff Nuttall who was a Boeing 757 Captain with Air 2000 at the time. My one-on-one course was being run by Primo Lonzardi, a very experienced pilot who was Ravenair's chief flying instructor. I hit it off with Primo right away and thoroughly enjoyed flying under his watchful eye. It was fun to be flying a basic aircraft again—a Piper PA-38—and it reminded me what I had been missing.

Soon after this, I started working part time as a flying instructor at a flying school based at Woodford, which was an airfield that was owned by British Aerospace. It was located very close to Manchester airport, which was very convenient for me. What with the flying instruction and my long haul flying with Virgin, I was as busy as I wanted to be, but instructing in the light aircraft didn't feel like work at all. I was thoroughly enjoying some good old stick and rudder flying again.

At the end of 1998, the news broke that Richard Branson was going to launch a new airline that would be flying Virgin Holiday passengers to popular European resorts. It was to be called Virgin Sun and the airline would be operating brand new Airbus A320 and A321 aircraft. Virgin Atlantic pilots who were interested in switching from long haul to European flying could volunteer to undergo a cross crew qualification (CCQ) course onto the 320/321. The plan was to have aircraft based at both Gatwick and Manchester airports. I was told they wanted me to be senior base captain and to manage the Manchester base. Then the company's training department told me that they also wanted me to be a line training and line check captain on the Airbus. It seemed that Christmas had come early this year. In January 1999, I underwent the CCQ course to get me reacquainted and requalified for flying the A320/321, and I did the base training at Prestwick with Roy Byway. We carried out three touch and goes, one approach and go-around and one full stop landing, and that was me back on the 'minibus.' I started my line training with Captain Ian Lund, operating Virgin's scheduled services between London Heathrow and Athens and London Gatwick and Athens. After twelve sectors of line training, I was given a final line check and line release check and signed off as being good to go.

At this stage, Virgin Sun was yet to start operating and all my A320 flying had been done on G-OUZO which was painted in the familiar Virgin Atlantic livery. Virgin Sun's first aircraft had been given the registration G-VMED and had been painted in the very distinctive and unmistakable new livery designed for that company. It was most definitely a 'Bovril' concept, in that people

G-VMED, an Airbus A320 of Virgin Sun

either liked it or loathed it. One thing was for sure, it wasn't subtle.

Every year, all the heads of the Virgin group of companies had a get-together. They discussed their company's performance over the past year, decided on plans for the year ahead and came up with group strategies and targets. For this year's get-together Richard Branson had a brilliant idea. He knew that Virgin Sun's first aircraft was currently sitting on the ground at Gatwick and not doing anything useful for a while. He suggested that all the Virgin bosses should be put onto it and flown to Majorca. Richard owned a hotel called La Residencia on the north coast of the island. With his excellent eye for publicity and promotional opportunities, he decided that was where the managerial get-together should take place. It would be an excellent way of 'flying the flag' and promoting Virgin Sun at the same time.

Anxious questions were asked, such as 'What happens if the aircraft crashes?' and 'What will become of the Virgin empire if the head of every company within the group is killed?' Richard dug his heels in and insisted that he wanted everyone on the Virgin Sun aircraft. The insurance people, realising that he wasn't going to be dissuaded, then insisted that the captain and first officer assigned to the flight had to be the most experienced Airbus pilots in the airline. A quick check with aircrew records showed that the captain with the most flying hours on the A320 was none other than me! The name of the first officer was Mike Kenny. I had flown extensively with Mike when we both worked for British Mediterranean, but I hadn't seen him since. When we got to Majorca, we were to spend two nights there with our VIP passengers and then we were to fly everyone back to Gatwick again. This promised to be a very pleasant reunion.

The day of the flight arrived and having met up with the cabin crew, we all climbed aboard the aircraft to get everything ready for the arrival of our passengers. Sometime later, we had all our passengers aboard, with one notable exception. Richard Branson. I had been told earlier that he'd been on holiday in the Caribbean with his family and was flying into Gatwick aboard a Virgin Atlantic B.747. The timing had been described as 'a bit tight' with regards to getting him off the Caribbean flight and onto ours. Unfortunately, it now turned out that his aircraft was running late, so arrangements had been made for a 'tarmac transfer.' This meant that as soon as his aircraft parked on stand, Richard was going to be brought across the apron by car directly to our aircraft. Because of his late arrival, our approved take-off time had passed, and I had been negotiating with ATC to try and get an extension on it. The controller was showing no signs of compassion and warned that we could expect a significant delay to our departure while a new slot time (approved take-off time) was arranged. I decided to try for the sympathy vote and began grovelling over the radio. I said, 'I'd really appreciate it if you could pull some strings and help me out here. We are actually waiting for the chairman of our airline who is currently on board another of his aircraft. That aircraft is on final approach to Gatwick as we speak. It is so vital that I get him down to Majorca that arrangements have been made for a tarmac transfer to get him over to us. Anything you could possibly do to help would be appreciated and would go a long way towards keeping me in his good books.'

This unashamed grovelling resulted in a moment of silence and then the controller said, 'I'll see what I can do.' A short time later, we watched the Virgin 747 taxi in and park a few hundred yards away from us. The air bridge was positioned into place at the forward entrance, and I noticed there was a car parked below the air bridge. There is an external stairway attached to the outside of an airbridge, at the top of which is a small access door into the airbridge itself. This access is normally only used by aircrew and engineers, but now I saw two figures appear through the access door and descend the stairway. Even from a distance I could see one of them had a distinctive mop of blonde hair. As he was bundled into the car, the radio burst into life and the controller asked, 'Are you ready for pushback?' I replied that we would be ready in two minutes. The controller then told us that if we were not airborne in ten minutes, he would have no choice but to cancel our flight plan. I tried to sound convincing as I replied 'Ten minutes? No problem!'

The car screeched to a halt near the nose of our aircraft and Branson climbed out. I should mention that when our other passengers had boarded the flight earlier, there had been a lot of PR nonsense going on with some young ladies dressed as giant sun flowers, serving champagne and canapés to our guests. As Richard appeared, they gave out a loud cheer and one of the girls thrust a glass of bubbly into his hand. A small crowd gathered around him, a barrage of camera flashes illuminated the area and Richard dutifully began posing for photographs. Someone then popped the cork on a huge magnum of champagne, whereupon Richard grabbed the bottle, placed his hand over the top and began shaking it vigorously. The wine began to shoot out like a fire extinguisher going off and Richard sprayed it all over the assembled crowd. There were shrieks and squeals from the sunflower girls as he continued to drench them in champagne, but just then our radio burst into life. The ground controller demanded, 'Can you confirm that you are actually pushing back right now?' I replied that we were indeed on the move. Glancing out of my side window I could see that Richard was in full swing and clearly determined to keep partying. I opened my side window, stuck my head out and shouted 'Richard!' Suddenly, everyone stopped in their tracks and turned to stare at me. 'I'm sorry but you have to get on this aircraft right now or we won't be going anywhere.' There was a moment of silence and then Richard, sheepishly handed back the champagne bottle and climbed aboard. The door was immediately closed behind him and moments later we were on our way. It's a good job there was nobody around brandishing a handheld radar speed gun, because we would have been nicked for speeding. We finally turned onto the runway with one minute to spare.

A few minutes after take-off, the stewardess came into the flight deck and said that Richard had asked if he could come and have a word with me. I turned to Mike the first officer and suggested that this might be the moment where I would be told to look for another job. However, when Richard appeared beside us, he apologised profusely for holding up proceedings and explained that he didn't realise we had been on the brink of having our flight cancelled. With apologies gratefully accepted, we soon settled into a pleasant and relaxed conversation.

We made good time en route and taxied in at Palma to be greeted by another excited crowd who were all busy snapping away with their cameras as they caught sight of a Virgin Sun aircraft for the very first time. There were some stretched limousines parked and Richard had told Mike and I that he wanted us to ride in his limo with him. We had handed our passports to an immigration official who came aboard as soon as we parked the aircraft. Now, after the briefest of glances at our documents, he handed them back to us, saluted smartly and left the aircraft. Clearly, travelling in the company of VIPs opened lots of doors.

Mike and I climbed into Richard's limo and I found myself

sitting opposite Steve Ridgway who was the managing director (later to become CEO) of Virgin Atlantic. Sitting in a limousine with Branson and Ridgway was definitely a bit of a 'pinch me' moment, but as the chauffeur swept us gently away from the aircraft, Mike turned to Richard and said 'Richard, I've asked my girlfriend to join us on this trip and she arrived in the terminal a short while ago. Any chance we could ask the driver to swing by and pick her up?'

I looked across at Mike in total disbelief and briefly considered throwing him out of our speeding car, but then Richard replied that it would be just fine. The driver pulled up outside the terminal and moments later a very attractive blonde girl with long legs and a very short skirt walked towards us. Mike jumped out to greet his girlfriend and Richard and Steve made room for her to sit between them. It seemed that my cheeky first officer had pulled it off and his girlfriend had the two VIPs eating out of her hand in no time.

It was a very pleasant drive to the mountains on the northern portion of the island, during which I chatted to Steve about his seafaring adventures with Richard. Virgin had commissioned the design and construction of a boat named the Virgin Atlantic Challenger, which was built specifically to carry out an attempt to win the Blue Riband contest. In this contest, the Hale's Trophy was awarded for the fastest crossing of the Atlantic Ocean and the title had been held by the American ocean liner *United States*. Richard was determined to bring the trophy to Britain and win his airline, Virgin Atlantic, a great deal of publicity in the process. In 1985, Richard and Steve had joined their fellow crew members aboard the *Virgin Atlantic Challenger* and set off from New York for the crossing. It nearly ended in disaster when the boat was badly damaged and sank while they were less than two hundred miles short of completing their journey. The crew had to take to life rafts and await rescue. Not to be deterred, a new boat named *Virgin Atlantic Challenger 2* was built and in 1986 they successfully smashed the record for the fastest crossing.

The Hales Trophy was in the custody of the American Merchant Maritime Museum (AMMM) at the time, but in a disgraceful display of sour grapes, they refused to hand the trophy to the Virgin team, branding their craft 'a little toy boat.'

Rather than responding to their snub, which had been viewed as unsporting and distasteful by most parties, Richard immediately created a new trophy. This was named the Virgin Atlantic Challenge Trophy and people from around the world were invited to compete for it by beating Virgin's 1986 record. In 1991, a boat commissioned by the Aga Khan and named *Destriero* set a new record that remains to this day. Presumably, the Hales Trophy custodians will have branded that another 'Little toy boat?'

Richard's hotel, La Residencia, is a beautiful retreat and we spent a pleasant late afternoon by the swimming pool and looking around the grounds. The whole crew had been invited to join Richard for dinner at his table in the restaurant and we had a terrific evening. It was a very relaxed atmosphere, and everybody enjoyed themselves. The Virgin management team held meetings throughout the next day and then relaxed and enjoyed themselves in the evening. The general idea was for it to be a brainstorming session that would produce new ideas and plans for the future.

After two nights in Mallorca, we flew everyone back to Gatwick. On the way, I asked Richard what the next big thing was going to be. He said it was going to be Virgin Mobile. This rather surprised me, because although mobile phones were becoming more commonplace and the market was clearly expanding, it looked to me as though others had got in there first and Virgin would be playing catch up. I suggested as much to Richard, but he told me that the experts were predicting that the mobile phone market was going to be massive. Not only would everyone want to have one, but new technology would enable them to send messages, listen to music, and even watch videos. Also, to make them affordable for young people, Virgin would be offering a pay-as-you-go option so that they could buy airtime as and when they could afford it. My pessimism underlines why Richard Branson is a billionaire, and I am a guy who used to fly his aircraft around!

Virgin Sun was yet to carry fare paying passengers and apart from Richard borrowing one of the aircraft for the brainstorming session in Mallorca, very few people were even aware of the company's existence. The A320 that we had used for the trip to Palma—G-VMED—was positioned to Manchester airport so people could get their first look at it. I was told that the company wanted me to operate a promotional sightseeing flight, starting and finishing at Manchester. My passengers were to be VIPs and guests from the travel industry. When I asked where I should take them, I was told, 'Just fly them wherever you fancy. Keep it under two hours duration, which will give the cabin crew plenty of time to do a meal and drinks service. The brief is to get the message across to our guests that flying with Virgin Sun is fun. So, Bob, off you go and have some fun.' It is not every day that someone gives you a brand-new Airbus to play with and tells you to go off and have fun in it. This was going to be another 'pinch me' day.

On 28 April 1999, I met up with my crew for our promotional flight. The first officer was Steve Dicksee, whom I hadn't met before. He had formerly been a flight engineer on classic Boeing 747s with Virgin Atlantic but had switched careers and retrained as a pilot. He was a real character who I would often fly with in the months ahead and whose company I always enjoyed. I told Steve that we had been cleared to fly wherever we wanted for up to two hours and I had decided we would head down to South Wales and overfly the town of Abergavenny. From there I planned to route directly to Land's End, and then we would make it up as we went along. ATC sounded intrigued and when they asked what it was all in aid of, I told them it was a promotional jaunt as part of the new airline's launch. What I didn't mention was that I had chosen Abergavenny—where my parents lived—so I could fly over their house and say hello.

We set off from Manchester and there was a real party

mood back in the passenger cabin. As we taxied out, I phoned my Dad and told him what time we should be overflying his house. He assured me he would be out in the garden with my Mum to give us a wave. We were really lucky with the weather because it was a lovely day with excellent visibility. We flew over my parents' house a short while later and continued down to Land's End. I had been giving the passengers a running commentary over the public address and we now manoeuvred the aircraft at quite low level so they could all get a good view of Land's End and the Scilly Isles. After circling around a couple of times, we headed up to St David's at the southwest tip of Wales. I handed control to Steve, and we flew over Strumble Head Lighthouse, then followed the coast all the way up to Snowdonia. We kept at low altitude throughout, and I was liaising with London Military ATC who were keeping a watchful eye on us. I took the controls back from Steve as we approached Snowdonia and flew us at a constant height above the ground as we followed the slope of mount Snowdon up to the top. The view was superb, and we could clearly see a train crawling up the mountain as we flashed past. We popped up over the top of the mountain, said goodbye to the military controller and switched to the Manchester radar controller. He made us laugh as he said 'Ah, there you are. I've been looking for you, but you were hiding behind Snowdon. Now that I can see you, I'll give you radar vectors to the ILS.' After a brief pause, he said, 'You guys have clearly been having some fun today. Was it good?' We confirmed that it had indeed been very good. A lot of people had been taking an interest in our magical mystery tour.

If that wasn't enough, when I checked in at the office later, they told me that they wanted me to operate another flight in much the same way the next day. Richard Branson would be hosting a launch party in Terminal 2 at Manchester airport. There would be a stage show, during which the new Virgin Sun cabin crew uniforms would be modelled. There would be music, dancing and a free bar for everyone. Virgin Sun was arriving in a blaze of laser lights, pyrotechnics, stage smoke and Branson razzmatazz!

We got stuck into a busy summer programme of holiday flights. I was thoroughly enjoying being back on European services and having a much greater variety of destinations. I also much preferred doing a round trip each day, as opposed to one ultra long flight taking me to yet another hotel room. Two take-offs and two landings, ending up back at home was far more satisfying to me than one take-off and landing ending up several time zones away from home. I was also being rostered with office days to carry out my base management duties and yet still had a decent amount of free time. That gave me the opportunity to spend a fair bit of time flying out of Woodford instructing flying students in single-engine aircraft.

I always found instructing very enjoyable and rewarding, it never felt like 'work.' This was partly because the students were all there because they wanted to be. They wanted to learn how to fly, and it was up to me to teach them. That was never a simple A-B-C process. Yes, there was a recognised syllabus to cover and yes, you had to develop certain skill sets within the student, but there are several different ways to achieve that. Every student is different, and they all learn at different rates. Some are naturally gifted in terms of their motor skills, while others must work hard to develop them. Some are under confident and need to be frequently encouraged. Others can be overconfident and need to be reined in to ensure their self-confidence doesn't tempt them try something that is beyond their current reach. It is this mixture of personalities and abilities that makes flight instruction so interesting and there are few things more rewarding than being able to help a student through a part of the syllabus that they had previously struggled with.

Virgin Atlantic, like all airlines, has a constant need to recruit pilots. When an experienced military pilot is about to retire from the service, they will usually be seeking a position with an airline and two of the airlines that are high on their wish list are British Airways and Virgin Atlantic. With that in mind, some years ago Virgin

Atlantic came up with a cunning plan. Any existing pilots in Virgin Atlantic who were interested were invited to put their names into a hat. Two names would be drawn from that hat at random. One would be sent to RAF Valley and the other would be sent to RNAS Yeovilton. At that time 208 squadron was based at Valley flying the BAe Hawk and 899 Naval air Squadron was at Yeovilton flying the BAe Sea Harrier. Each Virgin Atlantic pilot would be teamed up with a pilot from those bases who would take them for a flight in a Hawk or Sea Harrier. In return, those same two military pilots would be teamed up, at a later date, with their Virgin Atlantic partners, who would take them for a flight in a Boeing or Airbus. The idea was that it would give the military pilot an insight into what it was like to be a pilot with Virgin Atlantic. The hope was that they would be sufficiently impressed to ensure that when their time came to leave the military, they would send their CV and letter of application to Virgin Atlantic. The drawing of names from the hat was carried out at regular intervals throughout the year. As soon as I had heard about the scheme, I put my name forward, because I had never flown in a military jet and considered this to be my only chance to do so. I had heard nothing since and had quite frankly forgotten all about it.

One day, out of the blue, I received a phone call telling me that my name had been picked out in the draw and I was going to RAF Valley. I was over the moon and couldn't wait to get there. Flight Lieutenant Roger Goodrum and his family had kindly invited me to spend the night at their home which was near to the base at RAF Valley. I met Roger's wife and daughter and spent a very pleasant evening in their company. The next day I was taken to the base commander's office and asked what I would like to do on my flight in the Hawk. I said I was rather hoping to do the sort of things that would get me sacked if I attempted them in the airline. With a weary smile he said 'I was afraid you were going to say that. Okay Goodrum, take Captain Williams flying and make sure you bring him back in one piece!'

An RAF Hawk T2

The Hawk looked very sexy and business-like in its black paint scheme as I clambered up into the rear cockpit. A member of the ground crew helped to strap me in and then showed me that he had removed the safety pins from the ejection seat. With our seats armed, the canopy was closed, Roger and I established communications on the intercom, and he started the engine. The cockpit is very snug, and it felt like I was wearing the aircraft rather than sitting in it. The all-round view was superb, including looking directly forward over the top of Roger's bone dome. He continued to give me a running commentary to let me know exactly what he was doing. As soon as we got airborne and retracted the gear, he yanked the little aircraft into a steep turn to the left. I immediately felt the G-suit start to squeeze and hug my body, which felt strange at first, but I quickly got used to it.

We hadn't been airborne very long before Roger said, 'You have control.' The controls were so responsive and beautifully harmonised that I could hardly believe it. It handled like a dream, and it felt as though you merely had to think what you wanted the aircraft to do, and it did it. Roger demonstrated a couple of rolls followed by a loop and then invited me to do the same. The feedback through the controls and airframe made it easy and it almost felt as though I was a part of the aircraft. It was fabulous. Now it was time for some low-level flying in the Mach loop. Roger set our speed at 420 knots as we headed towards the ground in a shallow descent, I commented that I only had a basic pressure altimeter on my panel, so how was I supposed to accurately know when we were 250 feet above the ground. Roger replied that if I could see the legs on cows, we were about 500 feet up and if I could see the legs on Sheep, we were 250 feet up. It sounded like a good rule of thumb although I was pretty sure he was joking!

I swear that I had a huge grin on my face the whole time that we twisted and turned our way along the Welsh valleys. It was absolutely exhilarating, and I loved every second. We then flew back to Anglesey and as we headed for the runway at Mona, Roger told me what speed and attitude I needed to fly an approach. Following his verbal guidance, I did two touch and goes at Mona and then, as we climbed away again to set course for Valley, he took back the controls from me. He did a very impressive run and break, followed by a full stop landing on the runway at Valley. As we taxied in, I commented that the fuel remaining seemed alarmingly low, but I was of course thinking in terms of an Airbus' rate of consumption. As Roger cut the engine and the canopy opened, I just sat there for a while savouring the moment. I was still buzzing with adrenalin half an hour later as I started the journey home in my car. What a day it had been.

A few weeks later, I took Roger and his daughter Naomi for a flight from Manchester to Alicante and back. They sat on the two flight deck jump seats throughout and seemed to thoroughly enjoy their day out. However, I couldn't help thinking that it all seemed very tame compared to our flight in the Hawk. That really was a trip that I was never going to forget. I had come to the conclusion that flying a Hawk was the best fun a person can have with their clothes on.

Chapter Twelve

Life continued much as before for the rest of 2000 and the early part of 2001. As far as I was concerned, things were nearly perfect. I was as busy as I wanted to be with a good mixture of flying and office duties. The Manchester base was ticking along nicely with Virgin Sun aircraft whizzing around Europe and Virgin Atlantic aircraft crossing the Atlantic to Florida and the Caribbean. Because I was ex-roster—as far as pilot crewing levels were concerned—I was able to choose holiday dates during the school summer break, I could apply for days off for birthdays, Christmas and anniversaries. In the meantime, it was taking me just under fifteen minutes to drive from home to the staff car park at work. Shortly afterwards, I was either sitting down in the office or settling into my seat on the flight deck of an aircraft. Life didn't get better than this. What could possibly go wrong?

I was on a day off from work and had just walked into a shop in Wilmslow. I can't remember what I went in there to buy, but I do remember thinking that the two people who were behind the counter were being rather rude. They had heard me walk in, but instead of turning to face me to see what I wanted, they both stayed with their backs to me staring up at a television on the back wall. I glanced at the screen myself to see what was so riveting. The camera was focused on two skyscrapers silhouetted against a brilliant blue sky. I then noticed a rolling text banner at the bottom of the screen. Smoke was drifting from one of the skyscrapers and I realised that I was looking at the Twin

Towers of the World Trade Center in New York. Suddenly, I saw a large aircraft appear, briefly alter its course and slam into the second tower. Nobody spoke for a moment because we couldn't initially process what we had just witnessed. The date was 11 September 2001 and terrorism had just sunk to a new low.

I hurried home where Sara was staring in disbelief at the continuing television news coverage from New York. On an earlier trip to that city, Sara and I had gone to the top of one of those towers. As we had stepped out of the elevator and were confronted with a view right down the full length of Fifth Avenue, we had slowly absorbed the magnificent sight of Manhattan Island in all its glory. Like millions of people before us, that view had taken our breath away. It was a view that nobody would ever see again.

Apart from the immediate effect of grounding all air traffic in US airspace, it didn't take a genius to know that this terrorist attack would have a huge long-term impact on the aviation industry. Two days after it happened, I operated a flight from Manchester to Zakinthos airport on the Greek island of Zante. I was with my old colleague, Mike Kenny, and everyone was talking about the possible implications for Virgin Atlantic. The bottom had fallen out of the lucrative transatlantic market for now and it was hard to forecast how long it would take to recover. Fortunately, Virgin also had scheduled services to South Africa and the Far East, so the hope was that those routes would help to offset the decimated American market.

As far as Virgin Sun was concerned, the busy summer season was coming to an end and there were some disturbing rumours doing the rounds that the accountants were not happy with the company's financial results. We all knew that Virgin holidays had been late comers to the party as far as the European package holiday scene was concerned. Most of the major tour companies had been in the business for a long time. The startup costs of Virgin Sun had been higher than anticipated and a few glitches along the way had seen costs spiralling still further. Also, the events of 11 September could affect next year's European holiday market.

Our worse fears became reality when we learned that the whole operation was to be wound up at the end of the season. My last flight on behalf for Virgin Sun was on 31 October. We flew an A320 (G-VTAN) from Manchester to Larnaca, in Cyprus, and back. By then I had clocked up a total of 3,075 flying hours in A320/321 aircraft. All the cabin crew had employment contracts with Virgin Sun, so were now out of a job. The pilots, however, were employees of Virgin Atlantic, a company that still existed. We were told we were all going back to long haul flying, but our relief was short-lived. Because of the anticipated slump in long haul air travel—especially to America—the airline had decided to retrench over a hundred pilots. The redundancies would be based on a pilot's joining date: last in first out.

As I had only been with the company for five years, I assumed that I would be getting the chop. However, I was surprised to discover that well over a hundred pilots had joined the airline after me, so I might survive the cull after all, but there was more bad news to come. There were too many captains and not enough first officers. Tony Ling, the chief pilot, told me that, unfortunately, I was one of the people who would have to be demoted. Not only would I be losing my captain's salary, but also losing my extra pay as a training captain and manager. This meant that my salary would be dropping by more than 50%. When I asked Tony how long I could expect to remain a first officer, his reply was as expected; 'Not for a moment longer than necessary Bob, but your guess is as good as mine.' It didn't take me long to decide that I couldn't cope with the double whammy of a huge salary drop and having to give up my command for a second time. I then asked Tony if they had an offer for anyone interested in taking voluntary redundancy. They had, and it was a generous sum. Armed with this information, I contacted a former colleague.

In 1998, British Airways founded a short-lived low-cost airline called Go Fly. The chief pilot, John Mahon, had been with British Mediterranean when I worked there and—when Go Fly was set up—he asked if I was interested in joining the team. I visited their headquarters at Stansted and John gave me a guided tour. In the end, I decided that I would prefer to stick with Virgin, but John and I kept each other's contact details. Go Fly was sold by BA in a management buyout in 2001 and John moved on. He was now the Director of Flight Operations at British World Airlines (BWA) who were based at Southend. He had offered me a job as fleet manager of their Boeing fleet but, at the time, I was happy at Virgin Sun. I contacted John again and asked if he still had a position for me at British World. He did, so I took Virgin Atlantic's voluntary redundancy money and ran before they could change their mind.

I hadn't flown the Boeing 737 since March 1996, so my type rating had to be revalidated. Luckily, enough data remained lodged in my brain because the examiner awarded me a pass the next day, and Mario Fulgoni put me through my paces and carried out my licence skills test in the simulator. After flying 4,585 hours in Airbuses, I was now a Boeing pilot once again. I completed my line training on a flight from Liverpool to Vienna and return. A couple of days later, I climbed into the British Midland simulator at Heathrow and Hugh conducted my right-hand seat check ride. That now cleared me to fly the B.737 from both the left-hand and right-hand seats so that I could train captains and first officers in the aircraft on the line. Having been revalidated on the Boeing in record time, I was now ready for action. Unfortunately, that one round trip that I flew to Vienna and back turned out to be the only flight that I completed in a British World aircraft. My world was about to turn upside down yet again.

Before I joined the company, I knew they would have been badly affected by the September 11 terrorist attack, as were all the other airlines. However, with their previous experience in sub leasing activities, I had assumed they were sufficiently flexible to seize opportunities in the market as and when they arose. After all, the airline had been operating under various names since 1946, but I now learned that the company was closer to the precipice than I had realised, and their survival was far from assured. A

A British World Airlines Boeing 737 300

memo had just been circulated internally asking staff to take a temporary pay cut to help with the cash flow crisis, so nobody was under any illusions as to how serious the situation was.

BWA had their fingers burned a few months before when they had got involved in a leasing deal with National Jets Italia. Unfortunately, as we were to later discover, NJI had failed to pay their previous air traffic control charges and BWA were now presented with a bill for about a million Euros. John wanted me to go to Sicily to check out accommodation and facilities for the crews who were going to be based there and I flew out to Palermo the next day. While I was there, we learned that two of British World's aircraft had been impounded, all flight operations were suspended, and we were advised to get back to England as quickly as possible. Ideally before the news spread that the airline had gone bust. It was now 14 December 2001, and I was officially unemployed. Happy bloody Christmas!

Before driving home from Stansted to Manchester, I tried to phone John Mahon. When I finally got through to him, I learned that that some of the former British World management had persuaded Aberdeen Asset Management to finance a new charter airline called Astraeus. The airline would begin operations with two Boeing 737-300 series aircraft with bases at Gatwick and Manchester. John wanted me in on it, and I wanted to be in on it too!

On 6 April 2002, I taxied out in G-STRA to take Astraeus' first passengers from Gatwick to Malaga. Sitting alongside me was Chris Salmon and we felt privileged to be operating the airline's inaugural revenue earning flight. Over the next three days I would complete my line training. Then it was my turn to train captains and first officers and over the next few weeks I conducted forty-eight line training flights and seven final line checks. It was a very busy period indeed. By now, two Boeing 737-700 NGs had joined the fleet, and before the year was out, two more 737-300s would be introduced.

Towards the end of May, we were faced with an interesting problem. The company was due to start a series of weekly flights from Manchester to Calvi on the north end of the island of Corsica. Calvi is a Category C airfield which sits in a box valley and is surrounded on three sides by high ground. The French authorities insisted that the first landing there had to be done in an empty aircraft with only crew members on board. In the end, the solution was to fly our first lot of passengers from Manchester to Corsica landing at Bastia on the northeast coast, then take them by road to their destination. Having dropped them off, I then flew the short distance to Calvi and landed. Astraeus was now officially permitted to operate passenger flights into that airfield! The only restriction was that if an Astraeus captain had not landed at Calvi before, then his first flight had to be supervised by a pilot who had. It was obvious that I was going to be doing lots of trips to Calvi until I had checked a few more captains into the place.

The following Saturday we were approaching the south coast of France, when the first officer contacted Calvi for latest weather conditions and runway in use. The weather was fine with good visibility and no significant cloud, but the surface wind at the airfield was blowing from the north

G-STRA, a Boeing 737 300 of Astraeus

at twenty-five knots. Because Calvi was a Cat C airport, we had previously obtained a copy of an airfield briefing that had been prepared by British Airways. It was very straightforward, but the last part stated: 'UNDER NO CIRCUMSTANCES CAN A CIRCLING APPROACH BE MADE TO RUNWAY 36. LANDINGS ARE NOT PERMITTED ON RUNWAY 36.'

The wind was reported to be 360 degrees at 25 knots which exceeded our maximum permitted tailwind component for a landing on Runway 18. I called up Calvi tower again and asked for another check on the wind. He told me it was 360 degrees at 25, gusting to 30 knots. He added that the runway in use was runway 36 and that we were to establish on the localiser for runway 18 and then break off for a circling approach to runway 36. It seemed ridiculous that our only option appeared to be a diversion to another airfield when the visibility was gin clear and we could see both the runway and the surrounding terrain. I briefed the first officer that I intended to commence a visual circling approach. If, at any stage, either of us was unhappy, then I would abandon the approach and divert to Bastia. I asked him if he was okay with that, and he confirmed that he was.

I flew the aircraft towards runway 18 and then, at four miles, I banked it to the right to take us onto the downwind leg. I tucked the aircraft close to the valley wall and manoeuvred it gently to follow the contour of the terrain. The terrain loomed above us on all sides and I was flying with the starboard wingtip as close to the valley wall as felt comfortable. I kept tracking downwind until the windscreens ahead were filled with mountains and then, with the first officer shifting uncomfortably in his seat, I banked the aircraft steeply to the left onto final approach for runway 36. There were no VASIs or PAPIs for that runway, so it was a case having to judge it using the mark one eyeball. The fact that the runway had a pronounced downhill slope from this end made for an unusual visual picture. It was an interesting and somewhat challenging approach, and I made a note to that I would get captains to fly the visual circuit before releasing them to operate into Calvi without supervision. As the passengers were getting off, one of them said 'I see we had to do the circling approach in the valley. I always enjoy that as it is such a spectacular view.' I assured him that the view was even more spectacular from the flight deck. He added that Corsica was the 'best kept secret in Europe' and he hoped that not too many people would discover it and spoil it for him. Back in Manchester, I phoned John Mahon:

'Hi John. Can you authorise me to do a circling approach to land on runway 36 at Calvi?'

'Why?'

'I landed on runway 36 about three hours ago.'

'Consider yourself duly authorised'.

I then explained the problem regarding the British Airways briefing we had been using. John suggested that I was obviously the person who should write a brand-new revised briefing and that it should include details of how the circling approach to runway 36 should be flown. I sat down and wrote the brief before going home.

Over the next few weeks, I flew to Calvi every Saturday

The circling approach to Calvi Airport

and checked out several of our captains into the place. On each occasion—unless there was a strong southerly wind—I would request a circling approach and landing onto runway 36. Once I had explained to the Air traffic controllers that it was for training purposes and not because I was some kind of adrenalin junkie, then they were happy to oblige.

That summer almost every flight that I did was a training flight and I was either line training or checking captains and first officers. One of the reasons for this was because of a joint business venture between Astraeus and Bond Aviation Solutions Limited—whose managing director was Mario Fulgoni—and the company offered training for a Boeing 737 type rating. Historically, aircraft type ratings had been paid for by a pilot's employer. Although I had to pay for my training to obtain my Air Transport Pilot's Licence, I had not paid for any of the type ratings that were subsequently added to that licence. However, the airline industry was changing. As always, it all boiled down to supply and demand. At a time when there were more pilots than job vacancies, the airlines were able to call the shots. I first encountered this phenomenon when I was flying for British Mediterranean Airways. One of their first officers had paid for his A320 type rating through the airline Eurocypria and flown with them as an unpaid co-pilot until he had a couple of hundred hours of experience. He then approached British Mediterranean who offered him a job. He was an excellent pilot, so everybody was happy.

I understand the thinking behind a pilot buying their own type rating, but I don't like the idea. It excludes many good pilots, simply because they can't afford the additional expense. That can result in a person getting an airline job, not because they are the best, but simply because they can afford it. When times are tough, airlines will consolidate or even downsize. Rather than recruiting pilots, they are more likely to be getting rid of them. But when the industry is buoyant, they will revert to the 'traditional' practice of picking up the tab for the type rating. In 2002, pilots were queuing up to buy themselves a type rating. The Boeing 737 rating was the most useful one as it was the bestselling commercial aircraft in the world and a firm favourite with the airlines.

In Europe, one airline that was employing more pilots than anyone else was Ryanair. Even people who considered Michael O'Leary to be the Devil incarnate couldn't fault his business model. As the CEO of Ryanair, his ruthless and aggressive management style had made him plenty of enemies, but it had turned the airline into an incredibly successful company in the process. Their expansion in the market was huge and—as they exclusively operated the Boeing 737—they were constantly hiring pilots. That meant training organisations that offered 737 type ratings were very much in demand.

Pilots who were newly converted onto their first jet type had to follow it up with a minimum of 100 hours line training before they were fully qualified. This is where the Bond/Astraeus tie up came into play. Once Bond had completed a student's ground school instruction, they trained them in a flight simulator and the student would then fly an Astraeus Boeing 737 as a co-pilot on the line. This would always be with a training captain and initially, there would also be a safety pilot 'riding shotgun' on the jump seat. On rare occasions, if it all got a bit too much for the student on their first few training sectors, then they could swap seats with the safety pilot and spend the remainder of the flight watching the operation from the jump seat. Once a student had completed several flights and had gained competence and confidence, then the training captain would dispense with the safety pilot and all subsequent flights would be conducted with just two pilots. There was no hard and fast rule as to when this should be done because each student was different. My rule of thumb was to ask myself if the student could get the aircraft and its occupants back down onto the ground in one piece if I suddenly had a heart attack. A simplistic measure of a person's abilities, maybe, but one that seemed perfectly sound to me.

It was very satisfying and rewarding to train these young Bond students and see them progress from being somewhat overwhelmed during their first couple of flights, to becoming confident and able to do the job. Operating as a pilot on a multi crew aircraft requires discipline and teamwork. Whether performing as the handling pilot or the monitoring pilot, it is vital that they learn how to prioritise the various tasks they must perform, adhere to standard operating procedures and, because they are part of a team, learn how to delegate and communicate. As with most things in life, there comes a eureka moment when finally, after all the training and hard work, it clicks into place. That moment when the person sitting next to me finally slotted the last piece of the jigsaw puzzle into place. It always made me smile, and then I'd turn to the person and quote Rex Harrison's line from the film *My Fair Lady*: 'By George, I think you've got it!'

My busy flying programme continued in much the same way, but of course there was the occasional glitch. Such as the time when I took off from Manchester for a flight to Dalaman in Turkey. During the take-off roll, we got a master warning indicating that the right engine bleed air valve had closed automatically due to either excessive engine bleed air temperature or pressure. This happened occasionally when doing a full thrust take-off due to leakage past the closed high stage butterfly. It was normally possible to fix the problem by reducing thrust and then pressing a reset button on the overhead air system panel. I did so, but it failed to rectify the problem. I tried switching on the engine anti-icing to further reduce the pressure, but that didn't work either. Now I switched on the wing anti-icing and, at last, the system reset correctly.

We continued our climb, but a few moments later we got another master caution alert showing that the number one air conditioning pack had tripped off. With one pack unserviceable, you are restricted to a maximum altitude of just 25,000 feet and there was no way we would make it all the way to Turkey cruising at that altitude. I was relieved when we managed to reset the failed pack and getting everything operating normally again.

We recommenced our climb and I started explaining to the first officer that if an air conditioning pack failed during the climb before you had reached flight level 250 (25,000 feet) you were restricted to a maximum altitude of 25,000 feet for the remainder of the flight. However, if the pack failed when the aircraft was already cruising above flight level 250, then the remaining pack could maintain the cabin pressure and you could stay at that higher Flight Level. I was midway through delivering this pearl of wisdom when, suddenly, both our packs tripped off. The cabin altitude started climbing at about 3,000 feet per minute causing our ears to pop. Having donned oxygen masks and established communications, we made a rapid descent to a lower altitude. Things then got really busy while I liaised with the air traffic controller, made a reassuring public address to our passengers, briefed the senior cabin crew member and ran through various non normal checklists relating to our air system problems. Unfortunately, none of our efforts to restore the pressurisation were successful. The passenger oxygen masks automatically drop down from their stowage when the cabin altitude rises to 14,000 feet, but fortunately we had managed to get the aircraft below 14,000 feet before the cabin altitude had reached that point. Consequently, we didn't have a 'rubber jungle' in the cabin and the masks remained stowed. I had told ATC that I wanted to enter a holding pattern to the southeast of Manchester airport while we tried to work through the problem. I had contacted our engineers on our second radio, and they had come up with several suggestions for a fix. Unfortunately, none of them worked.

Our company operations department advised us that one of our aircraft was parked at Gatwick airport and wasn't due to fly again until the next day. The plan was for us to fly to Gatwick and transfer our passengers onto the other aircraft so they could continue their journey to Turkey. The engineers at Gatwick would then get to work on our sick aircraft so that it could be put back into service as quickly as possible. It was a good plan, but there was another problem. The flight from Manchester to Dalaman is quite a long one, and we were carrying a lot of fuel. With a full load of 148 passengers, we were at our maximum structural take-off weight, but the maximum allowable landing weight is always less. Short and medium haul aircraft such as the Boeing 737 are not fitted with a fuel dump system because the difference between the maximum take-off and landing weights is not usually great. If a return for a landing was required immediately after take-off, then the landing gear would accept the force of the touchdown, but engineers would have to carry out an extensive overweight landing check. This is time consuming, expensive and would almost certainly result in the need to replace certain some items including the tyres. If the check revealed overstressed parts of the structure, then the bill becomes eye watering! So, if the aircraft is not in immediate danger and there is no desperate need to get it back on the ground, you have to stooge around until the engines have used enough fuel to get the aircraft down to its maximum landing weight and then come in to land.

There is an old saying that the only time you can have

too much fuel on your aircraft is when it's on fire. Well, the situation we found ourselves in now proved that there is a second scenario when you can have too much fuel on board! We had to burn off a lot of fuel to get down to landing weight and because we had no pressurisation or air conditioning, the temperature in the passenger cabin was quickly becoming unbearable. There is no doubt that the passenger's anxiety was contributing to the rise in cabin temperature and despite my best efforts to keep them fully informed of the situation and to reassure them that they were not in any immediate danger, they were understandably nervous. I told the air traffic controller at Manchester that I now wanted to divert to London Gatwick and when he asked me what cruising level I wanted, I rather surprised him by replying 'As low as possible please.' I had already calculated that, even at low level, our short flight to Gatwick would still find us arriving on the approach well above maximum landing weight. I then turned to the first officer and played my only remaining card by telling him 'Gear down please.'

Lowering the landing gear would increase drag and we would burn more fuel. I made another PA to the passengers to tell them that we were about to lower the landing gear—which many of them would have realised from the aerodynamic sounds associated with that process—but pointed out that it didn't mean we would be landing imminently. Instead, I explained that the added drag would help us to get the aircraft's weight down quicker. As we set course for Gatwick— with wheels down and engine thrust high—the temperature continued to rise in the passenger cabin. If our passengers were planning to fly away in search of warmer temperatures, then we were certainly getting them off to an early start.

To cut a long story short, we landed at Gatwick—at maximum landing weight—with a plane load of very hot, but very relieved passengers. They were transferred to another Astraeus 737 and eventually arrived at their intended destination. Somewhat surprisingly, most of them were complimentary about the way we had handled the situation and appreciated being kept fully informed throughout.

I had thoroughly enjoyed flying the 200, 300, 400 and 500 series Boeing 737s during my career, but the New Generation Boeing 737s were to take my appreciation a stage further. Astraeus had added the 700 series to their fleet, and they were a significant step forward. This variant was known as the 737NG, which stood for New Generation. With a significantly larger wing, the 700s and 800s had improved performance both in terms of runway and climb ability, but also in terms of a higher cruise altitude capability. There were lots of improvements in the design of the aircraft's systems and in the flight deck—lovely big display screens had replaced the much smaller displays on earlier models. My only complaint is that when Boeing introduced the 737 NG, they missed a golden opportunity to radically redesign the cockpit. Instead, they bowed down to pressure from certain airlines that opposed radical changes to the cockpit design because they wanted to avoid retraining 737 crews onto the new variant.

Any pilot looking up at the overhead panel of an Airbus would see an uncluttered, ergonomically well-designed panel. Put that same pilot into a New Generation Boeing 737 and their reaction would not be as positive. Compared to an Airbus, the Boeing's overhead panel looks cluttered and untidy with switches placed where they would fit rather than where they should logically be sited. The basic panel layout was the same as the classic 737s, but a lot of additional modules and switches had to be added to the New Generation aircraft. A complete redesign would have been preferable but when a customer like Southwest Airlines tells Boeing that they want the changes kept to a minimum to ensure commonality with their existing fleet, then Boeing is going to listen. Southwest Airlines flies just one aircraft type; the Boeing 737. They currently operate an incredible 737 of them—coincidentally a very appropriate number—and they have another 437 aircraft on order. I think it's fair to say, a customer like that, is going to carry an awful lot of clout.

Life continued to be pretty hectic, and I had a very busy flying programme. A great number of my flights were training flights because, apart from the Bond students who were undergoing line training, I was also conducting routine line checks on Astraeus captains and first officers and clearing captains to operate into our category C destinations. I also carried out many command assessment sectors on first officers who were being considered for promotion to captain. It was always nice to see a pilot progress in this way and it was a real pleasure to conduct their final line check. I used to carry a set of captain's epaulettes in my flight bag when I conducted a final line check, and I would now pull these out, drop them onto their lap and say, 'You had better put those on and then sign the tech log captain.' It was a theatrical ritual that I always enjoyed. It's a big deal when a pilot gets promoted to captain and I reckoned anything that helped to highlight that moment was worth doing.

Astraeus continued to add to its extensive list of destinations and introduced transatlantic operations using the Boeing 737 from Gatwick to Deer Lake in Newfoundland. Some destinations posed interesting challenges such as taking oil workers in and out of Hassi Messaoud in the Algerian desert where high temperatures and sandstorms were a regular problem. At the other end of the scale, operating into Harstad-Narvik in Norway could have Jack Frost nipping at your nether regions. I operated a trip in and out of there in November and—at latitude 68 degrees north—there were very few hours of daylight, along with sub-zero temperatures and lots of snow.

We landed there without difficulty despite extensive snow coverage at the airfield and spent a few hours in a hotel on a split duty. By the time we returned to the airfield, our aircraft was completely covered in a thick blanket of snow. The de-icing operation took forever and, at times, felt like a losing battle. Just as fast as the airframe was cleared of snow and ice, fresh snow falls covered it once again. Eventually, during a brief lull in the snowstorm, the de-icing crew managed to get our airframe cleared. We quickly started the engines and taxied out to the runway before the de-icing holdover time expired. The snow clearance teams in their snowplough vehicles had been doing a great job of keeping the runway useable—just—in the appalling conditions. They would get into position in an echelon formation at the start of the runway and then all move forward as one, with plough blades and snow blowers doing their thing until they reached the far end of the airfield. Once they had left the runway and were trundling back along the taxiway, an aircraft would line up and take-off. No sooner had it lifted into the air than the snowploughs would begin their next sweep of the runway. It was superbly choreographed and impressive to watch. Thanks to their efforts and efficiency, we were able to take-off and climb away in weather conditions that would have closed the average British airfield for goodness knows how long.

Towards the end of 2004, Astraeus picked up a contract in Malaysia. The Kuala Lumpur based airline Air Asia was rapidly expanding and Astraeus provided them with two of their Boeing 737-300s for a six-month period. The aircraft were to be flown by Astraeus pilots who would remain in Kuala Lumpur for the duration of the contract. It felt good to be back in Malaysia. Over the next twenty-four days, I operated thirty-six flights, twenty-two of which were training flights with Bond students. Just when we thought that we had everything covered, on the very last day that we were operating scheduled services on behalf of Air Asia, things suddenly went very wrong. I had operated four flights finishing up in KL, but as I was about to leave the flight deck and hand the aircraft over to Mike King, who was operating the next service, I felt a thump and the aircraft suddenly rocked to one side. As I leaned across to glance out of the first officer's side window, my worst fear was realised—we had been hit by a baggage truck. I ran down the steps and around to the right-hand side of the aircraft's nose where I could see that the skin had been punctured leaving a long gash in the fuselage a couple of feet forward of the freight hold door. The driver was sitting motionless on his baggage truck, and I somehow resisted the urge to drag him off his vehicle and hit him, but it wasn't easy. Our aircraft, G-STRA, clearly wasn't going anywhere soon, and we had to come up with a plan B. The engineers inspected the damage and assessed what repair work was likely to be necessary. We decided that the captain and first officer who were due to ferry the aircraft back to the UK would stay in KL until it was serviceable, and our engineers would travel back with them. In the meantime, everyone else would travel back to England on the serviceable aircraft as soon as possible. The next day, we all headed back to the airport to fly to England in G-STRB.

I elected to fly the aircraft and to have David Snow as my first officer. I had done eight flights with him over the past few days and, based on his performance during those, decided he no longer needed a safety pilot supervising from the jump seat. The two of us went to the operations room to do our flight planning, while everyone else headed off to the aircraft to make sure our impressive collection of personal luggage was safely loaded aboard. In addition to the very extensive catering that we had procured, there seemed to be enough alcohol loaded in the passenger cabin to float a battleship!

It had been a very busy few months for me and it seemed likely that it was going to continue that way. Then something unexpected happened. When it was time to renew my class one medical certificate, I went to see my usual Aviation Medical Examiner (AME), Doctor Ronnie Reisler. He reminded me that the last time we'd met, he had recommended that I asked my GP for a Prostate Specific Antigen test to be done. Although I had no symptoms of any prostate problems, he explained that it was advisable for a person of my age to have the test done. Needless to say, as I had no symptoms, I'd done absolutely nothing about it. Ronnie gave me a stern look and said 'Get it done Bob. It is a simple blood test, so there is no excuse for putting it off.' He was right of course, so I promised him that I would arrange one. Ronnie then issued me with a renewed certificate for my medical and I went on my merry way.

The results of my PSA test showed an abnormally high

reading and biopsy was arranged. Events moved rather quickly after that as the biopsy showed cancer in three of the five samples. Further hospital appointments and tests followed and there was an anxious period waiting for the results to come back. Thankfully they eventually showed that the cancer hadn't spread to any other organs.

Having informed the CAA's aeromedical department of the situation by telephone, I soon received a letter from them on the first of June 2005 informing me that due to my medical condition, and 'Under the provisions of the Air Navigation Order', I had been assessed temporarily unfit to exercise the privileges of my licence and my medical certificate had been provisionally suspended. In other words, I was grounded. Although I knew it had been an obvious and inevitable action by the CAA, it still felt as though they had kicked me when I was already well and truly down. John Mahon was very supportive and told me to forget all about the job and to just concentrate on getting well.

I was placed under the care of Doctor Logue, the consultant oncologist at The Christie hospital in Manchester. He outlined the treatment options that were available to me, and I opted for brachytherapy. This involves implanting radioactive pellets inside a patient's body. CT and MRI scans had determined exactly where the pellets need to be placed for maximum effectivity against the cancerous cells, while at the same time, reducing the risk of unnecessarily damaging healthy tissue and organs. This accurate targeting of the problem area is one of the major advantages of the treatment. Another advantage is that there is normally a shorter recovery time, enabling the patient to get back to normal life again.

On 30 June I was wheeled into the operating theatre and had thirty radioactive titanium pellets imbedded into my pelvic bone. So now I had my very own built-in nuclear reactor humming away inside me. I was amused to read in some post operative literature that I shouldn't allow small children or family pets to sit on my lap for extended periods. Presumably they would start glowing in the dark.

I recovered quickly from the operation and then had to wait for the radio therapy to work its magic. Next, there were further tests to check my PSA levels and thankfully, when the results came back, they were good. On 14 September I received another letter from the aeromedical section of the CAA. This one informed me that they had received a report from my oncologist and having discussed my case they had decided to declare me fit for unrestricted JAA class one medical certification. On 22 September, I climbed aboard G-STRH and flew it from Manchester to Skiathos and back. It felt good to be back in the saddle.

The training programme was relentless. For most of my flights I was either line checking our own pilots or training Bond pilots. Some of the days were very long and tiring and looking back through my flying logbooks for that period I found plenty of examples of gruelling days and nights. One example was Manchester to Sharm El Sheikh in Egypt and then straight back to Manchester again. This was a journey of around 4,500 nautical miles (5,178 statute miles) and to be perfectly honest, it simply wasn't possible to complete it within the maximum allowable flight duty period. That said, with some incredibly 'tongue in cheek' and laughably optimistic flight scheduling, it could be shown as 'doable' on paper. We knew very well that even if everything went smoothly, we would have to use commander's discretion to get the job done.

Over a period of ten months, I completed one hundred and sixty-nine training flights, in addition to the normal non-training flights that filled my busy roster. Apart from flinging my body around the skies of Europe on a regular basis, I also had office duties in my role as the base manager. I shared the office with Ashley Chattaway, a lovely lady who was the cabin crew manager. Ashley was married to Chris Chattaway who was a training captain on the Boeing 757 with the charter airline Thomas Cook. Chris was a very cheerful guy with an infectious smile, and I soon got to know him as he frequently called into our office to say hello. One day Chris called in to the office shortly before Ashley and I were due to pack up for the day and suggested that the three of us went to a bar for a drink. A new long haul scheduled service airline was being planned and Chris was going to be the Director of Flight Operations. They were going to need a chief pilot and he thought I would be the ideal person for the job. I was interested and I signalled to the barman for another round of drinks.

The Boyle brothers, who owned the Canadian airline Zoom, had met with senior management at Astraeus to discuss a possible joint venture. Although those talks didn't amount to anything, the Boyles had been very impressed by Jonathan Hinkles, who was Astraeus' commercial manager. Jonathan's enthusiasm and ideas made such an impression that they made him an offer. They asked him to construct a business plan for starting a brand-new airline—Zoom Ltd—and he would be its managing director. Chris Chattaway was to be director of flight operations, I was to be the chief pilot, Ashley Chattaway was to be the cabin services manager and Jonathan's partner Adam Rowland was to be the cabin crew training manager.

Our airline was going to operate the Boeing 767-300 ER on long haul scheduled services from London Gatwick airport. It was to be marketed as a low-cost, full-service airline, with both economy and premium passenger cabins offering meals, drinks and in-flight entertainment. The plan was to operate services from Gatwick to the USA and Canada. Direct flights would also be available to Bermuda and with the introduction of each additional aircraft as the fleet expanded, a new destination would be added to the route network. Having seen at first hand the amount of work that had been needed to get Astraeus up and running as a new airline, I was under no illusions as to the size of the task ahead of us. That said, it was an exciting challenge, and I was eager to get started. I went to see John Mahon to tender my resignation from Astraeus and to agree on a final date of employment with the company.

Zoom Inc. of Canada and Zoom Ltd. of the UK were about to offer an extensive range of scheduled service destinations on both sides of the Atlantic. We—the fearless five—were keen to get started. We were also about to discover that sixteen hour working days would become commonplace and days off a rarity.

I had a meeting in the Six Bells pub, close to Gatwick airport, with five of the Astraeus captains that I was hoping to tempt across to Zoom. I gave them my sales pitch, following which four of them decided to make the jump. Eventually, I poached seventeen pilots from Astraeus—ten captains and seven first officers—following which I feared there might be a limousine with tinted windows searching for me. Chris had poached a total of eight pilots from Thomas Cook, his previous employer, so we figured that the bounty on my head was twice as much as his.

I would have to do a type rating on a Boeing 757 and then undergo a 'differences' course that outlined the differences between the 757 and the 767, as we were going to operate both types. I can confirm that as you get older, absorbing the very considerable amount of data that you are expected to learn during the ground school phase of a type rating does not get any easier. I ploughed through it all and thankfully passed the exam at the end of it.

I enjoyed the simulator phase of the course because the 757 was a delightful aircraft to fly. Similarities between it and the 737 were obvious, but at the same time, there were many significant differences. I quickly felt comfortable with the aircraft. One of the instructors who ran some of our simulator sessions was Captain Hassan Nejatbakhsh, a very experienced pilot and an absolute gentleman. I was delighted when we were able to recruit him as a training captain with Zoom and he later conducted some of my line training flights.

The first time that I flew the actual aircraft was on 13 June 2007. I completed my base training at Doncaster, where I flew four circuits. A few days later I started my line training when I flew from Gatwick to Bermuda and then onwards to Kennedy airport in New York. I did a total of six sectors of line training and then, on 12 July, Hassan conducted my final check on a flight from New York to London.

We were obliged to take delivery of our next aircraft—

A Boeing 767 300 of Zoom

another Boeing 767-300 ER—much earlier than we had planned. This was because we had been told that if we didn't take it now, the leasing company was going to pass it on to another airline. Because we couldn't start our next scheduled service for some weeks, Jonathan managed to secure a series of charter flights. These were very long flights from Copenhagen to Phuket and from Billund to Phuket.

I started the ball rolling on 6 December, when I flew from Copenhagen to Phuket, which all went to plan and took us twelve hours and thirty-five minutes. By now, we now had a good variety of scheduled service destinations from Gatwick including Halifax, Calgary, Vancouver, Bermuda, New York, Fort Lauderdale and San Diego.

Our aircraft, although they were being worked hard, were proving to be extremely reliable. We had excellent engineering back up and reaped the benefits. Needless to say, there were exceptions such as an occasion when I departed Gatwick with Phil Noyes whom I was line training at the time. After take-off, when attempting to retract the flaps and slats, the leading-edge devices jammed in the extended position. To cut a long story short, following numerous attempts to resolve the issue, we had to return to Gatwick. Luckily we had only set off with the intention of flying to Glasgow, so we were able to return without dumping fuel.

In June 2008, John Boyle announced that he was getting married in Bermuda. He would fly his guests to the wedding reception and put them up in a hotel at his expense. I was assigned to take them out there, so I took my ex-Astraeus colleague, Spencer Meakins, along as my first officer. We took all John's guests from Glasgow to Bermuda and then positioned the empty aircraft to Fort Lauderdale. We spent three nights in Florida and had a great time, following which we returned to Bermuda, picked up John's wedding guests and flew them all back to Glasgow. It really was a great trip, and a good time was had by all.

During the months of June and July, we were all as busy as ever. The aircraft were running reliably back and forth across the Atlantic serving our various destinations and, to a casual observer, everything would have looked fine. In fact, everything was *far* from being fine. Sometimes, an airline can suffer a setback due to something that is completely beyond their control. We had just such a setback when one of our aircraft went in for a routine maintenance check to be carried out by KLM at Schipol airport, Amsterdam. The maintenance staff were preparing to remove the walkways mounted close to the aircraft's fuselage and tail area, when an engineer accidentally activated the hydraulic system causing the rudder to kick across and strike the gantry.

Our aircraft wasn't going anywhere until a replacement rudder assembly was sourced and fitted. This ended up being a hugely expensive incident because there wasn't a replacement Boeing 767 rudder available anywhere in Europe, the only one we could find was in America. So now, a cargo aircraft had to sourced and chartered to fly the very large rudder unit from the USA to the Netherlands. In the meantime, we hadn't got an aircraft to operate our scheduled service between London and New York, so we had to sub-charter. Believe me when I say that they charge

The author in the left-hand seat of a Boeing 737

eye watering rates for that. By the time the replacement rudder had been flown to Amsterdam and fitted, the bill for the sub-chartered jet was astronomical. The incident wasn't our fault and KLM would be picking up the tab for flying the rudder over from America, but the outgoings and incidental costs generated by the delayed return of our aircraft would be disputed and argued over by insurance companies and lawyers. That would drag on but, in the meantime, Zoom had to pay for everything up front.

That incident was a 'one off,' but there were two much more persistent and worrying problems that were refusing to go away. In 2008 there was an economic downturn that was having a negative effect on passenger numbers. This was being felt by all the airlines but, of course, an airline like Zoom that offered a low-cost, full-service product, had to achieve a very high passenger load factor. In other words, they couldn't afford to fly around with many empty passenger seats. The realistic aim for an average all-year-around passenger load factor would be ninety percent. Worryingly, because of the economic downturn, our load factors were less than expected and, as if that wasn't bad enough, we had an even bigger problem.

Between July 2007 and July 2008, the average price of aviation fuel had increased by eighty-two percent. In fact, in the four years leading up to July 2008, the price had increased by a staggering 244 percent. Zoom didn't have deep enough pockets to 'hedge' by buying long-term fuel contracts, so we were forced to keep buying our fuel at the ever-spiralling prices that were being charged in 2008. Our fuel bill had increased by £15 million and, to put it bluntly, we were running out of money.

Zoom's senior managers had been working on a financing deal for several weeks and appeared to be making progress. At a management meeting, we were told that an investor was due to inject a large sum of money into the company's account the next day and that this would see us through the lean patch. Rumours of our financial plight had been circulating amongst some of our staff for a while and naturally they were worried. Early the next day, the director of flight operations and I met with the pilots who were due to fly out of Gatwick later and reassured them that the crisis had been averted. We told them that the new investment money was due to be deposited later that morning and that they could fly off to their respective destinations knowing that all was well. Looking relieved, they thanked us for the update and made a start on their pre-flight planning. We didn't know it at the time, but the rug was about to be pulled from under us.

On 27 August 2008, one of our aircraft landed in Calgary from Paris and was impounded by the leasing company due to non-payment of bills. The next day the CAA grounded another aircraft at Glasgow because of failure to pay outstanding European air traffic control charges. Both these events involved Canadian registered aircraft being operated by our sister company Zoom Inc. The speed at which that news spread, and the resultant chain reaction was astonishing. Perhaps not surprisingly, nobody was interested in differentiating between Zoom Inc and Zoom Ltd. All they knew was, Zoom hadn't been paying their bills so fuel supply companies, catering companies and passenger handling companies all started phoning to ask for outstanding bills to be settled. Then we received the devastating news from the bank that the money from the new investor had not been deposited and that all subsequent attempts to contact that investor had failed. Finally, we learned that all Zoom's aircraft were going to be seized and impounded wherever they landed. 4,500 British passengers were now stranded abroad, a further 60,000 passengers had unusable Zoom tickets, and 710 employees were out of work.

It took a while, but we got all our crews home eventually. We were painfully aware that our great team would now be disbanded and would eventually be re-employed in different companies and in different parts of the world. It had been a great team of highly professional, enthusiastic, and dedicated people and I knew I was going to miss working with them. One thing was for sure, it had been a hell of a good gig while it lasted.

Chapter Thirteen

I heard on the grapevine that the Irish airline CityJet was looking for captains and first officers for their newly opened permanent base at London City airport. CityJet had started operating in January 1994 between Dublin and London City under a franchise agreement with Virgin Atlantic. In 1996, that franchise ended when Virgin started their own airline, Virgin Express. CityJet struggled to survive and by 1999, were on the verge of collapse. Fortunately, Air Foyle stepped in and covered CityJet's debts in exchange for a percentage share in the airline. Air France also took on shares in the company and made a substantial cash injection. The thinking behind Air France's involvement was that they had traditionally been shackled by extremely powerful labour unions. The unions had now agreed to allow the airline to outsource the operation of any aircraft with less than 100 passenger seats. In an attempt to dramatically reduce their operating costs, Air France decided to take sole ownership of CityJet and to build up its network of European destinations.

Those destinations were served by CityJet's fleet of BAe146 aircraft, most of which were rebranded in Air France's colour scheme. In December 2006, they purchased 23 Avro RJ-85 aircraft from Mesaba Airlines to replace their older BAe146 aircraft. The STOL capability of the RJ-85 made it ideal for operations in and out of London City with its 1,500-metre runway and very steep approach path for landing. With eighty-five passenger seats, it also kept Air France's labour unions happy. Apart from expanding

An Avro RJ-85 of CityJet

and updating the CityJet fleet, the decision was also made to maintain CityJet's headquarters at Dublin, but with additional bases at Paris and London City airport.

I told all my Zoom pilot colleagues that CityJet was recruiting and gave them contact details. I also applied myself and received a surprisingly prompt response inviting me to Dublin for a simulator assessment. When I got there, I discovered that the flying assessment was to be carried out on the old BAC1-11 simulator that I used to use many years before. The poor old simulator was showing its age by then, but weren't we all? The examiner was dry and rather humourless; when I asked if he had failed the hydraulics—the controls felt incredibly heavy—he didn't bother to reply. I must have fooled him into thinking that I knew how to fly a plane, however, because a short while later, I was invited to attend an interview.

The airline VLM operated a scheduled service between Manchester and London City using Fokker 50 aircraft and I had taken this into consideration when choosing to apply to CityJet. It meant that I could use VLM as a means of getting to and from the London base from my home, but at this stage I needed to know more about the terms and conditions of the job, always assuming they would offer it to me in the first place. I met up with a couple of ex-Zoom colleagues whose interviews were scheduled close to my own. Just a few weeks before, I had been interviewing them as the potential employer and now we were all sitting alongside one another waiting for an interview in the hope of being taken on as employees. When my turn came it was a pleasantly relaxed affair and the guys joked that I probably knew how to interview people better than they did. That wasn't true of course, but it did help to break the ice and I have to admit that I actually enjoyed the whole process from there on. Much to my relief and surprise, they contacted me soon afterwards offering me the job. And so it came to pass, that I embarked on yet another bloody type rating course!

I found myself sitting in a classroom at CityJet's Headquarters at Swords, Dublin. Among my classmates were some former Zoom pilots and a former Astraeus pilot, so I was in familiar company. As always, we quickly engaged with the other course members and got to know them. Being very familiar with the process by now—having done so many type rating courses—I knew that we would end up being quite a tightknit group. As a course progresses, individuals will inevitably find some parts difficult. That's when you offer words of encouragement to a colleague who is flagging or feeling a bit overwhelmed with the workload. Nobody is immune and there were times when we all needed some words of encouragement.

One day I was sitting in the classroom listening to our instructor, Pete Smith, as he tried to explain the mysteries of yet another system on the RJ-85. Peter had been a test pilot with British Aerospace and was involved with the BAe146 and RJ-85 from the very beginning. He told us that he had never had anyone fail the type rating examination following one of his many courses. We all hoped that we weren't about to ruin his unblemished record. It suddenly dawned on me that today was my sixtieth birthday, and

I hadn't even noticed it. On the day I reached the age when captains had formerly been forced to retire, I was desperately trying to absorb all the technical information to get myself yet another type rating. What else would a person want to do on their sixtieth birthday but learn about the quirky design features of the Avro wonder-jet?

We had a couple of people on our course who had previously flown small commuter aircraft, but most of us had flown larger jets and had a lot of experience between us. Our instructor was a very patient man, which was just as well because, inevitably, as the course progressed and he explained the various aircraft system design features to us, someone would comment, 'That's a strange way to design the hydraulic system. On the Boeing, it's designed differently and seems much better.' It has always been an unwritten rule that you shouldn't drone on about your previous aircraft type when undergoing a new type rating course, but some people needed to be reminded. These unwelcome comments are affectionately known as WIWOBs—'When I Was on Boeings.' Having said that, it was fun to wind up Pete now and then.

One of the pilots was standing next to an engine that had been removed from an aircraft and was now mounted on a moveable frame. He said, 'This is really great Pete. Seeing this here makes so much more sense than seeing a picture in the classroom. What scale is this model of the engine?' Pete fell for it and spluttered 'This isn't a scale model, it's the real thing!' A couple of seconds later he realised it had been a wind up and he laughed along with everyone else. Everyone used to joke that the Avro was powered by four hair dryers rather than jet engines, or they said it was the only aircraft to have five APUs (Auxiliary Power Units). Much to our collective relief, Pete Smith's record for getting all his students to pass the exam remained unblemished. It seemed that my sixty-year-old brain cells were still functioning reasonably well.

I clocked up a total of forty hours in the simulator, and on 22 January 2009, I flew the aircraft, EI-RJP, from Dublin to Shannon to do my base check. I was delighted to discover that it was actually very nice to hand fly and had well harmonised controls. The line training passed reasonably quickly and was mostly enjoyable apart from the fact that there could be some horribly early starts to the day. I have never been a morning person and when people cheerily tell me that 'it's the best part of the day' I have no hesitation in telling them that they are talking nonsense. When those same deluded individuals say to me, 'Once you have finished your day's work following an early start, you have the whole of the remaining day to do whatever you want.' I point out that following an early start, all I want to do for the rest of the day is collapse back into bed.

When I was approaching the end of my line training sectors, the line training captain announced, 'I'm not going to put you forward for a final line check on your next trip, because I think you need a few more sectors under training.' That bombshell took a moment to settle in my mind and when I asked why he thought I needed some more training sectors, he said 'I didn't like the way that you liaised with the ground personnel at the other end of the headset when we were due to pushback and start our engines. You used some nonstandard phraseology, and you must remember that very often with the ground staff, English is not their first language.' I asked him if he was being serious, and he assured me that he was. I then pointed out that while the ground staff member on the pushback team at Edinburgh was not English, but Scottish, I had every reason to believe that he understood what I was bloody well saying. He replied that nonetheless, I should get into the habit of sticking to standard phraseology. I somehow managed to refrain from issuing a stream of nonstandard phraseology right there and then.

The next day, I was teamed up with a French line training captain and we were due to fly from Paris to Birmingham and back. Before we set off, he read the notes in my training file, including the comments from the previous day. He frowned and gave me an enquiring look as if to say, 'What is this all about?' I merely shrugged and we got on with the day's business. We had a very pleasant couple of trips at the end of which he said, 'I see no problems at all.' I was put forward for my final line checks, cleared to the line and, finally, let loose.

The beauty of being based at London City airport, was that we got every weekend off due to the airport being closed. This was part of an earlier agreement to keep neighbours happy when the airport was being developed. No night flights and no flights over the weekend. As most of the people using the airport were travelling on business, this worked well for everyone concerned. It also worked well as far as I was concerned. Not very long after I started with CityJet, the company asked if anyone was interested in working a seventy-five percent, part-time roster and I quickly volunteered before they had a chance to change their mind. In November 2011, I heard the sad news that my former employer, Astraeus, had gone into administration. Yet another airline gone, and all its hard-working employees were now out of work. It wasn't going to be a happy Christmas for them in 2011.

I flew the Avro RJ-85s for three and a half years and clocked up fifteen hundred flying hours in them. Anyone who flew that aircraft soon became blasé about master warnings and master cautions. The 'Bong' audible warnings and illuminated warning captions on the central panel soon became all too familiar, but usually they were either transient faults or things that could be easily rectified. I suppose that it all added to the quirky character of the aircraft. I certainly preferred Airbuses or Boeings to British Aerospace offerings for a quiet life but, having said that, the RJ-85 wasn't a bad old girl really.

Someone once asked me if I ever felt like quitting the flying game. I replied that several setbacks had really hit me hard. Finding myself unemployed after nineteen years with Dan-Air had left me stunned, but with a big mortgage to pay and my wife expecting our first child, there was only one thing to do in response. I had to pick myself up, dust myself off and move forward again. That meant moving halfway around the world to get the next job, but I had no choice. Subsequent events beyond my control continued to knock me down and, each time, it was a little harder to shrug it off and move forward. A boxer will keep getting up off the floor after being hit, even though he knows there will be more blows coming. At least I could convince myself that if I got off the floor again, there couldn't be any more blows coming. Unjustified optimism, maybe, but it kept me going. The person who asked me this admitted that he was seriously thinking about quitting himself. I told him that if I was no longer enjoying flying, I would know that it was time to quit. At first, he didn't say anything in response, but merely nodded. He resigned from the company very soon after that conversation.

In June 2012, Air France announced that they intended to sell CityJet, but first, they needed to make the company more attractive to potential buyers. Suddenly, we kept hearing the word 'streamlining'. Anyone who had worked in aviation outside the CityJet 'bubble' knew that the company was overstaffed, and productivity was poor. The fleet of ageing Avro regional jets needed to be replaced with aircraft that were more fuel efficient and less labour intensive from a maintenance standpoint. The fleet replacement would, of course, be very expensive, and that sort of major investment would need to be triggered by the new owners. In the meantime, to attract new investors, the company needed to increase their aircrew productivity. The solution was to reduce the number of crews and roster those that remained more efficiently. Of course, in Air France—the monolithic bastion of inefficiency that currently owned CityJet—overstaffing and low productivity was a way of life. In comparison, CityJet was already efficient. I knew that if the company did away with part time rosters, I would not be happy. I was away from home and family far too much as it was. I was also just fifteen months away from my sixty-fifth birthday: the compulsory retirement age for commercial flying. I asked myself if I was still enjoying the job, and the answer was no. When CityJet asked if any pilots were interested in taking voluntary redundancy, I gratefully signed on the dotted line. For once, I was in the right place at the right time.

On 21 September 2012, first officer Carrie Imlach and I took off from Amsterdam's Schipol airport bound for London City. The aircraft I was flying was EI-RJH and when we landed in London forty minutes later, I concluded my last ever commercial flight. I had clocked up 1,500 flying hours on the RJ-85 and a total of just over 21,000 hours on all types. It had been quite a ride.

Chapter Fourteen

My wife Sara had noticed an unusual swelling in my neck and had, for some time, been urging me to have it checked. Feeling out of sorts anyway, I finally made an appointment to see my doctor. He immediately made an urgent appointment for me at our local hospital. Over the weeks that followed, I had two biopsies, both of which were inconclusive. I then underwent an excisional biopsy, and this confirmed the problem: I had stage three Hodgkin Lymphoma.

This is a type of cancer that affects the lymphatic system, which is part of the body's immune system. There followed a full body PET scan and further blood tests. Over the next three months, I underwent chemotherapy at the excellent cancer unit at Macclesfield hospital. A few weeks after completing the chemo course, I was given another full body PET scan, at Christie's hospital, following which, I'm delighted to say, I was free of cancer and in remission. From the initial diagnosis to the 'all clear' had taken seven long months, but thanks to the excellent team who had cared for me, the final outcome was good.

With each generation that has come along, pilots have said that this is the best time to be in aviation. The early pioneers would certainly have said it, believing—correctly—that they were at the forefront of an industry that would go on to change the world. The quirky flying machines of that period had dubious handling characteristics and unreliable engines that required people with excellent motor skills and steely nerves to fly them.

Those early pilots were highly regarded by the public, who considered them to be bold masters of the sky. Those pilots loved their job and wouldn't have changed it for anything.

Today's pilots would rightly point out that computers and advanced engineering techniques have enabled aircraft and engine designers to produce machines that are incredibly reliable and efficient. Huge advances in technology have improved safety, navigational accuracy, fuel efficiency and ease of operation. So, today's pilots would argue that now is the best time to be in aviation because they can be a part of that exciting technological advance.

In between those bookends, there was me. When I first flew in an aircraft at the age of five, few members of the public had ever been up in an aircraft. Airline passengers were usually colonial administrators, government envoys, businessmen or wealthy people. The pilots, of course, we're almost exclusively ex-military and had flown during World War Two. Growing up, I eagerly soaked up any aviation related stories and frequently dreamed of adventures flying to far flung locations. Little did I know that, over the years, many of those dreams would come true.

When I first started with Dan-Air, I found myself flying with former World War Two pilots like Paul Ashpitel and Ken Mackie and being with them and learning from them was an absolute privilege. Once they had guided me along the way and helped me get comfortable in my role, then I think my golden period began immediately after I got my command on the Boeing 737. I was flying for a well-established and respected airline and that gave me the freedom to run the show completely once I took to the air. I knew that they would back me up and support me until the job was done, but then, quite rightly, jump down my throat if I screwed up. That's the way it was then, and I really enjoyed being entrusted with that responsibility. The captain's authority has been seriously eroded since and, in my opinion, that is a bad thing.

In terms of my own flying career, it is interesting that one single decision that I made had an enormous impact on subsequent events. When I was a Birmingham based captain with Dan-Air and they decided to close the base, I was offered a transfer to Gatwick. Because members of my wife's family lived in the Manchester area, I opted to go there instead. Had I gone to Gatwick then a few years later—when the company was taken over by British Airways—my seniority position would have guaranteed they kept me on as a Boeing 737 captain. I would have continued in that role and on that same aircraft type until my sixtieth birthday on 4 December 2008.

Financially, in terms of uninterrupted salary and pension, I would have ended up much better off. Because I chose to transfer to the Manchester base all those years ago, my career took an entirely different path, but it ended up being a far more interesting one. Although it meant that Sara and I were forced to move overseas for a while and had to endure numerous times of stress and uncertainty due to job insecurity, it also meant that I had the opportunity to experience a far more exciting and varied career. I flew lots of aircraft types, I went to lots of new and interesting destinations, I flew long haul and short haul, I became an airline manager and experienced all the responsibilities that entails. I trained lots of pilots who have gone on to become the 'next generation.' Maybe it's that last point that pleases me most. Hopefully, I have managed to teach and influence many of the next generation of pilots in a positive way. Maybe they will now think they too are experiencing the 'Golden days of Aviation.' I certainly hope so.

During my time with Dan-Air, I enjoyed nearly nineteen years of stable employment as a pilot. When that ended, I spent the next twenty years trying very hard to stay employed. I succeeded, but it wasn't easy. It called for lots of hard work, sacrifice, and financial hardship. Most of the hard work involved aircraft type rating exams when moving from one aircraft type to another. Also, learning new standard operating procedures and company specific procedures when switching airlines. I then had to go through the slow but enjoyable process of getting to know another group of people in yet another airline. While doing so, I sincerely hoped that my new employer didn't end up joining the ever-expanding list of airlines that went out of business. Unfortunately, out of the ten airlines that I flew for as a pilot, only two still exist. Job insecurity was very much a way of life.

As for the sacrifices, my wife Sara deserves a special mention. I had to leave her—pregnant with our first born—back in the UK while I headed off to Malaysia at very short notice to find a temporary home for us in that country. Meanwhile, she made all the arrangements to rent out our house and have our belongings placed in long-term storage. A few weeks later, she left friends and family to join me in Kuala Lumpur. A couple of months after that, our son Joe was born, and Sara had to learn how to cope with being a new mum without the benefit of help from our families who were thousands of miles away. A few months later, we were on the move again. Another airline, another temporary contract, and another temporary home.

Having been a captain for twelve years, I then had to go back to being a first officer for one of my job changes. That obviously involved a significant drop in salary but was considered a necessary forfeit to get a permanent contract with an established airline. Having later regained my command, that airline ceased operations and we were picking ourselves up off the floor yet again. After some more job changes—each one punctuated by personal financial cost, insecurity, and worry—we knew that we were not destined to enjoy a settled way of life.

Over the years, I missed many of the family birthdays, anniversaries, kids' school sports days and important family events. I often couldn't take time off during school holidays because that was when the airline was at its busiest. 'Next Christmas? Ah … I meant to tell you about that, Sara. Unfortunately …' It takes a special sort of wife who, when faced with all that uncertainty and disruption, decides to stick around: a wife who can single-handedly sort out car repairs, washing machine repairs, house maintenance problems and other typical day-to-day issues while simultaneously raising two kids. With the time I spent working away from home, ours was almost a single parent family. Sara coped with it all and kept her patience and sense of humour throughout all the many ups and downs. I know that I could not have coped with all the hard knocks and setbacks without the support and encouragement that I received from my lovely wife. Thank you, Sara. You deserve a medal!

We decided, at an early stage, that it was important to establish a home base where the kids could grow up and go to school and we could build a circle of friends in the local community. That home base is in the town of Wilmslow, Cheshire, where we have lived for over thirty years. We love taking foreign holidays, going to the theatre, and meeting up with friends. I also enjoy playing the guitar, writing stories and articles, and taking long walks with my dog Betsy.

Sadly, my two eldest children Nicole and Paul, live on the other side of the world in Australia, but my other two live near our home. My son Joe has his own business—a fitness studio—and my daughter Phoebe works for the British Heart Foundation. I'm extremely proud of them and love them dearly. I am a lucky man.

When I finally slip the surly bonds of Earth, the atoms that formed my body will float up the chimney of the crematorium and be carried away on the wind. They will, of course, be returning to an environment that I was once very familiar with. I find that rather reassuring. As they float away, I hope they enjoy the journey.

SunRise

Feminism in Aviation

PETER PIGOTT

The Golden Age of Flying Boats

Peter Pigott

Printed in Great Britain
by Amazon